# I Will Praise Thee

## JoAnne L. Keini

Edited by Kay Coulter

*I Will Praise Thee*
by JoAnne Lewis Keini

Printed in the United States of America

ISBN 1-594671-98-2

Unless otherwise indicated, Bible quotations are taken from King James, THE NEW OPEN BIBLE, STUDY EDITION version of the Bible. Copyright © 1990 by Thomas Nelson, Inc.

Reference(s)

Holy Bible, The Book of John, The New Open Bible Study Edition, King James Version, 1990, p. 1191

Holy Bible, The Book of Psalms, The New Open Bible Study Edition, King James Version, 1990, p. 696

This book is fiction. All characters and/or situations in this book are fictitious. Any similarities to persons living or dead is merely a coincidence.

Xulon Press
www.XulonPress.com

Xulon Press books are available in bookstores everywhere,
and on the Web at www.XulonPress.com.

# TABLE OF CONTENTS

# ACKNOWLEDGMENTS

First, I would like to thank Father God through my Lord and Savior Jesus Christ for giving me the ability to understand his love for mankind and family enough to write this book.

My heart is filled with gratitude for the many people that have supported me through prayers and/or encouragement. I thank all of you, but I must name a few publicly. Vanessa Andrews, Joyce Fuse, Barbara Young, Bonita Shelby, Evelyn Ryles, Corenne Labbe, Doreen Rollins, Kathy Lewis, William Johnson, Barbet Bryant, Mary Haygood, Marcia Hooks, Ellen Brinson, Alexis Saucedo, and Stella Johnson. Special thanks to Terri King and Vanessa Andrews for taking time out of their schedules to read my manuscript. I thank Mary Haygood and Lauren Jones for doing the initial proofreading and/or editing of this book.

My sincere thanks to Reginald Sanders and the media staff of Woodson Regional Library located in Chicago, Illinois for their computer knowledge and assistance, and Judith Blake-Littleton of Starr Travel for the use of her equipment. I acknowledge Mr. Nash for telling me, "don't sweat the small stuff."

Last, but not least, I acknowledge my family with overwhelming gratitude for supporting me in all my endeavors. Jay Keini, my husband; Dolores Green, my mother; Darlene Lewis, Sharon James, Janet Sellman, and George Green Jr., my siblings, I thank God for choosing you to be a unique and special kind of people and to play a very important part in my life.

To God be the glory!

# PREFACE

E ven though this book is fiction, God's truth in this book is real. As you read this book, if there is anything in this book that gives you food for thought, raise an eyebrow or make you say hum, then I have done my job. I have tried to make this book as realistic as possible to give you the reader a better understanding and/or appreciation for the importance of making the best choice for your life. Dating is a serious undertaking and choosing the right mate is even more serious. The decision you make will not only affect you but your family and others as well.

ENJOY!!

# DEDICATION

This novel is dedicated to Jay Keini, my husband, who has made significant sacrifices to support me while I have pursued my endeavors. I thank God for uniting us, Jay. I could have never selected a husband like you without God's direction. Only God knows our hearts and he has shown me through you, just how much he knows and understands our needs.

Dear Reader: As you read this book for enjoyment, ask God to show you his truth and to let you understand the importance of the word "trust."

# GOD LOVES YOU

# CHAPTER 1

# I NEED A DATE

As Marquetta walked to work, she thought, *It's a beautiful summer day, the sky is a powder blue, the birds are chirping, and the leaves on the trees are swaying to the warm summer breeze. It would be nice to enjoy the day with someone special. Why is it so hard to find Mr. Right? I haven't had any good prospects recently. That's bad. But I know one thing—I'd rather be by myself before I go out with Bobby Rhinehart again. That brother was tripping. He picks his dates by looking at their anatomy to make a determination on how his children will look. To think I would be flattered to know I passed his test. I don't think so. Um, um, um, he was arrogant, too.* Marquetta often walked to work enjoying, the tree lined streets in this progressive rural town. As she walked near the construction sites, she heard the sounds of progress, the jack hammer break ground through the old paved street. Horns blew and tires screeched as drivers' tried to avoid the closed lane. And, of course, you cannot leave out the usual remarks and/or greetings from the construction workers who decided to take a break as she walked passed. The non repeatable remarks she ignored but she spoke when the greeting was friendly and respectable. Since some of the trees were deciduous, the tree lined street scenery changed with the seasons. This allowed Marquetta to enjoy each season as she walked. Marquetta welcomed change. She moved to this rural town some ten years ago when she heard the local correctional institution would be enlarged to house an additional 200 offenders. She was 21 years old and just out of college. After cancelling her engagement she decided she should dive into a career. Since she wanted to start a business working with the offender population, she decided Growth town would be the ideal place to live. She developed relationships with the local and federal correctional agencies and through that relationship received her first group of trainees. The brick building with a rectangular shape that sat on top of the hill was where her office was housed. She leased the entire first floor. The building has two entrances, but each entrance has its own key or buzzer for access. Security officers were at both entrances. The entrance to her offices was away from the main thoroughfare. As she neared her building, she looked at the two-story red brick building, smiled, took a deep breath then walked toward it. As she entered her building she walked toward the elevator then turned a left pass the water cooler and into the door that read SCI. She opened the second door with a key. Upon entering her office she determined, *Well, no need to look back—I have work to do.* When she walked passed Barbara's office, the door was cracked as usual to let Marquetta know she had arrived. Acknowledging the crack door, she spoke. "Hi, Barbara."

"Hi, Marquetta." Barbara replied as she rose from her desk to follow her with her calendar. Her eyes sought out her favorite chair in Marquetta's office and she walked directly to it and, took a seat. "Do you realize you need a date by Friday to escort you to the banquet?"

"Thanks, Barbara, I really needed to hear that this morning," Marquetta said sarcastically.

"You are the guest speaker. You have two days left, not counting today. What are you going to do?"

"I don't know. I guess, look for a date."

"Do you want me to cancel your appointments for Thursday and Friday to prepare for the affair?"

"Yes, I think that would be best. Barbara, being single and trying to abstain is tough."

"I know what you mean."

"But you have Phillip. That's different, he understands."

"Getting the date isn't the real problem. The problem is making sure I'm not going to be fighting off someone's hands all evening. They say they understand, but I guess being men, they still have to try. You know—just to let you know they're interested. Hey, that reminds me, I need a vacation!"

"A vacation! How did you get that from this conversation?"

"Well you know date equals man, man equals relaxation, relaxation equals rest and rest equals vacation. When have you tried to figure out my logic?"

Barbara smiled and said, "Oh yeah, that's right, I don't!"

"I really need a vacation. Please make reservations for me. I'll leave on Saturday. I never knew developing an organization to help the offender population could be so demanding, yet so challenging."

Ring, ring. "I'll get the phone. You type my speech, please. Thanks Barbara." Marquetta said as Barbara left the room.

"Hello, Second Chance, Inc., Ms. Logan speaking. May I help you?"

"Hi, Markie, its Sam Brooks from high school. Remember, I said if I ever get to Maryland again, I would look you up. Well, I'm in Maryland. I thought maybe we could go out on Friday, if you're not busy."

"Sam, I am busy. I have a speech to give at a banquet, but I do need a date. Interested?"

"Sure."

"You'll need a tux. Is that okay?"

"That's fine. Great, we have a date. Good bye."

As Marquetta hung up the phone, she covered her face with her hands and asked, "Oh no, what have I done? I must be really desperate. I have no idea what this man looks like. It is a must that I go home and check my yearbook."

As she walked to her condo, her mind wandered back to her old neighborhood in Maryland. Marquetta thought, *I love the people there but I had to move. Although my family loves me, living there could be somewhat controlling. It's still nice to go to the 'Day of Celebration' that the town has every summer for past and present residents. I wonder what the theme will be this year, since it's a different theme each year. Knowing Mrs. Peabody, she put it in the town paper she mails to past and present residents.* Marquetta made a mental note to check the paper for upcoming events. As Marquetta continued her stroll down memory lane, her face lit up with a smile as she envisioned the casual struts and varied strides of the people. Her eyes beamed and her smile broadened as she continued on this path. The men tipped their hats and the women nodded their heads as townspeople passed each other on the streets. Those in vehicles got customary waves as they passed residents sitting on porches or stoops. The lack of hesitation each person had in approaching one another for assistance or when admonishment was in order, made you think it was a small rural town, but it actually was in the suburbs, minutes from city limits. It wasn't a neighborhood. It was an extended family that surpassed bloodlines. But what single woman in the late 1990s could live in a town filled with family? Of course, Mrs. Peabody, the owner of the town's paper kept the neighborhood abreast of any and all events. She also helped to keep this fellowship in tact. Mrs. Peabody is a short scrawny woman that keeps her hair in two braids, which she wraps around her head as if forming a braided rope. The braided rope forms what appears to be a circle around her head and from that circle protrudes a number two writing pencil—poised for quick access. Marquetta snickered when she stated, "Mrs. Peabody is something else." *That woman seems to know everybody's business in town, accept for my family. I wonder why? I'm not going to complain because she helps where she can. If it weren't for Mrs. Peabody's putting my idea of developing a business to assist the offender population in the town's paper, Second Chance, Inc., would not be in operation today. That was ten years ago; now we're self-supporting. Wow. Time does fly. God is good."*

Marquetta lived in a garden style condo with a total of three floors. She lived on the top floor. Her unit was the last one to reach on her level. The entrance to her building was glass. There was an elevator but Marquetta preferred the stairs. The rest of the building was stucco. To reach someone in her building you had to enter the last four digits of the residents phone number. To purchase a condo in her development, each prospective buyer would have to meet with the board members of the condo association for approval. Her unit consisted of two bedrooms, a small eat-in kitchen and a living room/dining room combination. Whereas Marquetta's office furniture was a combination of traditional and contemporary furnishings, her condo reflected more of her personality and that was traditional.

She entered her condo, walked to her guest room, opened her storage closet, and looked in the boxes for her yearbook. She queried, "Why can't I find a loving, gentle, caring man like Daddy? *Whenever I ask Mom how did she know Daddy was the one for her, she says she just knew. She prayed for a husband and, finally, when she met him, it all came together. 'Pray and trust God, honey,' that's what she always says. I've been praying! I know— patience. It's not our time. It's His time. Well, at least I know when God does it, he does it right. Grandpa Tom and Grandma Kate, Ma and Daddy are still in love and boy, do they know how to share it! Now that I think about it, I wonder if they got together at night to decide who I was going to spend time with and where I would go, how much candy I could have, and how many times to let me know each one loved me? Every time I turned around someone was kissing or hugging me except when the spankings came. I remember, Grandpa Tom and Daddy would say, with love comes discipline. You must learn right from wrong. Oh yeah, I'll never forget the lecture on the word 'nigger' from Mom. "'I don't care what the dictionary says or what other people say the word 'nigger' means, a nigger is a dumb ignorant person. Since all people can be dumb and ignorant from time to time, anybody can be called a 'nigger.' Remember, it is used in a derogatory sense, so you shouldn't use it at all. However, it will tell you something about the type of person who is using it. Analyze things for yourself."' Marquetta smiled, then reasoned, "I can't complain. Being on my own has made me realize that I was blessed to have a family that loved me enough to sacrifice their time, money , and resources. That's probably why I do what I do–show and give love to those less fortunate. I must admit, I'm discovering most people let others analyze things for them instead of for themselves. That is where the real problem lies. God gives each of us a mind and the ability to make choices. If we want to make the best possible choice, we need to seek God for direction.* Loudly she asked, "Where is the yearbook?" As she continued her search, her thoughts wandered to the church's singles ministry. *I'm glad I joined the singles group at church, she thought. It has really helped me with my Christian growth and development. I know I'm not perfect, but at least now I'm reading the Bible to live in a way that is pleasing to God.* Her thoughts drifted back to her yearbook and she said, now frustrated, "I can't find it!" She calmed down and said, "I guess this will be a blind date of sorts, because I don't remember him. What does it matter? It's just a date. She noticed the mirror on the closet door, stood up, and decided to take a look at herself. She said, "Physically, I'm in shape. At one time my size was the thing, but I still believe there is a man for me, and my size will be just what he wants, not, too fat and not, too skinny. My measurements have stayed the same since college. I don't think 36-26-36 is, too bad. I think my husband will be pleased with his wife in every way."

# CHAPTER 2

# WHAT IS IN A CONVERSATION?

R ing, ring. Marquetta answered the phone, "Hello."
"Hi, Marquetta. This is Barbara. We have a problem.
"What is it?"

"Mr. Greely, from Greely's Towing Service called about one of our clients. He said he stole a tow truck from the company's tow yard. He's going to press charges." William Greely was a short, pudgy man with a pouch for a stomach. His overactive sweat glands caused him to perspire frequently so he constantly reached for his handkerchief that he always kept in his back right-hand pocket.

"Who is the client?"

"The client's name is Tony Davis and he's still at the job site." Tony Davis was a young man in his early 20s. His skin tone was dark brown and he had very dry skin. He had small beady eyes and a mustache with a full beard which hid a great part of his face. Anyone seeing him for the first time would believe he had criminal ties. He was often picked out of a police line up even when the real perpetrator was in the line up. Most victims would admit to choosing him because he looked guilty even through they thought it was the other guy. The police would get a kick out of the situation then release him and question the other guy. When he became a SCI client, he no longer participated in police lineups. Marquetta's professional reputation was excellent. She respected the police and they knew it. Some of the officers knew her personally because of her friendship with Todd. So when Marquetta requested that Tony not be used for line ups unless the police believed he was involved, the Chief agreed without hesitation. She suggested to Tony that he could improve his appearance by shaving his mustache and beard. When he shaved, he looked less guilty and much younger. He has a small frame. He weighs 140lbs and stands 5 feet 8 inches in height. As a teenager he was constantly in fights. He proved he could hold his own with the older and larger boys by fighting all who discussed his size. The only two boys that seemed to accept him was Gilbert and Carlos Huggs. Gilbert and Carlos spent most of their time stealing cars. Tony's involvement with them introduced him to the penal system.

"He's still at the job site? Did he steal the truck and go back to work?"

"Mr. Greely said he brought the truck back."

"Barbara, this smells. I need to talk to Mr. Greely and Tony. Call Mr. Greely, tell him I'm on my way to the job site. Ask him if he would wait until I get there before he calls the police. If he won't, tell Tony we will meet him at the precinct. Contact his parole officer and brief him on the situation. Make certain the parole officer understands it's an allegation, nothing more. As the information comes to us, we will relay it to him. Call our attorney and have him meet me at the tow yard. After you do that, bring the cassette and meet me at the tow yard. That is the job site location, right?"

"Yes that's it." Barbara replied.

"Give me the address, please." Marquetta requested.

Barbara gave her the address and said, "I'll meet you at the tow yard. Good bye."

Marquetta was almost out the door when she heard her phone ring and hurried to answer it. She answered it on the fourth ring. Slightly panting Marquetta said, "Hello."

"Hi, Marquetta. This is Barbara, again. It's a false alarm. Mr. Greely said he was just letting the kid know that working for him was serious and if he broke any rules he'd be back in the slammer before he knew it. He was sorry if he inconvenienced us, but the boy needed to know he doesn't play games."

"What? False Alarm! Are you serious?"

Barbara heard the anger in her voice and said, "I asked him to let me speak to Tony. He did and I told Tony to report to our office as soon as he gets off. I also told him not to worry about anything— it would be all right."

She heard the calm in Marquetta's voice when she said, "Thank you. You knew exactly what to do. How many of our clients are working for Greely's Towing Service?"

"Tony was our first."

"Good, mark Mr. Greely's employee request folder red for caution. We need to be careful of the type of clients we assign him."

Barbara understood completely and said, "I know. I'll draft an office memo for your signature stating the status change on Mr. Greely's folder."

"I want that memo to reach the staff today. Type it for your signature and put a copy on my desk. I won't forget the meeting with Tony Davis this evening. I'll see you later. Good bye."

———

Barbara hung up the phone and began to prepare the memo. Her mind drifted back to the early years of Second Chance, Inc., (SCI). She thought, "Working with Marquetta has really changed my life. I would have never thought a job announcement placed on the grocery store want ads' board would turn out so good. I love this job. I enjoy working at SCI because this company really helps people. I think it's because we provide Christian-based life skill classes in addition to job training and placement. Some of our clients have their own businesses now, like John Wordsler. I know one thing if Marquetta wasn't a dedicated and praying woman, John Wordsler could be in jail. To think a company would deliberately set out to sabotage another company just because it's helping the offender population. It's hard to believe this stuff happens, but it does. At least that's what happened to John at Boyd's Lumber Company. They assigned him the responsibility of monitoring the company's books knowing he had no experience in that field. They assigned him that position in order to frame him. Boyd's Lumber

Company didn't expect SCI to get involved but when we did, we blew the cover off their scheme. Now, we understand the game. We won't allow any of our customers to frighten our clients into committing crimes for them. It turned out to be a blessing. After the incident with John and proving his innocence, our clients have no problem confiding in us. They should feel confident in our staff because Marquetta screened me and then the two of us screened all the others. Recently, I found out what Marquetta looked for when she hired SCI's employees. Knowing her, I should have guessed it. She is very careful when it comes to our clients and their sensitivities. She will not hire anyone that she believes has a prejudice against our clients, no matter how slight. Another thing we do because of Mr. Boyd's behavior, is investigate every employer who wants to participate in our program."

The phone rang and broke Barbara's thoughts. "Hello, Second Chance Inc."

"Hi, Barbara," said Marquetta. "I'm at Todd's office. I'm going to treat him to lunch. Do you want me to bring you anything?"

"No thanks. Have a nice lunch. Good bye." Marquetta hung up the phone and sat down.

Todd inquired, "Marquetta, did I hear you say that you are treating me to lunch?"

Marquetta smiled, then responded, "Yes."

"Uh oh, I knew this wasn't a social visit. I'm in trouble, lunch and a smile. You want something, don't you? What is it?"

"It may be nothing, but do you remember how we met? You were a Police Detective determined to seek out the truth. You helped me. I should say Second Chance Inc., keep its doors open by discovering a plot to set up one of my clients."

"Yeah, I remember."

"I think I have a similar situation in the making."

"What makes you say that?"

"I think we got our first clue this morning."

"What happened?"

"Barbara received a call this morning that one of our clients stole a truck. When Barbara called back with our response, they told her 'false alarm.'"

"False alarm? Really?"

"Yes, really! I'm wondering if we should go to the employer and talk with him. I feel like I should do something. Maybe we should start by praying."

"Okay," replied Todd. Todd pushed his chair away from his desk and rose to his feet. He then walked around his desk and, took a seat by Marquetta. He then put one of his hands in hers and they prayed. After prayer, Marquetta's uneasiness was lifted. She smiled as she said, "Now I can eat."

As they walked out of Todd's office and neared Myrna's desk, Todd said, "Myrna, I'm going to lunch." On the drive to the restaurant Todd suggested, "Let's wait until we have more to go on. See how the trap is being set. That way we'll know how to defend Second Chance Inc. and you, if necessary. Right now, we can't rule out this being an innocent mistake. I hate to bring this up, but everybody doesn't feel comfortable dealing with your clients."

"That's a good idea. The key word is 'wait.' With patience we can watch the scheme unfold. Todd, that's the answer! We have to thank God for it." Simultaneously they said, "Thank you, God."

As Marquetta walked into the restaurant, the owner said, "Hi, Marquetta. Is Todd with you today?"

Todd appeared in the doorway and said, "Yes, I am. You know I wouldn't miss an opportunity to eat one of your pizzas. Where's your wife?"

"Marcy's in the back helping out," Frederico said, as Todd and Marquetta followed him to a table near a window. After the order was placed, Marcy came out to greet Marquetta and Todd. She said, "I knew you were here. Nobody orders a pizza like you." She smiled and said, "Married yet?"

Marquetta responded, "Marcy, behave. You always ask us that question. How many times do I have to tell you we're just friends and he's SCI's attorney?"

"I hear what you say but I know what I see with my eyes," replied Marcy. Marcy winked at Todd.

Todd said, "She keeps fighting my affection, Marcy, but keep up the good work."

Marquetta, a little embarrassed, said with a smile on her face,

"The two of you are ridiculous. Is our pizza ready?"

Marcy laughed and went to check on the pizza. Marquetta tried to get down to business, but couldn't resist peering out the window. Immediately she noticed a family of feathery white creatures with orange bills and web-like feet waddling single file toward the pond. As she watched for the ducks to emerge themselves into the water, she noticed a gull-like bird hovering over the pond. In an instant the Herring Gull swooped into the water, bringing out a fish in his beak. Marquetta was astonished at the deftness of the bird, but realized it was time for her to get down to business. She turned to look at Todd and said, "Todd, I brought us to Frederico's Pizza Parlor because it is a good distance from the office, not, too busy this time of day, and good for privacy."

"I know, you prefer to talk to me with the least amount of interruptions as possible. That's fine," Todd replied. "I needed a change. Recently, I've had working lunches with Myrna. But now that we have brought everything up-to-date, I wondered what I was going to do today. This is a pleasant surprise."

"I'm glad." Marquetta replied, then stated frankly, "Todd, I need a favor. Although you're an attorney now, would you help me follow up on the problem we discussed earlier? By the way, I'm going on vacation to the Caribbean. I'm leaving on Saturday. I would like to tell Barbara that if she has any problems with any of our clients or customers she should contact you. She may need some advice or assistance. I realize this does not come under your duties as the organization's attorney, but you're also a friend and someone both of us trust—at least from a business standpoint." Both laughed just as Marcy brought the pizza to their table. Marcy smiled and said, "Enjoy, you two lovebirds."

Marquetta said, "Thanks for the pizza, Marcy."

Todd said, "Thanks for the comment, too."

Marquetta looked at Todd and said, "Stop encouraging her."

"I will not!" Todd said with a grin that would bring most women to their knees. "To answer both your concerns, I will just say one word, yes. However, you realize you're asking me to work closely with Barbara. Are you sure you want me to do that? Suppose she falls for me." Todd said as sincerely as he could muster.

"Fall for you and dump Phillip, never!" Marquetta smiled then remarked, "Todd, stop dreaming. Anyway, we're friends remember. No romance! It would spoil everything. Think about it. When I need you, I know where to find you, usually. I can come to your office or your home anytime without feeling the pressures placed on relationships. People act crazy in the dating scene. Besides, I'm abstaining from sex and I know you can't handle it. The next time I am with a man in an intimate relationship, it will be as his wife. Why am I telling you this? You already know how I feel. We've known each other for ten years."

"I know. I can't believe its been so long. But I think you're wrong."

"Wrong about what?"

"In thinking I can't handle dating you, knowing how you feel. I think I can."

Marquetta changed the subject as she reached for her shoulder bag which she hung on the back of her chair. "Are you ready to leave?" She then looked at the bill, put the exact amount of the meal in the leather folder that the bill was in, closed it and placed it back on the table.

"Yes," Todd stated as he, took money from his wallet and rose from his seat. As he and Marquetta walked toward the door, Todd handed Marcy the tip in her hand, along with a dollar for each of her children. As they exited, Marcy realized the amount Todd placed in her hand, walked over to the door, stuck her head out of the doorway, and shouted, "Thank you, I'll give the boys their money when they get home from school." Todd and Marquetta were so involved in conversation, they never heard Marcy. But waved to her as they saw her head peaking out the door as Marquetta drove off. Todd, took a quick glimpse of Marquetta as she pulled out of the parking lot onto the road, knowing she was too occupied to notice him. He couldn't help but comment. "I would love to get my hands on that guy who changed your mind ten years ago."

Marquetta chuckled, then replied, "Todd, it wasn't a guy. I made that decision. When I began to grow spiritually and started reading the Bible regularly, I realized that my fornicating wasn't pleasing to God. I thought, God is always there for me but what thanks do I give him? That's when I realized I could show my love for Him and my gratitude by trying to live a life that's pleasing to Him. Although I know I'm not perfect, I know that God knows I'm doing my best. You know, Todd, I really don't miss that lifestyle. Too many problems come from it."

"Seriously, Markie, what can I do to convince you to go out with me again?"

"I think we both know that's not a good idea." They drove the rest of the way in silence.

Marquetta pulled her car close to the entry door of Todd's office and jokingly said, "Get out."

He said, "You're using me, Markie, you're using me."

Marquetta smiled and said, "I'm not using you, you're helping me."

"Right, I hear ya." Todd walked to his office with a grin on his face.

---

Marquetta activated her car phone and called her office. "Barbara, I'm on my way to the office. I'll see you when I get there. Good bye."

---

Myrna noticed the grin on Todd's face when he entered his office so she asked, "How was lunch?" Todd composed himself, then said, "Fine, how was yours?"

"Fine, although I have to admit we've been eating in so long, I missed eating with you."

"Well, Myrna, that proves I've been working you, too hard. From now on, I'm going to insist that you have lunch outside the office. It will be good for you. Do me a favor. Hold all my calls, please."

"Yes sir, I will."

"Thanks."

Todd's office was in a contemporary style building. The building was of cedar exterior with visible wood rafters hanging from the roof. There were four offices in the building. Todd's office was located on the first floor. Clients pushed the buzzer by the name of the company they wished to visit, before they could enter the building. The foyer was decorated with hanging plants. The skylights in the ceiling were designed to give light to the foyer. Todd's office was to the right of the main door. The name of Todd's company was on the door, Todd Parker and Associates. When you entered, his office Myrna's desk was in the center of the room. Her desk was shaped in the form of a half circle. The desk was made of mahogany. The charcoal grey, padded chair was made to protect her back and give her comfort. There were times when she worked 12 hour days to get briefs ready for court. Todd believed the chair was an investment and not a waste. The lamp on her desk was made of stainless steel. The lamp shade was silver and had a circular shape with a whole in the center. To the left of the entryway, closest to the door was a seating area for guest. A soft dark-blue leather sofa with matching chairs sat at this location. Coffee tables were in the center of the sofa and in the middle of the two chairs. Magazines were on top of both tables. Against the wall near one of the chairs was a credenza. On top of the credenza sat a coffee machine and hot water for tea. A basket with sugar, cream and saccharin packs was also on the credenza. Todd's office and the associate's office had similar desks. However, Todd's was bigger with locking file cabinets on both ends of the desk. His built in bookcases were filled with law books. He sat in a dark blue soft leather arm chair. The sitting area in his office was identical to the sitting area in the lobby with the exception of the credenza. Seated at his desk, trying to peruse a file, his mind wandered to Marquetta. He thought, "What is wrong with Markie? Doesn't she realize I really like her? Maybe I play with her, too much and she doesn't know when to take me seriously. I had my chance to show her I was serious about her, but I blew it. I must admit, I wasn't accustomed to dealing with a woman of her caliber, but now I am. How can I get her attention? There has to be a way! I know one thing—I can always be her friend. But is that all I want to be to her?"

Myrna buzzed in, "Mr Parker, I know you said you didn't want any calls, but Ms. Smith insisted I check to see if you would receive her call."

"Myrna, when I say to hold all calls, that's what I mean. Tell

Ms. Smith I'll call her back near the end of the day, please."

"Yes sir, I'm sorry."

"That's okay. I know she can be insistent. But don't let her bully you.

"Yes sir." Todd released the buzzer.

Todd thought, *How can I forget Juanita? Markie probably won't believe I'm serious as long as she knows I'm escorting Juanita places all over town. She also knows I have contemplated living with and marrying Juanita more than once. I don't know why I tell her so much about me. Being with Juanita isn't the same as spending time with Markie.* He smiled and thought, *Juanita is a good catch from a financial perspective, and she's good in the sack, too. The fact that her father is one of the richest men, if not the richest African-American man in this area, is a big plus. I meet a lot of business people with Juanita. She makes it a point to publicize my law firm and to keep me in front of people who could use my services to build my business. What's wrong with me? Why can't I commit myself to her? She'll be good for my career, but she's no different to me than any other woman I've been with, except she has money and prestige in the community. Marquetta, on the other hand, has personality. She's special. She stimulates me. Just being with her can be enjoyable. She is voluptuous, too. There's not, too many voluptuous women around who dress as modestly as Markie. I'd love to see her in a bathing suit, a bikini. No, I don't. That means someone else would see her, too. I want her for me. She's just one of a kind. She has determination and courage, too. To know the pleasure of sex but to decide not to have it again until she's married is serious. That takes willpower. She stands up for what she believes, even in adversity. She'll make a good wife and mother. The question is: Will she have me as a husband? Let me get some work done. Markie Logan, you have taken up, too much of my time today, even if you don't know it."* Todd forced himself to take care of the work at hand. Time flew by. Involved in his work, Todd was interrupted by Myrna with a buzz. Todd answered, "Yes Myrna."

"Its 5:00p.m.. Do you want me to stay late?"

"No, wait for me. I'll walk out with you." Todd grabbed his briefcase and walked to the outer office. Just as he and Myrna were about to walk out the door, the phone rang. Todd said, "Go on Myrna. I'll get it." Todd placed his briefcase on the floor near Myrna's desk, sat on the corner of the desk, close to the briefcase and near the phone. He glanced at his watch, then picked up the receiver. "Hello, Todd Parker and Associates." As Juanita spoke she was sitting in the chair at her desk with her legs crossed at the ankle on top of the desk—displaying her stocking feet. "This is Ms. Smith. Did you get my message? I wanted to catch you before you left the office."

"Hi, Juanita. What do you want?"

Enticingly she declared, "You...my father is having a few business partners over for dinner and he told me I could bring a friend. I think he's just checking to see if we're still together. I really would like you to be there, tonight. Can you make it?"

Todd acknowledged her declaration with an emphatic tone, "Oh, I'll be there. You can tell your father you're not available yet."

Juanita's voice, took on a concerned note. "Yet? What do you mean by that?"

"I mean we're still going out together, right?" Todd stated soothingly.

Juanita's fear of losing Todd began to surface. She uncrossed her legs, took her feet off the desk, and put on her high-heeled shoes. She was no longer in an alluring mood. It was time to fight for her man. Anxiety crept in and she lost her composure. She was now sitting at her desk with one hand gripping the phone and the other forming a fist resting on her left thigh. With both feet firmly planted on the floor under her desk, she was ready for battle. Although she was talking to Todd, Marquetta was in the back of her mind. "Oh yeah, sure. Are you going to pick me up?"

"I usually pick you up, don't I?" Todd sensed the mood change but was unable to detect the reason. He knew she would eventually disclose it. "Yes, but I know you had lunch with Marquetta today. Oftentimes, you act differently after you've been with her. I know she's your friend, but she's a little, too religious for me."

"What do you mean by that?" Not waiting for an answer, Todd continued....: "Because she doesn't just go to church on Sunday, she tries to live according to her understanding of the Bible."

Juanita, with disdain in her voice, said, "I'm sorry, I forgot you get so testy when I say anything about her. But I have to say this, she needs to get out more often. She needs a man."

"How do you know what she needs? You don't know her." Todd said defensively.

"Wow, getting hyper, aren't you? She's not perfect you know!"

Todd realized he needed to make a point, but a defensive tone wasn't going to accomplish anything so he regrouped and spoke in a relaxed manner. "I never said she was. However, I don't try to find fault in others to cover my own." The style was relaxed but the blow hit hard.

She spouted, "What do you mean by that remark?"

Todd used his courtroom prowess to disarm her. He contended, "I'm saying that whenever Marquetta's name is mentioned, you suggest she's not perfect. I never said she was perfect. She's a friend of mine, that's all. But you've known me long enough to know I don't like anyone talking about my friends, male or female." Recognizing the battle was won and this wasn't the time to linger in his victory, he looked at his watch and said amicably, "Hey, I better get off this phone if I'm going to pick you up in a timely fashion. I should be at your place in about an hour. Better yet, I'll call you when I leave my house. That way you can time my arrival to your place."

Juanita, bewildered, managed to muster up the words, "Okay, bye-bye." Todd hung up the phone, grabbed his briefcase and left his office.

---

He listened to a jazz tape while he drove home and thought, *Two more days and then the weekend. What's wrong with me? Why am I looking forward to the weekend? This is my law firm. I have worked hard to get my clients and their accounts. Why am I not motivated by the opportunity to pick up new clients? Maybe I'll ask about my feelings tonight when I say my prayers.* He pulled into his parking space, got out of his car, locked his car door with his automatic lock, and went into his townhouse. Standing at the foyer, Todd looked around in admiration. He contemplated, *If I must say so myself, this is what a bachelor's pad should look like. To start with, dimmer switches on every switch in the house to set the mood. An open fireplace that faces both the formal dining room and the living room to give off a warm cozy feel. A gourmet kitchen to promote togetherness and a family room with a built-in aquarium to relax the mind.* He smiled as he reflected, *"I've convinced many women to say 'yes' in this place. Well, I don't have time to reminisce, I need a shower."* Todd went upstairs, walked into his bedroom, put his briefcase on the top shelf of his closet, then searched for his tux. Once he found it, he laid it on the bed and went into the bathroom that adjoined his bedroom. Todd looked in the mirror and decided to trim his mustache and facial hair on his chin and said, "I know I'm appealing to Markie. I'm a handsome, caramel colored African-American man. Six feet tall, light brown eyes with a thin mustache, and a nicely trimmed goatee. I exercise regularly, and most women love laying their heads on my chest. I have a grin that make most ladies melt. That's it! Markie is determined to ignore my qualities."

---

Myrna walked to her Volkswagen bug her father gave her as she pondered, *I better hurry up so I can stop and get something to eat before class starts. I don't care who thinks I'm wasting money getting a degree in Secretarial Management—it's a good field.* Myrna opened her car door and got in. She closed her door; put on her seatbelt, and buckled it before she put her key in the ignition and started the car. When she drove out of the parking space her thoughts drifted back to the reasons she picked her major. *With my skills, I can help businesses stay together. Mr. Parker understands his company couldn't function properly without my assistance. That's why he gives me a pay increase every time he gets a new client. Mr. Parker is a nice guy, but his problem is that he loves women. At least he did. I don't know what happened about two years ago with him and Ms. Logan, but he's changed. She's the only woman that can make him smile no matter what kind of day he's having. He stopped dating a lot of women, too. I think she's the one he's going to marry. Although he's still dating Ms. Smith.* Myrna said with hope in her voice. *Ms. Smith, honey, I think you lost him.*

She stopped near the campus to get a bite to eat and saw Marquetta.

Marquetta walked up to her and said, "Hi, Myrna. What are you doing in this area? Do you live around here?"

"No, I go to the University."

"Oh, you're in school. What's your major?"

Because of the flack Myrna received from friends about her major she hesitantly said, "Secretarial Management."

Marquetta, not understanding Myrna's response, asked, "Why did you say it like that? Don't you like your major?"

"Yeah, I like it, but most people make a negative comment about it."

"There's nothing wrong with your major. If you're pleased, don't worry about anyone else's opinion. Secretaries are critical in the work place. If I didn't have my secretary, Barbara, I don't know what I or my organization would do. You are your own person and you know why you want to major in Secretarial Management. One thing I learned a long time ago—do what makes you happy."

"Thank you for your comment. You've made me feel a lot better. I mean—a woman who has her own business and doing well appreciates my major!"

"Myrna, I'll let you in on a secret. I used to be a secretary and I think it allowed me to better understand the inner workings of operating a business."

"Really, that's good to know. Thanks a lot. Good bye."

"Good bye," said Marquetta. Myrna watched as Marquetta got into her car and drove off—then strutted to the store feeling more confident then ever about her major. Her strut resembled that of a peacock.

Myrna ruminated, *That's the first time I held a conversation with Ms. Logan. She's really nice. Now I see why Mr. Parker has a smile on his face when he talks to her. She encourages you. Now, I'm sure Ms. Smith doesn't stand a chance.*

---

Marquetta drove home contemplating the taped meeting with Tony Davis. *I'm glad Barbara stayed to be a witness and, took notes. I must make a note to reward Barbara for always being there for me. She doesn't have to stay late but she does without my asking. Poor Tony! He was so frightened. I could sense it in the tone of his voice as he spoke. Let me listen to this tape one more time before I contact Todd.* She put the tape in her cassette player in her car and pushed "play." Marquetta listened intently as the tape played. "Mr. Davis"

Tony interrupted, "Ms. Logan, please call me Tony."

Marquetta said, "Okay. Tony, we are asking your permission to tape this conversation. It may be used in a court of law at a later date. However, if you tell me that you do not want this conversation taped, we will not tape it, and it will not affect your current position in this company as a client. Now, having said all that, will you permit us to tape this conversation?"

Tony responded, "It's okay Ms. Logan, I have nothing to hide."

"Why are you smiling?"

"Because this is the first time I said it and meant it."

"Oh, okay. Tony, do you mind Ms. Barbara sitting in on this meeting? She will witness it."

"That's fine, I trust her. She's okay."

"Tony, tell me what happened when you reported for work at Mr. Greely's tow truck service. Let the record show that the name of the company is Greely's Towing Service."

"Well, I reported to Mr. Greely like you told me. I told him my name was Tony Davis and I was told to report here by Ms. Logan from Second Chance Inc. He said..." Marquetta interrupted him. "Who said?"

"I'm sorry, I should have said Mr. Greely introduced himself to me as William Greely, and his son as Robert. He told me I would be reporting to Robert and Robert would give me my work assignments. I said 'okay,' and then I said I meant 'yes sir.' Ms. Logan, I remembered you said to show that you have manners and respect for others and they will know you also respect yourself." Good—go on Tony, what happened next?"

"Oh yeah, Mr. Greely reminded me that I would be paid $7 a hour. He seemed pleased with that because he asked me if this was the first time I made that much money legally. I smiled and said 'yes sir.' Then Robert told me that I was to wash all the tow trucks every morning. They prided themselves on having the cleanest tow trucks in the area. Robert told me to broom sweep the trucks and throw away all trash found in them. If I found any, he instructed me to give them to his father. I said 'okay, but how do I get in the cars if they are locked?' Robert said, 'Sometimes the owners give us keys; other times we may have a master key that will fit them, or we may have to bust the locks. When you check the cars, check to see if the doors are open. If they are locked, check the office for keys. Busting the lock is the last resort on any car. Before you bust the lock, come get me.' I didn't tell him my mode of operation was grand theft auto. Do you think I should have?"

Marquetta said, "No, you did fine. He has no reason to know that information. Mr. William Greely, the owner, has been told and made the decision to hire you. You don't need to inform him or any of his employees about your past history even if he happens to be his son."

"I thought that was what you told us. I was just making sure because it was his son."

Marquetta said, "Go on Tony, what else happened?"

"A tow truck came in and Robert told me I could practice washing it. So I did. Robert was pleased with how quickly I washed the truck and said I was faster than he thought. When I finished. Robert said that would be all for the day. I had the job and he would see me tomorrow. Then Mr. William Greely called Robert and Robert told me to wait. He would be right back. When Robert came back, he asked me to move the truck I had just finished washing to lot 2. I told him I never drove a tow truck before. Robert asked me if I drove stick shift. I said 'yeah.' I thought, I may be a tow truck driver for them some day. Robert told me I could drive and how to put it in gear. I parked the tow truck on lot 2. Robert was with me the whole time. Robert told me to punch out and that I would get paid for the day. When I went in the office that's when things went crazy. Mr. William Greely told me I stole his tow truck and he was calling the police. I said, 'No sir, I didn't, I parked it on lot 2 and Robert has the keys. You can ask him.' William told me not to put his son in this situation. Then William told me he never said I should drive any of the trucks anywhere. Ms. Logan he was all in my face. I have to admit, I lost if for a second.

I said, 'Look, Man, it's not my fault you and your son got your wires crossed. But don't accuse me of stealing your truck.' I realized I was yelling, and prayed silently. After that I noticed I calmed down. Then, I asked to use the phone. I said I needed to call Ms. Logan. That's when William Greely called SCI. When Ms. Barbara called back and spoke with Mr. Greely and me, he changed his tune. William told me he concocted this scheme to let me know how serious he was about auto theft. He reminded me he was the boss and his word was final. I asked if I still had the job? William said, 'Report tomorrow, and you'll get paid for your time here today as well.'"

Marquetta said, "Is that everything that happened?"

"As far as I remember, yeah."

Marquetta said, "If you remember anything else, you can tell us and we will add it to this report, okay?"

"Yes ma'am."

"Tony, are you keeping a record of everything you're doing in the book given you by SCI?"

"No ma'am. I thought I would start when I get a job."

"Well, I want you to write down everything that happened today. I also want you to continue keeping a log of daily activities. Remember you recently were released from prison. You need a record of your daily activities. It will be for your benefit in the long run. Just think! You can look back and read your accomplishments."

"Okay."

"That will be all for now."

"Okay. Oh yeah, do you want me to report to work tomorrow? Remember, I have the job."

"You can report to William Greely tomorrow to start work or you can be reassigned to another employer, if you want. It's your decision. What do you think is best for you?"

"I like Robert. I think I'll enjoy working with him. Besides, I stole cars. Can you think of a better way to do it–than to work around all those cars daily and not take one? That would be an accomplishment I would love to read in my log book."

"Well, that's your answer. You can go back to Greely's Towing Service tomorrow. Now, if you change your mind later and want to be reassigned, you can be reassigned."

"Okay, thanks a lot. Oh yeah, Ms. Barbara and Ms. Logan, thanks for believing in me. Bye now."

"Good bye." Marquetta and Barbara responded in unison.

The tape cut off. Engrossed in the tape, Marquetta drove past her home. She mused, "I can't believe I passed by my condo, but I'm close to Todd's place. Instead of calling him tonight and playing the tape for him on the phone maybe I can catch him at home." She drove to his townhouse, saw Todd's automobile in his parking space, and stated, "Good, his car is here."

---

"Who is that ringing my doorbell? Let me hurry and dry off, then put on my robe," thought Todd. He said, "Coming! Who is it?"

Todd closed his robe and secured it with the belt as he ran down the steps. He went to his front door and peeped through the peephole then said, "Markie." Todd opened the door, smiled and said, "Hi, Markie. What's up?"

Marquetta asked, "Are you surprised to see me?"

"Yeah, but I shouldn't be. Come in and have a seat." Marquetta entered Todd's house but wouldn't take a seat. She opted to stand by the closed door, holding the tape in her hand. After Todd closed the door, he stood in front of her to make certain she noticed him as he continued talking. "When you want something, you can become a persistent little pest." Todd's lips closed gently and formed a slight smile which exposed a deep dimple. His intoxicating eyes began to dance and his face, took on a sensuous appearance. He used his infamous grin to try to draw her.

Marquetta replied nonchalantly, "Thanks a lot. You sure know how to make a lady feel wanted. Why don't you go upstairs and get dressed? I can talk loud enough for you to hear me."

Todd, recognizing he struck out again, shrugged his shoulders then said, "Thanks," to her suggestion. Todd ran upstairs and shouted, "Go on." He left the bedroom door open so he could hear her. "I've been listening to the tape of my meeting with Tony Davis. I think you'll want to listen. It could be innocent, but I don't think so. Call and tell me what you think after you hear it. Thanks, I can let myself out."

"Wait, I can walk out with you." Todd stated as he came down the stairs in formal dinner attire. "Markie, you are my favorite pest. Come by anytime. If I'm not home, leave a message for me. You know you mean a lot to me, don't you?"

"Thanks, Todd." Marquetta thought it best to change the conversation, so she inquired, "Where are you and Juanita going tonight?"

"How do you know I have a date with Juanita?"

"She's the only girl you date with money. You're wearing formal dinner attire. Come on, give me a break."

"Are you sure you're not a detective?"

Marquetta laughed with her mouth closed but her smile was broad and her eyes glittered. In a sincere voice she said, "You look very handsome. Give me a call later and tell me what you think of the tape." Not wanting to leave her presence, Todd followed Marquetta to her car. Neither uttered a word but both had contented smiles on their faces. Once at the car, to remain in her presence a while longer, he knew he had to speak. "May I ask you a question?"

"Sure. What is it?"

"You never told me what you think of Juanita, Markie. Why?" This time when Todd called Marquetta by the nickname he gave her, her mind went back to the conversation she had had with Sam Brooks. She realized the only person she knew that called her Markie was Todd..

Marquetta gasped, then said, "That's right, you're the only person I know that calls me Markie. You tricked me. Who is Sam Brooks?"

Todd hesitantly confessed, "He's my brother. He's coming into town on Thursday. Since I told him so much about you, he asked me to put in a good word for him. He wanted to go out with you. I told him no one could convince you to date anybody. It has to be your choice. He asked me what I knew about you. I told him I knew you loved the people in your old neighborhood. That's when he came up with the 'old high school buddy coming back in town,' routine. Are you angry? I'm sorry. It was one of those days I was frustrated again about our not going out, and I complained to Sam. I needed a shoulder to cry on and he was there. Now, he's using it against me. I love my brother, but sometimes he can be a trip.

"Boy, you're not giving me a good opinion of him. Anyway, it's just a date to the banquet. But I think I have an idea why my dating him may make you uncomfortable. Especially since I refuse to date you again. We usually discuss everything, except we haven't discussed what happened two years ago. I think it's time we discuss it. It will probably do us both a world of good. Let me know when you're free."

Todd, wanting more time with Marquetta, smiled and asked, "Do you want to talk now?"

"No, you have a dinner engagement, remember? I'll talk to you later." As Todd began to walk away Marquetta queried, "Oh, by the way, do you have a picture of your brother?" Todd was very confident in himself and his walk made that statement. His head positioned to focus straight ahead as he, took even strides while his arms moved in unison with his legs. Todd had been instructed to walk by his father. Todd walked back toward her car, pulled out his wallet and showed Marquetta a picture of him and his brother at the beach. Marquetta commented, "He looks just like you, except he's a little heavier and has a deeper hue. He's very attractive, Todd. He's probably more of a ladies' man than you. Marquetta was looking at Todd when she made that statement and saw the concern in his eyes. She said, "Oh, so that's what's bothering you. Todd, I'm not having sex with anyone. I will make love to my husband only! If your brother wants to have sex with me, he's going to have to marry me." She smiled and said, "Stop looking so concerned—this is just a date. I'll talk to you tomorrow. Good bye."

"No, wait! You never answered my question about Juanita."

"Todd, it's not for me to give you advice about a person you date. You know her better than I do. I only know what you tell me or what I may have observed being around the two of you. Besides, her behavior around me could be different because I am a female. Let's face it. The two of you are having sex, and not, too many women enjoy their sex partner's having a female friend. Do you know what I mean? I'm not going to try to bias your thinking."

"Why do you always know what to say?"

"I'm being truthful. When I was living that lifestyle there was a connection—a type of ownership I felt with some of the men I dated. With those men, I didn't like other women around. Although, I was so caught up in the lifestyle of having sex whenever I felt the need, sometimes I slept with a guy to satisfy my physical need and had no personal interest in him at all. It's a terrible lifestyle. I never want to get involved in it again. I thank God for opening my eyes and for forgiving me of the sin of fornication. God is good." She smiled and said, "Go to your engagement. I'll talk to you later. Good bye."

"Good bye. I'll call you."

———————

Todd opened the door to his car and got in, then put the key in the ignition to start the car. The second the engine began to purr, Todd's car phone rang. He answered it. "Hello."

Juanita said, "I thought you were going to call and let me know when you were leaving!"

As soon as she began to talk he put the phone on speaker and commenced driving out of his parking lot and onto the main thoroughfare. He replied, "I'm sorry. Something came up. I'm on my way to you now."

"I'll be downstairs in the lobby waiting for you," said Juanita.

"I should be there in about 20 minutes. Good bye."

———————

"Suzette, who is it?" Juanita inquired. Those who met Suzette often referred to her as a woman's woman. Meaning… she had everything that made her a woman twice over. She was a large breasted woman with a hefty rump and weighty calves. She stood six feet one inch tall, yet was a very modest lady. Suzette covered the phone receiver with her hand and said, "I keep asking her, but she won't tell me."

"I'll take it!" Juanita, took the phone from Suzette and stated harshly, "This is Juanita Smith. Who is this?"

"Hi, Baby, it's your mother," Loretta mentioned cunningly as she sat at the table in her hotel room glimpsing through a tourist brochure on the state of Maryland. Juanita, took the phone with her as she walked onto her balcony. She sat in one of the lavender cushioned patio chairs, near her patio table with matching lavender umbrella, as she placed the phone on the table. Incensed that her mother called her at her home, Juanita blurted, "I thought I told you not to call me here!" With her high heels firmly planted on the balcony floor, one hand was gripping the phone and the other formed in the shape of a fist on her leg. She was ready for battle. Juanita was fearing her mother would disrupt her life again.

Loretta anticipated Juanita's reaction to her call. With a conniving look on her face she proceeded. "I'm sorry, Baby, I didn't give her my name. I just want to know, are you going to help me?"

Juanita responded sharply, "The account I have with a sum of money that large is a joint account with Daddy. I'll see what I can do. Why did you come back here, anyway?"

Loretta gave a sentimental response, "I thought you would be glad to hear from your Momma. After all, you haven't seen me since you were a little girl."

Determined she wasn't going to buy into her mother's mush, she disclaimed, "I was eight, Mother, eight. That didn't seem to bother you much then, me seeing my Mother. Because you left."

Still trying to sound sweet, Loretta declared in a softer tone, "I explained that to you when I called your office. Your Daddy made me leave and he wouldn't let me take you with me."

Juanita said sarcastically, "You forgot to tell me how much you fought Daddy for me."

Loretta remarked, "You know your Daddy is a powerful black man in this area and was, even back then. I had no money to fight him."

"Look, don't make my daddy the heavy," Juanita said defensively. "The way I heard it, you had an affair with his junior partner. He caught you!"

"Honey, your daddy was so absorbed in his business and making money, he forgot about me and my needs. Warren was his flunky. He owned less than 10 percent of the company, so whenever a problem arose at the office, Earl would stay to handle it and send Warren to check on me. So I decided I might as well make use of Warren's services, too. Your father happened to walk in on us one day."

"So you were willing to sacrifice living as a wealthy woman for a lay in the hay. Mother, you're not smart, are you? You think I should trust $50,000 in your hands. I want Daddy to check out this investment. I don't want to loose my money dealing with a woman who was willing to throw hers away for a one-nighter. Basically, that's all it adds up to. You had nothing to gain from it."

"My dear daughter, I don't need any lessons from you. Are you going to lend me the money or not? If not, I'll just make myself more visible around these parts. I'm sure someone will remember me as Earl Smith's ex-wife and Juanita's mother. You do understand that I've been out of money for some time. My clothes are tattered and torn. My shoes have holes in them and my hair is uncombed. I'm sure that would make juicy conversation in your circle of friends."

"Mother, I'll see what I can do. Bye."

"Bye, Baby."

---

"I cannot believe my mother. She would try to embarrass my father by looking like a bum around his business associates and clients. Knowing Daddy, he wouldn't have the sense enough to see how humiliating that could be, not just for him, but for me, too. Just what I need—as if this is the only thing plaguing me right now. I'll check with Todd to see if I could pull from my joint account with Daddy without his getting a copy of the statement. To get back to more important things, let me take one more look at myself before I go to the lobby and wait for Todd." Juanita walked to her bedroom and closed the door. The walls in her bedroom were panels of mirrors. She looked at herself from different views, smiled sensuously and thought, "I'm a beautiful chocolate brown African-American woman. Five feet, three inches of ecstasy—with a butt that men go wild over. Todd better get his act together and marry me soon or I'll find me someone who will."

---

Todd came into the lobby of the building and said, "Hello, Juanita, you look nice." The lobby's carpet was so thick that you could sink your feet into it and not see the heel of a man's shoe. The furniture was traditional. Looking as if it came straight from Ethan Allen's showroom floors.

"Thanks Todd. Where have you been these days? I haven't heard from you in a while."

"I've had a lot on my mind, in addition to working long hours."

"I hope I've been on your mind, too." Juanita said as she batted her eyes.

"Yeah, I have been thinking about you, but I think we better continue this conversation in the car."

"Todd…oh nothing. You're right. We're running late." Juanita started to ask Todd about the joint account she had with her father, but decided against it. She didn't want him to know about her mother, at least not now."

---

Marquetta drove home, content in knowing the real name of her date. She thought, *I can't wait to tell Barbara that Todd's brother is taking me to the banquet.*

As soon as Marquetta got settled in her condo, she sat in her over-stuffed light blue leather chair with accompanying hassock and phoned Barbara. The second Barbara picked up her phone Marquetta said, "Hello, Barbara. It's Marquetta, what are you doing?"

Barbara could hardly stay seated on her sofa when she heard Marquetta's voice. She felt like she was going to burst with joy. She replied happily, "I've been trying to reach you. Before you say anything, guess what?" Without pause, Barbara continued, "I'm getting married. Do you believe that? I'm getting married to Phillip James."

"Jubilantly, Marquetta asked, "Are you serious?"

"He asked me tonight."

"I thought he was out of town for a month on business."

"He is! He called to tell me he was in his hotel room and was so lonesome that he went to the bar hoping to find someone there he could talk to, to pass the time. He then realized he wasn't really lonesome, he just missed not being with me. That's when he said it, 'Barbara, will you be my wife. I mean—would you marry me?' I was so surprised that I said, 'What did you say?' He repeated it. I said yes. He wants to get married very soon. So it won't be a big wedding but that's all right with me. Five years without sex! I'm ready for a husband. More importantly, I love Phillip. He is the nicest man I've ever known. So patient and kind, too. I feel so comfortable around him. You know I've been praying about Phillip, asking God if he is the one. I got my answer tonight. I'm so happy."

"I'm so happy for you. You know I love you both. You're like the brother and sister I never had. Let me know how I can help."

Barbara heard the sincerity in Marquetta's voice and said, "I had to tell you. I knew you would be genuinely happy for us and I wanted you to share in our joy. We are sisters you know. We are sisters in Christ."

Tears swelled in Marquetta's eyes and her voice was squeaky with emotion as she said, "That's true, we are." She cleared her throat, collected herself then continued. "Barbara, since you and Phillip participate in the singles group at church, do you think Pastor Green will still have the two of you go through counseling? After all, we discuss marriage and its responsibility in our meetings."

"Knowing Pastor Green, we will."

"You're probably right. Have you told him yet."

"No, you were the first person I told. I'll call him tomorrow."

"Oh, that's good. Barbara, I want to thank you for staying late with me and keeping the office running smoothly. I want to treat you. Would you like to go shopping with me tomorrow evening? That way, I can treat you to dinner or buy you something."

"I would love to go shopping tomorrow and have dinner out. Dinner out would be a treat. I haven't been out in almost a month— ever since Phillip left town. But you don't have to treat me. You know I love my job. I like the free reign you give me, and the last look at our staff salaries revealed I'm the highest-paid employee."

That's because you can run Second Chance, Inc., as well as I can. I've been thinking about making you my Executive Assistant, but I'm going to need you to train the new secretary. Also, on cases like Tony Davis, I'll still want you to be the only person handling the tapes and the reports. That means from time to time, you'll still have to type and file. Will that be okay with you?"

"Marquetta, that's fine. Thank you for the confidence in my work ability, but I can't run Second Chance, Inc., the way you do. I may be able to keep things running smoothly, only because you showed me how. But you're the businesswoman. That may be why Mr. Greely changed his tune."

"Oh, Barbara, thank you for reminding me what I called to tell you?" Barbara bringing Marquetta's thoughts back to work reminded her of the phone call she had with Sam.

"What?"

"That Sam Brooks is really Todd's brother Sam."

Barbara scratched her head as she pondered Marquetta's statement. She then replied with a question, "You mean the guy that called and said he was a guy from your high school was really Todd's brother?"

"Exactly. Todd told me this evening. Well, really I guessed it and he confirmed it."

"You guessed it? How?" Barbara asked curiously.

"I kept trying to place him and couldn't, so then I started thinking about people I knew who called me 'Markie.' I couldn't think of anyone. I dropped the tape at Todd's townhouse and when we started talking, it hit me. Nobody that I know calls me 'Markie' but Todd. So it had to be someone he knew. So I asked him."

"Do you really think it's fair for you to go out with Sam, knowing he's Todd's brother? You know how Todd feels about you."

"Barbara, Todd's a ladies' man. What I mean by that is, no matter how much he says he thinks he cares for me, I don't believe he's willing to wait until we marry to make love. He wants sex. But the interesting thing is, I think the reason he is attracted to me is because I'm abstaining. This date with Sam may be what Todd and I need to clarify our relationship. Barbara, I'm glad I'm abstaining, although it can be difficult at times. I'm able to view things differently. Think about it, when we were in that lifestyle how many times were we willing to, and/or *did* compromise our standards, just to say we had a man?"

"Don't remind me. Phillip was a welcome change—a man who cares about my needs as well as his own, and willing to satisfy me rather than himself. Thank you, Father God."

"That's what I'm talking about, a man of God. You can't beat it."

"But I think Todd knows the type of woman he wants. He just needs to find out the kind of man he needs to be to have her," said Barbara.

Marquetta asked, "Do you know who I empathize with?"

"Who?"

"Juanita. She's putting all this time and energy in him and I don't think he'll marry her. I think he likes the contacts and the prestige she brings him and his company, but I don't think he loves her."

"Why do you say that?"

"Well, he asked me how I felt about her? But now that I think about it, maybe he is thinking about marrying her again. That could be why he wanted my opinion."

"What did you tell him?"

"You know it wouldn't be right for me to give my opinion of her. Basically, that's what I told him."

"That was the right answer. But I have to admit I don't empathize with Juanita. I think she's using her prestige and contacts to pull him and once he gives in, he's in trouble. We know Todd has scruples; Juanita has none. Remember, Juanita thinks she's every man's heartthrob—which means—she picked Todd; he didn't pick her."

"That's probably true. However, we can't excuse Todd's part in this. He understands marrying her could increase his business immensely."

"Marquetta, you and I have discovered something about Todd that not, too many women have, and that is, he wants to play the field but he wants to marry someone that doesn't."

"Well, I have to agree with you there. In these times you wouldn't think men still thought like that, but some do."

"Maybe more than we think!"

"That's true. Oh, Barbara before I forget—Todd is going to be in touch with you while I'm gone concerning Mr. Greely or any problems you may have. Thanks for the itinerary. Note on your calendar that I won't be in the office until that following Monday. You did keep a copy of my itinerary for yourself, didn't you?"

"Of course. Marquetta, I have to say this!"

Marquetta detected concern in Barbara's voice, so she responded immediately. "What?"

Barbara posed a thought provoking question. "Why would Todd's brother want to go out with you?"

Marquetta sat up more attentively in her chair, bit her bottom lip lightly, and squinched her eyes a little as if trying to remember her conversation with Todd on the subject. Then she spoke, "Todd told me I was on his mind one night when he was talking to him, so he mentioned me. I guess it made Sam curious."

Barbara felt disquieted. She sensed a motive. She explained, "I don't like it. I think brother wants to show Todd the way to treat a lady—if you know what I mean!" When Barbara said the last sentence, her head went down, then up, in slow motion.

With both lips turned inside, Marquetta nodded her head, understanding the profoundness of the statement. "That could be it. Todd seemed to be worried, but I'm not going to be troubled by it. I tell you what, you pray for Sam and me and this date, and I'll do the same."

Barbara looked at her watch, then said, "Okay. Look at the time. I better go. I have to be at work tomorrow."

Marquetta laughed and said, "Good bye."

# CHAPTER 3

# LOOK WHAT HAPPENED!

Barbara remembered her conversation with Marquetta as she prayed and said, "Father God, please let Marquetta marry the man you have for her. In Jesus' name. Amen." She read her Bible and went to sleep.

---

Marquetta dressed for bed, then knelt down beside the end of her bed and prayed, "Father God, please lead and guide me. Please protect me on my date with Sam and let me marry the man you have for me. Please give me strength to continue to wait on you. In Jesus' name. Amen." She read from her Bible and went to sleep.

---

Once Juanita and Todd left her father's home, Juanita knew she had to make known her feelings on how she wanted the evening to end. She hated the fact that he had bucket seats because she couldn't get close to him so she decided to use her left hand to play with his ear lobe closest to her, as Todd drove. Todd didn't respond, so she said, "It's late. You don't have to drive me to D.C. tonight. The last time I was over at your townhouse, I left an outfit. I can wear that tomorrow," said Juanita.

Todd smiled to himself, then said, without taking his eyes of the road, "No bother, I'd rather take you home. I have work to do, so I won't be good company for you. Besides, I have to be at the airport by 6:00 a.m. to pick up my brother."

Since you have to go to the airport—why don't you stop by your townhouse, pick up a change of clothes, your work and stay at my condo? It's closer to the airport and if you bring him by my place, I can have breakfast waiting for both of you."

"Juanita, I don't want you going out of your way for my brother and me."

"No problem. I insist on helping a friend in need. What do you say?"

Hesitantly Todd said, "Okay." Todd drove to his townhouse, picked up some clothes, the tape Marquetta gave him, earphones, and a tape recorder. *I really don't like Juanita in my business, especially when I'm helping Markie. But I can't hurt her feelings after the evening I had at her father's house. I picked up three new clients, even though Earl Smith doesn't use my firm. Not bad, if I say so myself. But, I'm still not sleeping with her. I'll make that clear on the drive to her condo, thought Todd.* As Todd was preparing to leave he heard his car horn and thought, *She can be so thoughtless at times. Blowing the horn this late at night. Let me get out of here before she wakes all my neighbors.*

Juanita leaned over to open the door for Todd. She hoped he noticed her breast pushing out of her dress and was aroused. As Todd got in the car he noticed the tightness of the dress and said, "Is that dress comfortable?"

"Why do you ask?" Juanita inquired alluringly.

"Oh, no reason," Todd said impassively. He thought, *I don't want to offend her, but can she breathe comfortably in that dress?*

Juanita smiled and thought, *He's jealous because the other men at dinner saw so much of me. But it was worth it to get Todd to notice me.* To Todd she said, "Don't be jealous, all this is for you to enjoy." She put her left hand on his right thigh and squeezed it.

Unrelenting, Todd explained, "I told you not tonight. I have work to do. In fact, I was thinking I should sleep in the guest room. That way, I can do my work without disturbing you."

Juanita pouted and said, "I want you to sleep with me. We haven't had sex in months. What's going on? Are you seeing someone else? Don't tell me Miss Goody-two-shoes has convinced you to abstain!"

"Juanita, I told you, I have a lot of things on my mind right now and I have work I want to do tonight." Todd, recognizing her frustration, leaned over and kissed her on the cheek as he stopped at a light. Todd hoped that kiss would quiet her. The rest of the way to her condo Juanita plotted ways to change his mind once they arrived at her place. But, to her surprise, she suddenly couldn't stop yawning. By the time they actually arrived at her condo she realized she was very tired. When Todd put her key in her condo door and opened it, she walked in yawning. She thought, *I'm so sleepy. Todd's decision to sleep in the guest room was a good idea, after all.*

---

As Juanita undressed she threw her clothes on the chair in her room, put on a silk night gown, and dived into bed Her eyes closed the minute she covered herself with a pink satin sheet. Her eyes sprung open when she remembered she hadn't set her alarm clock. She reached for her clock on the night stand by her bed, set the alarm, and put the clock back on the night stand. As she dozed off, she thought, *Suzette will hang my clothes up tomorrow. I just want to go to sleep.*

---

Todd, took off his clothes, hung them up with the clothes he had brought over to Juanita's, with the exception of his pajamas. He, took the pajamas off the hanger and put them on. When he finished putting on his night clothes, he sat on the side of the bed closest to the night stand and put the tape in the tape recorder. He inserted the earphones in his ears, which he was happy he remembered to bring, and hit "play." With a probing attitude, he listened to the tape twice. Then he ejected the tape and put it inside his pillowcase. He didn't want Juanita to get her hands on this tape. He put the tape recorder and earphones in his duffle bag. Todd got on his knees and prayed. "Father God, I am so confused. Help me sort out my life. In Jesus' name. Amen."

---

Todd awoke by the humming noise of a vacuum cleaner. He stretched, gathered his thoughts as he looked around then remembered he was at Juanita's. He also remembered Sam would be at the airport waiting for him by 6:00 a.m. He looked at the clock on the dresser and saw it was 7:30 a.m. He grabbed the tape and put it in his pants' pocket. He put on his clothes hurriedly and walked out the door as he shouted, "Miss Suzette, tell Juanita I'll call her later. I have to get my brother from the airport."

To Todd's surprise, as he entered the parking lot, he noticed Sam in Juanita's car. They had just arrived. He looked straight at the car with his mouth opened. Juanita loved having surprised Todd by picking up his brother, whom she knew he respected. Juanita thought, *I scored big this time.* As she got out of the car she said to Todd, "I surprised you, didn't I? I told Sam you were probably still sleeping and I would let him wake you. Well, I underestimated you, you're up and dressed."

As soon as she parked, Sam got out of the car and walked toward Todd. When Sam was near Todd he said, "Oh, by the way, Little Brother, close your mouth." Once Todd closed his mouth, Sam embraced him with a hug, a kiss on the cheek, and a hand shake.

Todd said, "Hi, big brother don't start giving me orders already, I don't care if they are needed. Both laughed and walked toward the building where Juanita's condo was housed.

Once in Juanita's condo the three took a seat on the sofa. Juanita liked the idea of having a man on each side of her. When Suzette heard the voices she came out of the kitchen and said, "Mr. Todd, I'm glad Miss Juanita caught you. You ran out of here so fast I couldn't tell you Miss Juanita wanted you to stay here. She went to get your brother."

"I'm sorry Miss Suzette for not asking you any questions. That's my fault."

"That's okay, Mr. Todd. Miss Juanita, should I prepare breakfast now?"

"Yes, but first show Sam to the guest room so he can freshen up. Sam followed Suzette to the guest room. Todd said, "Excuse me, Juanita, I dressed so hurriedly I didn't have time for a shower and shave. I'll take one now." Todd went to the guest room where Sam was to apologize, "I'm sorry I overslept. I'm glad Juanita remembered and picked you up. Were you waiting long?"

"No, as a matter of fact, she was there when I arrived."

Todd exclaimed. "Really?"

"Why that response, Little Brother?"

Todd, in a calmer tone reasoned, "Nothing really—it's just that Juanita is not noted for her promptness unless it will benefit her. I don't know how she figures you could benefit her. I never told her what you did for a living. I told her your work involved meeting with and working for top businessmen."

"That's all she needs to know." Sam put a Cheshire cat grin on his face before he continued. "Little Brother, you didn't tell me that you're thinking about getting married." Is this true or is this another one with her nose wide open?"

"Man, I don't know. I have contemplated it. Juanita has been pushing me to live with her, but that doesn't seem right to me. Plus, you know Ma and Dad are not modern parents, and I am getting up in age. I might as well get married. I want a family. Anyway, nothing is definite."

Sam asked, "So, are you telling me that Markie is free game?"

"You haven't met her. How do you know if you're going to like her? Anyway, I doubt if she gives you a second thought."

Sam inquired excitedly. "Do you want to bet?"

"No, Sam, I don't!"

Sam tried to persuade Todd. "Come on, Little Brother. Let's see if she gives me a second thought. If she does, her abstention period will have ended. You know how I love to break them in, but in her case, in again."

Impassioned, Todd declared, "Wait a minute, Sam! Markie is a close friend of mine and I'm not going to watch you try to destroy her and her beliefs."

Sam decided to pry. "What's the problem? Do you want her?"

Todd, refusing to let Sam know his feelings toward Marquetta, responded in a serious tone. "Markie and I are very close. I'm not looking to write her down in my book of conquests. You know, Sam, I don't think you respect any woman except Momma."

"That's not true. I respect Aunt Rita, too." Sam chuckled.

"Sam, really, two women out of all the women in the world. You're a sick man."

Sam decided to irritate Todd by whining as he spoke. "What's the fuss? Do you want me to respect Markie? I can't promise you that, but I can say if we get together, she'll respect me. Ya know what I mean?"

"There are plenty of women that you can go out with while you're in town. Why are you so determined to go out with Markie?"

"I just want to be with the woman that has my brother's heart in her hand."

"Because I respect the woman, she has my heart in her hand. Todd, not wanting to hear any more of Sam's comments, turned away from his brother and walked out the door as he said, "Sam, I'm going to use the shower in Juanita's bedroom. I'll see you at breakfast."

Sam laughed and said, "Okay, Little Brother, I hear ya." Sam thought, *Juanita is right. This woman is trying to prevent Todd from having the best things life has to offer. Not, too many African-American males have an opportunity to marry into money. Earl Smith is considered an insurance magnate around these parts, not to mention the power he has acquired from the consortium he developed. This man carries a lot of weight in the community. His daughter has a lot to offer in the looks department, too. She sounds like she likes to please her man. Now that I think about it, Little Brother, better make a decision fast, she may be put on my list, too. He gave a loud laugh.*

Todd thought, *He won't like Markie. I'm almost sure of it. Oh, he'll like her looks, but if they talk for more than five minutes he's going to find out she is serious about her Christianity. She'll probably invite him to church.* Todd laughed loudly and thought, *He never liked a woman who was active in church. I have nothing to worry about. Sam, my brother, you are in for a surprise.* Sam and Todd seemed to finish showering and dressing around the same time. They met in the hallway leading to Juanita's breakfast room. Once they were seated at the table Suzette brought each a plate topped high with hot pancakes and surrounded with eggs, sausage, and bacon strips. Todd, Sam, and Juanita had polite conversation as they ate. When Sam noticed Todd glancing at his watch he said, "Breakfast was delicious. Thanks Juanita for such fine hospitality. Todd, does Suzette fix you breakfast this good every time you spend the night?"

"Yes, Miss Suzette feeds me well whenever I'm here."

Sam tried to charm Juanita when he stated, "Juanita I just don't understand that boy. I don't think I would go home if I had the opportunity to eat this good and be with a beautiful woman like you."

Juanita smiled and said, "Thanks, Sam. If your little brother isn't careful, he could lose some fringe benefits to you."

"Little Brother, did you hear that? Hold on to your good thing!"

Todd rose from his chair as he said, "Sam, come on, we have to go. He walked to where Juanita was seated and kissed her on the cheek, then said, "Thanks, I'll call you."

Sam said, "Juanita, it has been a pleasure meeting you. Perhaps the three of us can get together before I leave."

"That would be nice," replied Juanita. "Good bye."

———

Hearing the phone ring, Suzette answered, "Miss Juanita's residence. How may I help you?"

A woman with a brash voice said, "Is she in?"

"Yes ma'am."

"Let me speak to her!"

"Just a moment, I'll see if she's available, but first, may I ask who's calling?"

"Loretta Smith, her mother!"

"Hold on." Suzette went to the balcony where Juanita was seated and said, "It's Loretta Smith, your mother."

Juanita, perturbed because her mother gave Suzette that information, picked up the phone and said angrily, "What do you want? Didn't I tell you I would call you? This is going to take some careful planning on my part, if I'm going to be able to help you at all. I just can't pull $50,000 out of my joint account with Daddy without his finding out about it."

"I know that much would take some time. But you can give me

some money now, can't ya? You do have your own company. Can you give me a couple of thousand to tide me over?"

"What do you mean 'tide you over?' Do you mean that you need money to put down on a contract or something to help sustain you? Because, I need to check out this business transaction before I commit myself to a contract. Whether you like it or not, I respect my father's opinion in business. I want him to look at the contract and check the books before I commit. So, if you think this is going to be an easy ride, you are sadly mistaken." Loretta still trying to remind Juanita of their relationship replied, "Regardless of what you think of me, I am your mother and I love you. I wouldn't try to waste your money. I'm trying to become a businesswoman you'll be proud of. One you can discuss at your high-falutin' meetings and dinner parties I hear Earl is always having at the mansion. But if you want people to always refer to your mother as a loser, that can happen, too. Especially if you won't help me. Think about the future—when you have your children. What are you going to tell them when they ask about your mother? She's a loser, a tramp, or she's a businesswoman?"

Juanita thought, I *sure like the idea of her becoming a business-woman before Todd meets her. He has such respect for his parents.* She said, "Mother, I told you I would help you. Give me your address. I'll mail you a check today for $500. Bye, Mother." After Juanita hung up the phone, her thoughts immediately went to Suzette and her father. *Suzette is going to tell Violet that Momma called and Violet will tell Daddy. Sometimes they're so loyal to Daddy I could scream! I realize they have been working for Daddy for years, but he doesn't need to know everything. Really! It's bad enough I couldn't move into this condo unless Suzette was willing to move with me. To think how much money I spent convincing her, we could have a good time living together. A woman old enough to be my mother! I still have to take her to a movie every once in a while or she'll remind me by saying, 'when you asked me to move with you, you said we would go to the movies a lot together. I haven't been to the movies in a long time.' Daddy treats them like family. Although, he is good to all his employees. I heard he even gave Warren a good job reference after he caught him with*

*Momma. Of course that could have been a condition of the buy out. He did own a small percentage in Daddy's company. Daddy's parents must have been wimps, because they didn't teach him how to be ruthless. He became an insurance magnate and founder of the consortium only because he's smart and has good business sense, not because he's grim. I'm pugnacious. People who work for me know I want only one thing and that's the deal. If they cannot cut it then they have fired themselves.* She loved that last thought. That was her motto. She, then, looked at the glare of the sun on her red finger nails with a small gold leaf on each finger and smiled.

---

Myrna was on the phone talking to Earl Smith when Todd and Sam walked into the office. Myrna wrote Earl Smith's name and a question that said, "Do you want to speak to him?" on a blank sheet of paper and gave it to Todd. Todd read the note, then threw the paper in the trash. He turned to his brother and then looked at Myrna and said, "Yes, I'll take it, but first, Myrna, I would like to introduce you to my brother Sam Parker. Sam, I would like you to meet Myrna, my secretary. Myrna, make Sam comfortable in the lounge area, please. Offer him something to read and drink. Thanks. I'll buzz you when I'm ready for you to escort him to my office. Okay?"

"Okay," responded Myrna.

Todd went to his office and made himself comfortable before he answered the call. "Hello, Mr. Smith, what can I do for you?"

Earl Smith answered briskly, "Todd, I want to know if you are serious about my daughter? I don't want her reputation smudged because you enjoy playing house. My name does carry some weight in this area and people have a tendency to listen to my suggestions. So, I'm sure you'll understand when I tell you my daughter is no toy, young man!"

Todd was taken aback by Mr. Smith's boldness. To him this was a personal matter, so he was determined he wouldn't let Mr. Smith make him sweat. He said, "I'm not, I mean 'not' in the sense that I'm ready to marry her. However, Mr. Smith, I must admit I have contemplated marrying your daughter. Unfortunately, this is the best answer I can give you right now."

Earl, astonished at Todd's blatant honesty had, to rethink his next response. Once collected, he said, "I would like to meet with you on a business matter. Call my secretary and schedule an appointment for some time next week." Click.

Todd held the phone a moment in disbelief. Then he did what he had been doing for years when he needed clarity and understanding on a subject. He pushed his private line that had a direct dial number on it. The phone rang.

Marquetta answered, "Hello."

"Markie, you're not going to believe this! Guess who called me this morning?" Todd continued non-stop. "He was on the line when I got in the office—Earl Smith. You know, Earl Smith the insurance magnate. Mr. 'I am the man and everybody should want to know me.' He had the audacity to ask me how I felt about his daughter. Whose business is that? I'm telling you, Markie, he made me so angry. I don't know what to do? What are your plans for the day? I need to see you. I need to unwind."

The minute Marquetta heard the tone in Todd's voice she stopped packing her suitcase and sat on the corner of the bed near her suitcase. She held the earpiece of the phone pressed to her ear, as if trying not to miss a single word. Her right arm formed a L-shape across her stomach and her left arm that was holding the phone seemed to be resting on her right fingers. This was her pose whenever she was listening intently on the phone. As she listened attentively to his conversation, she heard a pause. She knew he was ready for her to speak. She said, "I'll be home until 4:00 p.m. Barbara and I are going out this evening." Her voice filled with compassion said, "Todd, don't let Earl Smith get to you. He's a man that loves his daughter that's all. I think you need to count to ten slowly. Better yet, say a prayer."

There was a long pause, then Todd said, "I did, just now. Thank you for reminding me."

"You're welcome." Marquetta remembered Todd was to pick up his brother from the airport so she inquired, "Todd, you can come over, but what time do you have to pick up your brother from the airport?"

Marquetta's question jolted Todd's memory. His fingers covered his forehead in a worried pose as he closed his eyes for a quick minute then replied, "Oh, he's in the lounge area in my office. I was so mad I forgot all about him. Do you mind if I bring him?" Marquetta smiled then responded, "After all, he is going to be my date tomorrow night. He may be looking forward to meeting me. Of course, you can bring him. What time should I expect you?"

Todd said, "I need to talk to you about business, too. I'll do that later tonight, okay?"

"Well I could come to your office. That way we can talk and when you're ready to introduce Sam to me, you can."

"Good idea. What time should I expect you?"

Marquetta replied, "Let's say 1:30 p.m.. Is that good for you?"

"Fine, see ya then. Good bye."

"Good bye," said Marquetta.

---

As Marquetta entered Todd's place of business, she was cheerfully greeted by Myrna. "Hi, Marquetta."

You're prompt as usual. Mr. Parker is with his brother. Do you want me to interrupt?"

"Have they been together all morning?"

"Mostly, Mr. Parker had a 12:30 p.m. appointment, so his brother just went back in his office.

He's been sitting out here with me. He's not like my boss. He's arrogant."

Marquetta laughed and said, "Thanks for telling me. He's my date for a banquet I'm speaking at on Friday. At least I know who I'm dealing with now."

"I didn't think you knew him, because of his remark, 'I want to meet this Markie person. When is she coming here. She'll probably be late—typical woman. Always wanting to make you wait.'"

"Thanks, Myrna, for the information. How would you like to get together with Barbara and me one evening at my place?"

"That would be great. Thanks for the invitation."

Marquetta said, "I'll tell Barbara, but it won't be for a couple of weeks because I'm leaving for the Caribbean on Saturday."

"That's fine. Oh yeah, before I forget, thank you for the

encouragement. That was just what I needed."

"That's wonderful! I'm glad I could help. You can call me anytime. Do me a favor, announce me now. Thanks."

When Myrna announced Marquetta, Sam came out of Todd's office with a big grin on his face, to hold the office door for her. As she walked through the opening in the door, she smiled and said, "Thank you." She sat in her favorite chair near the door.

Todd smiled at her admiringly as she, took her seat. He thought, "She looks beautiful. She always knows how to dress modestly, yet appealingly. Her feminine characteristics exude her." Todd searched Sam's eyes for a response. Sam's eyes were dancing. Todd believed they said, "I want her." Todd was not pleased.

Marquetta, unaware of the affect her appearance was having on the brothers, said nonchalantly, "Hi, Todd."

Todd responded, "Hi, Markie."

By this time, Sam had positioned himself close to the chair where Marquetta was sitting which made Marquetta uncomfortable. She asked, "Am I in your seat?"

Sam acknowledged his closeness to her and apologized, "Oh, I'm sorry. No, I was sitting in the seat closer to the wall." Todd, trying to rectify an awkward moment, chimed in, "I think it's time for a formal introduction. Marquetta Logan, I would like you to meet, my older brother, Samuel Parker, Jr. Samuel Parker, Jr., I would like you to meet Marquetta Logan. As you discovered, he will be your escort to the banquet tomorrow."

Marquetta then spoke, "Hi, Samuel, it's nice to meet you."

"Please call me Sam. Hello, Marquetta, I'm pleased to meet you. I beg your pardon for calling you 'Markie.' You're, too beautiful of a woman to be called 'Markie.' I must say, I'm happy to escort you to the banquet."

"Thank you," said Marquetta.

Sam looked at Todd and inquired, "How could you wait so long before you let me meet her?" Before Todd could answer, Myrna buzzed him. Todd responded to the buzz, "Yes Myrna."

"Ms. Smith is on the phone. Do you want to speak with her? She said it's important."

"Thanks, I'll get it," said Todd. Todd excused himself, then pushed down the button to receive his call. "Hello Juanita."

Juanita braced herself as she blurted, "Todd, my Daddy told me you don't sound like a man who is getting married. What did you tell him?"

Anger swelled in Todd the moment Juanita questioned him about his talk with her father. "I didn't think it was his business so I really didn't tell him much of anything, other than I had considered it at one time."

Marquetta could tell by Todd's facial gestures that he was not pleased with the conversation he was having with Juanita. So she said, "Sam, I think we should give Todd some privacy. Let's sit in the lounge area until he's free."

"That's a lovely idea," replied Sam.

As they walked to the lounge area Sam stated, "I'm scheduled to be here for two weeks. I would like to spend every day with you. Is it a date?"

"No, I'm sorry it isn't. I leave for vacation on Saturday."

"How long will you be gone?"

"Five days, but I don't think I'm your type, even if I stayed in town, Sam."

"You couldn't be more wrong. I love a real woman; one I can enjoy hugging, kissing, and caressing. You have just enough of everything. I can tell it's all you—nothing fake."

"It's apparent you don't know who you're talking to, because I don't get excited by a man discussing what he wants to do with my body. All you know is my name. So, don't try to familiarize yourself with my body, when you don't know me. Personally, I don't find the comment romantic I find it disgusting and disrespectful."

"Oh I'm sorry, I didn't mean to offend you. Maybe I can redeem myself if you'll spend the entire day with me tomorrow. That way, we'll be better acquainted by the time we leave for the banquet."

Before Marquetta could answer, Todd came out of his office, walked to the lounge area, and interrupted, "Markie, may I see you—alone."

"Okay." Marquetta still steaming from Sam's remark got up from her seat and left the lounge area with Todd.

Todd closed his office door, waited for her to have a seat in her favorite chair, then queried her, "Well, what do you think of my brother?"

"Todd, I'm just going to be blunt. He's obnoxious. He has no respect for women and I'm not sure if I want to go out with him."

"Markie, what did he say to you? I have never seen you this angry at anyone."

"Todd, I'm sorry, but he had the audacity to tell me that he wants to hug, kiss, and caress me. I could tell he thought I enjoyed hearing that garbage. Is this the kind of mess women are putting up with today? I hope not!"

Todd laughed loud and long. Finally after regaining his composure, he commented, "I'm sorry. It's not funny, but that is one of his favorite lines. I don't know if he'll use it again now."

Todd's laughter calmed Marquetta so she began to smile. Then she stated, "I'm glad you're enjoying this, however, we do have business to discuss. Are you ready to tell me your opinion of the tape, or do you want to laugh some more?"

"No, I'm finished laughing, at least for now." Todd smiled, then put a grave look on his face as he continued talking, "Markie, you don't know how worried I was about losing you to Sam. In growing up whenever I met a girl, she liked me until she met Sam. He's usually much better at talking to women than I am. He liked competing with me for women so much that he developed a game for us to play. 'See who could keep the girl the longest,' and of course Sam's favorite part of the game, 'or take the girl from the other one.' Sam usually won, but as I grew older I realized it was because he developed the game and kept changing the rules. Needless to say, I was worried when he told me he wanted to meet you. It reminded me of the old days. But, it was all for naught."

"Todd, you forgot one thing. I'm not your girlfriend. Shouldn't your concern be geared toward Juanita?"

"Markie, you are my close friend. Sam doesn't understand that kind of relationship with a man and a woman. Plus—you know I want us to be more."

Deliberately changing the subject, Marquetta said, "Did you have time to listen to the tape?"

"Yes," Todd said, as he gave a slight grin.

By Todd's reaction, Marquetta knew he knew something and wasn't going to share it. She prompted, "What do you know that you don't want to tell me?"

Todd tried to play it off . "Wait a minute, Markie. You're jumping to conclusions. I only said one word, yes. You are a client, but more than that, you are a friend. I would do whatever I could to help you and will, if there is a problem. I did have a chance to listen to the tape. In fact, I listened to it twice. There are a couple of things that concern me. Let me hasten to say—that's all it is—my concerns! If something turns up, I'll let you know, even if I have to fly to the Caribbean to tell you personally."

Marquetta thought, *You're holding back, but I will find out what you know, with or without you.* She said, "Right," with uncertainty in her tone.

Todd picked up the skepticism in her tone but believed it would be inappropriate for him to reveal his thoughts without solid information. As nonchalantly as he could, Todd queried, "How long has Mr. Greely been accepting clients from Second Chance, Inc?"

"I don't know how long he has been accepting our clients, however, I do know that Tony Davis was the first client we assigned to him. I need to check with Barbara to see if he turned down any of our clients before accepting Tony and if so, why?"

Todd chimed, "Good idea."

"Any other questions we need answered?"

"No. Stop trying to find a needle in a haystack. These are good questions any investigator would ask in an initial investigation."

"May I use your phone?"

"Sure," said Todd.

Marquetta rose from her seat, walked around to the corner of Todd's desk where the phone sat and reached for the receiver. Instantly, Todd's phone rang. Without thinking she answered it, "Todd Parker and Associates, may I help you?"

"Not making enough to support yourself in your small company that you're answering phones for Todd, Marquetta?" Juanita said sharply.

Refusing to be provoked by Juanita, Marquetta's response was cool. "Thanks for the concern about my financial status, Juanita.

I'm here on business and I answered the phone because I was in the process of using it."

As if disinterested, Juanita said, "Whatever. Is Todd available? I need to speak with him." Marquetta put Juanita on hold and asked, "Todd, do you want to speak with Juanita?"

Without hesitation Todd replied, "No, we're busy. Tell her I'll call her later."

Marquetta pushed down the hold button so she could speak with Juanita. Nicely, she stated, "Juanita, Todd will call you later. We are in a meeting."

Todd's refusal to speak to her while he was with Marquetta annoyed Juanita. But what really vexed her was Marquetta's indifference to the fight. "Is she, too stupid to realize we are at war?" Juanita wondered. She surmised, "I may have lost this round, but I won't lose the next. Wait a minute! Now that I think about it, that may have been a blow to the chin, but I'm not knocked out, yet She inquired, "Is Sam there?"

"Yes, just a moment." Marquetta put the call on hold and gave the phone to Todd as she said, "She wants to speak to Sam." Todd transferred the call to Myrna.

Marquetta commented, "Not wanting to change the subject, Todd, but Juanita asked to speak to Sam. You mentioned a concern earlier—you may want to intervene."

"If anything happens there, that's their business. They both love to play games."

"I'm calling Barbara," Marquetta said, changing the subject back to business. She dialed the number to SCI.

"Second Chance, Inc., Ms. Biggins, may I help you?"

"You're more cheerful than usual today. This is Marquetta. I'm at Todd's office. I need to ask you some questions about Greely's Towing Service. I'll hold until you get the file."

"I have it on my desk, awaiting your call. I know you, too well. When I called your condo this afternoon and you weren't there, I knew where you were and why? What's your question?"

Marquetta laughed and said, "You're, too much. What would I do without you? Wait a minute; let me get the questions from Todd. She looked at Todd and said, "What are the questions again?"

Todd said, "How long has Mr. Greely been accepting SCI's clients? Has he turned any down before accepting Tony, and if so, why?" As Todd read the questions off his paper, Marquetta held the phone to his mouth. After he finished stating the questions, Marquetta put the receiver to her ear.

Barbara said, "He didn't turn any down, per se, but he has a hiring stipulation in his contract agreement. He only wants men who can drive vehicles with manual transmissions. So far, Tony was the first one who qualified. His contract agreement with us has been in operation approximately three months."

"Barbara, do me a favor, check and see how much of a background was done on his company and bring it with you this evening. I'll review it when I get home tonight."

Barbara said, "Okay. See you at 4:00 p.m.. Good bye." Marquetta hung up the phone and, took her seat. Todd said, "Markie, we need to talk about us—what happened two years ago and what we want to happen now?"

"Todd, now we are friends. We see things differently."

"Not really, Markie."

"Oh, so you're willing to wait until you're married before you make love to your wife?"

"No, I mean, I don't know. I'm thinking about it."

"Really, what brought this on?"

"Who brought this on? You did."

"I did, how?"

There was a loud knock on the door. Todd responded firmly, "I'm in a meeting."

Sam ignored Todd's comment and opened the door, then said, "Excuse me. Juanita said it's urgent."

Todd was disturbed by Sam's actions. He stated harshly, "I'll call her back in five minutes."

"Brother dear, the woman had breakfast prepared for us this morning. The least you can do is talk to her for a minute on the phone. Right, Marquetta?" Sam said empathetically.

Todd sighed, excused himself, picked up the receiver, then pushed the button down that was blinking and, took the call.

Marquetta responded to Sam by changing the subject. Sam

wanted to be near Marquetta so he, took a seat on the sofa so he could be next to her as she asked, "Sam did you enjoy your flight?"

Sam still wanted to reveal Todd's presence at Juanita's last night. He said, "It was okay. I was glad Juanita was waiting for me when I got off the plane. She left Todd sleeping at her condo. I thought that was nice."

Marquetta laughed to herself as she thought, *He thinks I don't know Todd sleeps with Juanita.* She said, "That was thoughtful."

Sam was surprised at Marquetta's calmness but was determined to get her angry. So he said, "I don't know how he does it, keep two beautiful ladies happy. The only way that's possible is one isn't as demanding as the other. Which one are you, more demanding or less demanding?"

Now perturbed, Marquetta looked directly in Sam's eyes when she spoke. "Sam, let's forget about our date tomorrow. I think it will be, too demanding for you." Marquetta unflinching continued to pierce him with her eyes as she sent the message she doesn't play games. Sam, impressed by her no nonsense response, replied with a flirt. "No way! I'm looking forward to this date and all the demands that come with it."

"Good, you can start by knowing I'm not going to have sex with you and I don't want to have to fight your hands all night to prove I mean what I say. Secondly, I am not attracted to the type of behavior you have been displaying today. If it continues, I will cancel the date. I can and will go to the banquet without one. If we do go to the banquet together and your behavior becomes intolerable, I will leave you where you stand. Now, do we understand each other?" Marquetta said, securely.

Neither Marquetta or Sam noticed Todd was off the phone until Sam said, "Understood," with a snide grin.

As Todd waited for the perfect opportunity to interrupt Marquetta and Sam's conversation, he enjoyed watching Marquetta demonstrate her quick wit. Todd didn't want Sam to know he overheard their chat but he couldn't get the smile off his face that was put there by hearing their exchange of words. "Excuse me, Sam, I need to talk to Markie. I won't be long. Okay?"

Sam noticed the smile on Todd's face as he spoke and knew he overheard some of, if not all of, his and Marquetta's dialogue. He refused to look at either Todd or Marquetta as he rose from his seat and opened the door to leave. "Yeah, all right," Sam said, embarrassingly, and left.

Todd knew Marquetta was still angry because the top of her nose had perspiration balls on it. He decided to make clear his conversations with Sam. "Markie, I never gave Sam any indication I slept with you. I don't know why he said that to you."

Calmly, she said, "I do. He's trying to find out what's going on with us. He really can't believe that a man and a woman can know each other for as long as we have and be as close as we appear to be to him, without having sex. I haven't been able to abstain for ten years without running into men who thought like Sam. He doesn't bother me. That's his problem."

Todd was looking at Marquetta with admiration in his eyes. He couldn't believe how mild her tone was toward him, when he knew she had just had a bout with Sam. What was more incredible to him was he knew this was no act. He'd seen her in action before, but he still marveled at her control. "Your attitude amazes me sometimes. Markie, I guess that's why I like you as much as I do. We have known each other for ten years and understand so much about each other. I want us to be close in all areas."

Marquetta saw through the white wash. "Todd, give me a break. You want sex. My mind will not change. I mean, you're different to me than Sam, in that you are a good friend. I can usually call on you and you'll help me if you can. However, sex is not negotiable in our friendship."

"How would we know if we are right for each other sexually if we don't try before we're married? Todd explained. "For me, marriage is serious."

Marquetta exclaimed. "It's serious for me, too! Since I'm trusting God for a husband, I have to believe he knows what we both need in each other."

"Oh, so that's how you see it."

"Yeah, that's how I see it. That's why I told you earlier, we see things differently. I will not compromise my standards, no matter how much I think I love you. Todd, to me this is bigger than you and me. This deals with my relationship with God. In my life, my goal is to do things that will please God. Fornicating with you will not be pleasing to God. That's why I know you have no idea how I felt when we almost had sex two years ago. That was a night I don't think I'll ever forget. Thank God I got through it victoriously."

"Do you think it's easy for me? I'm trying to respect your views, but we can't continue this way." Before Todd could continue a knock came on the door. Todd knew it was Sam. He said, "Markie, we need to discuss this further." Todd rose from his seat to escort Marquetta to the door. As he walked toward her, he said, "I'll meet you at your condo this evening, alone. Right now I need to let Sam come in." At that moment Todd was standing less than two feet in front of her and both of them could feel the passion emanating from each other. Containing her emotions, Marquetta asked solemnly. "Todd, do you think meeting at my condo this evening is a good idea?"

Todd responded gravely, "Yes. We have to get it all out—everything that's on our minds. Look, I'm getting pressure to marry Juanita. I need to know if there's an 'us.' He, took her hand and began to rub it gently as he said, a little above a whisper, "I'll see you later."

Fighting back her desires, she knew she had to be frank with him. As she removed her hand from his with a sincere voice, she commented. "Todd, there comes a time in everyone's life that he (she) has to make a decision that will change the rest of his (her) life. You are going to have to review your priorities and decide what you can and can't live with. Only you can make that decision. Good bye."

As Marquetta walked out of Todd's office, Sam was expected to enter. Instead he decided to follow her to the entrance door of the outer office. He wanted her to know as far as he was concerned, the games had just begun. He said, "I love to see a woman squirm after acting so tough."

Marquetta stated, with determination in her tone and steadfastness on her lips, "Sam, this is not a competition. If I said something to make you think I want to compete with you, you are sadly mistaken. I am merely telling you, if you think there is going to be some type of compensation given you by me for this date, you are wrong! I'm telling you again, if you want to back out gracefully, that's fine with me." Marquetta's stance was that of one ready for battle. Each hand was on a hip; her right leg was a foot away from her left pointing straight forward while her left leg was close to her body. Her back was slightly arched and her facial expressions emphasized each word..

Marquetta's feisty behavior stimulated Sam. He knew he had to have her. With controlled excitement he said, "No way. I told you I'm looking forward to this date. I'll see you tomorrow evening promptly at 7:00 p.m.." He grabbed Marquetta's hand, kissed it, and walked back toward Todd's office. As he walked, he pictured himself taking a leap into the air and clicking his heels before touching the floor. He had been challenged and he loved it. As Marquetta left the office, she stated, "Myrna don't forget to put me down on your calendar an evening of fun with the girls. Choose the night, call Barbara, and give her the date."

"Okay," replied Myrna.

"Good bye," said Marquetta.

---

Marquetta arrived at her condo promptly at 4:00 p.m. She noticed Phillip sitting in Barbara's car. She walked over to the car to speak, "Hi, Phillip. I hear congratulations are in order."

Phillip smiled broadly as he responded, "Yes, we're meeting with Barbara's parents this evening. I'm sorry I'm interfering with your shopping. I hope you understand. Marquetta, after I asked Barbara to marry me, all I want to do is get married as soon as possible. I finished my work and came home early."

Phillip and Barbara had arrived a few minutes early because they wanted to leave from Marquetta's promptly at 4:00 p.m. for Barbara's parents home before the traffic got heavy. When Barbara discovered Marquetta wasn't home, she decided to slide the folder under Marquetta's door, but to her dismay, it wouldn't slide. Frustrated, she looked at her watch to see what time it was. When she realized it was 4:00 p.m. she decided to walk back to the parking lot and meet Marquetta there. She knew Marquetta was very punctual. Not noticing her shoe lace was untied, she almost fell as she tripped over the lace. She knew then she was moving, too fast and had to stop and calm down. She prayed silently for peace as she bent down to tie her left sneaker. Smiling as she walked out the door onto the parking lot, she noticed Marquetta talking to Phillip. She walked back to the car, gave Marquetta the folder she requested, and declared, "That's all I could find."

"That's fine. I'll review it and if I think it means anything I'll give it to Todd to check out. Let me know the steps you take in planning your wedding. Who knows? I may need the information someday."

Barbara responded, "It may be sooner than you think."

Phillip inquired, "Did Todd propose?"

Marquetta exclaimed, "Why did you say that?"

"Really, Marquetta, do you think he will propose to you? Phillip continued without waiting for a response, "I think you may want to consider someone who respects you, your values, and is looking for the same kind of lifestyle. Todd gives me the impression that his goals are very different from yours. Remember, he has been dating Earl Smith's daughter for some time now. Don't tie your feelings up with him unless his views change."

Marquetta listened intently, then replied, "Phillip, it's interesting that you said that, because I shared some of what you said with Todd today. You know, I didn't realize it until today but I think I have allowed myself to get attached to Todd. Phillip, I know better. Thanks for the advice. I needed to hear that today. Do you think I should get another attorney?"

"No, Marquetta, you handle yourself fine around him. It's just that I know you and I don't want you getting hurt on a personal level. You understand what I mean, don't you?"

"Yeah, Phillip, I understand. Thanks. See ya later." Marquetta walked into her building, climbed the stairs to her condo and went in. She walked to her sofa, laying the folder on the coffee table near her as she sat down. The minute she kicked off her shoes, her phone rang. The phone in her living room set on an end table which also held a lamp and was near the sofa. She reached for the receiver and answered it. "Hello."

"Hi, Markie, I need to see you. May I come up?"

Marquetta's thoughts went back to her conversation with Phillip as she said, "Todd, I don't think I should see you tonight."

"I'm on my car phone in front of your building."

"Okay, come up," she said reluctantly. She carried her shoes to her bedroom and came out wearing a pair of soft pink fluffy slippers. Having acknowledged her attachment to Todd, she felt vulnerable and weak. She prayed. "Father God, I need your help. Please strengthen me. In Jesus' name. Amen."

She remembered the folder on the coffee table when she heard the knock on the door and moved it to the dining room table close to the window. Marquetta gathered her composure and opened the door. Todd walked past her as he entered her condo and spoke with his back toward her. "I need to talk to you now!"

"What's going on? You seem so tense."

"Everybody's pressuring me to marry Juanita. He turned around, looked Marquetta in her face and said, "How would you feel if I married Juanita? I mean, would it affect our friendship?"

Marquetta prayed silently, "Please don't let the expression on my face change." She said calmly. "What brought this on?" Without pause for an answer, she continued, "Todd, I hate to say this, but you're fickle."

Both laughed. Then Todd asked, "Why did I come over here, anyway? You're right. I have to admit that question made me appear fickle." Todd felt the stress leave him. He realized he just wanted to be with Marquetta. Now feeling comfortable in his surroundings, he said, "Markie, may I have something to drink?"

"Oh, sure. That reminds me, I have something I would like you to taste." As she walked toward the kitchen she said, "If you're ready to sit down, you may have a seat." Todd sat in his favorite chair that had a hassock in front of it. As he propped his feet up on the hassock, he shouted to her in the kitchen, "Thanks, may I put in a tape?" Not waiting for an answer, he put in a jazz tape he gave her for Christmas.

Marquetta walked out of the kitchen carrying a tray with two beautiful crystal wine glasses on it. Todd, astounded, said, "When did you start drinking wine?" Marquetta, forgetting her folder was on the dining room table, responded to Todd without looking down on the table. She placed the tray on top of the folder on the dining room table, then walked with the glasses in her hand to the living room. As soon as she gave Todd a glass, she reached for her coasters under the coffee table and placed two on top of the table. Then she sat on the love seat which was adjacent to the chair where Todd was sitting.

"Taste it and tell me what you think."

Todd, took a sip. "It's good."

"It is, isn't it? This is the first time I tasted it. It's been in my refrigerator for about a month."

"You're drinking now?" Todd said disapprovingly.

Marquetta laughed and said, "You really can't tell the difference, can you?"

"What do you mean, I can't tell the difference?"

"This is non alcoholic wine. I have such beautiful wine glasses, I thought I may as well use them. So I bought some non alcoholic wine."

"I should have guessed it," Todd said with a smile.

"Todd, you're ridiculous. I don't believe you. You drink, but when you thought there was alcohol in these glasses, you were upset. I could tell it in your voice."

"I know, Markie. I don't know what's wrong with me. I'm getting so particular about things when it comes to you. You've been on my mind so much recently. Now Earl, Sam, and Juanita want me to make a decision about her, and I can't because you are the one on my mind. I've been thinking while driving over here, if we decide to get married, set the date and send out the invitations, then could we have sex. One time, just to tide me over?"

Marquetta laughed and said, "No way."

"Markie, I just want to see if it fits."

"You don't get to try me out before you take me home. I'm not a shoe. I'm a human being. Anyway why are you so anxious? What's going on with you?"

"I feel so confused. I don't know what to do. I think I know what to do but Sam doesn't think I'm thinking clearly."

"I hate to ask but I feel I should. What did he say?"

Todd laughed, then said, "He said I have an opportunity to live a life that a lot of people dream of, if I marry Juanita. You know—marrying into money. Through Juanita's…well… her father's businesses and his associates, I could acquire a lot of rich clients. He also said Juanita knows how to play the game, because she learned it from her father, which makes her a great business asset. He reminded me she's an attractive woman and loves to please her man. Let's not forget, Earl hinted that the clients I picked up at the dinner party could easily decide to take their business elsewhere. He informed me that his name carries a lot of weight in our community and he doesn't want his daughter's reputation smudged by me. He told me it seemed I like to play house, but his daughter isn't a toy."

Marquetta queried, "Todd, what do you want?"

"What do you want, Markie? I mean—would you marry me?"

"No."

"No?"

"Yes, no! You're not ready. You need to be sure about what you want to do. Back up. How does Sam know that Juanita loves to please her man?" Marquetta snickered.

"Oh, he said he listened as she shared how much she tried to please me and how I ignored her gestures. She told him she was afraid I was going to leave her for you. Markie, I don't know why she said you. I never told her anything about us. Not even about that night."

"I should think not! She dislikes me as it is. If she ever finds out that she almost had a reason, I don't know what she will do—probably try to destroy my company."

Todd, with concern, looked at Marquetta and asked, "Why would you say that? Do you think she would go that far?"

"I don't know. She's used to having her own way. You never can tell."

"Markie, about that night two years ago, I still think about it."

"Todd why make such a big deal about it? You spent the night over Juanita's, remember. I'm sure you were able to finish there what was started here."

"That's what you think happened that night?"

"Todd, it's your business. I don't know why I agreed to go on a date with you that night."

"I know why. You felt guilty because I had been volunteering so much of my time helping to paint your offices."

Marquetta's mind drifted back to that day. She smiled and said, "That's right, you and Phillip were our hardest workers. Both of you supervised groups and brought food for everyone who helped. I thought I could go on a date with you because you were so nice and helpful. Besides Phillip and Barbara were going with us."

"The evening was great, wasn't it? Juanita heard about the supper club and asked me to take her but I couldn't."

Marquetta knew she had almost crossed the line that night from being Todd's confidante to being just another one of his many conquests. The thought of that pained her deeply. But what infuriated her more was Todd's attempt to act as if that night was important to him. After all, he left in the midst of a conversation that could have changed their relationship, to assist Juanita. Marquetta said harshly, "Oh, you can't take her to a restaurant but you could sleep with her that night!" She regrouped and said, "I'm sorry. That's not my business. Besides, the two of you do sleep together. I know that I was wrong. I never should have agreed to go on a date with you, anyway." Marquetta realized she had just revealed her heart to Todd. She never wanted him to know how hurt she was when he left to take Juanita home. Although that move helped her put things into perspective.

Todd walked over to Marquetta and sat beside her. He tried to console her by putting his arm around her waist but she rejected him. She removed his hands from her waist and turned her head away from him as if she saw something on the wall that needed her attention. Todd, took his right hand and put it on her cheek while turning her face to his. He requested, "Look at me."

"Why?" Marquetta questioned as she tried to turn her face from his.

"Look at me!" Todd's tone was stern.

Without thinking, Marquetta adhered to his request. "Okay, I'm looking. Now what?"

Todd looked into her eyes as he spoke. "That evening was a very special evening for both of us. I didn't have sex with Juanita that night. I didn't even sleep in the same bed with her. Think about what happened that evening." Unable to continue to look into Todd's eyes as she thought about the events of the evening, she rested her head on his chest. Todd wrapped his arms around her waist as he continued talking. "I didn't remember to pick her up from her father's house. Earlier that day I remembered because Phillip teased me and said I was playing chauffeur. He remarked that her father had a chauffeur and he could give her a ride home. He inferred that the chauffeur didn't give her the same benefits. Then Phillip and I laughed. You and Barbara overheard the conversation because Barbara told Phillip and me to be nice. Then we all laughed."

"That's right, we did."

"That night was the best time I had had in years. Ever since then, I've thought more and more about us but not to the extent it has been recently. Markie, I think I love you but I don't know if I can marry a woman without having sex with her first."

Marquetta's body during a quiet moment acknowledged Todd's closeness and wanted to respond to him passionately. At that moment, Marquetta jumped off the love seat and said, "I thought you liked sitting in the chair."

"Markie, I'll sit in the chair. We need to continue this conversation. If my holding you was distracting, I'm sorry. Being around you and holding you feels natural to me." He moved to the chair, propped his feet on the hassock and continued to reminiscence. "The food was delicious, the music was nice and smooth. I really enjoyed the jazz band. It was the best I heard in a long time. Would you like to go there, tonight?"

Marquetta stated soberly, "No, thank you. I remember the evening was wonderful. The dinner and music wasn't the problem. In thinking back, what happened afterward was. But it was my fault. I let my guard down. When Barbara and Phillip left my condo, I should have asked you to leave, too. But I didn't. I should have never let you kiss me, but I did." While looking in Todd's direction, Marquetta was wringing her hands as she spoke.

Todd, trying to make his point, used hand gestures. He opened his hands and spread them flat, moving them from time to time to bring emphasis as he gave his explanation. "Markie, at the time, we had known each other for eight years. We had eaten lunch together for years. We had worked together on committees and had dinner meetings when it was just the two of us, both here and at my place. I would say my kissing you that night was inevitable."

"Todd, you don't understand. I don't kiss. I mean—on the cheek, that's fine—but I'm talking about fervently."

"So, you let me discover that you are human and have emotions. That you can be passionate. That's not bad."

"Todd you are not my husband and with you that passion was turning into lust, which means I could have..."

"You could have what? You didn't. We didn't. Is that why you tense up every time I reach for your hand? Just like you did today in the office. Markie, I would never force you to do something you don't want to do. I realize I should not have tried to caress you that night. I guess the kissing became so intense I acted on instinct and fondled you. I'm sorry."

"You don't understand! I should've never let it get to that point. I should have stopped kissing you, but it was so hard. If I hadn't prayed for help, we would have had sex. I realized I had lost control. Only because of God was I able to regain it."

Todd grinned, then said, "That's what happened! I thought you were at the point of no return, but all of a sudden you were resilient. I remember you said quite firmly, 'No, I mean it! Stop now! You have to leave.' I knew you were serious, so I left you alone. I moved to the chair because I couldn't leave. I was enjoying your company and I wanted the night to continue for as long as it could. I really wanted to start dating you. That's why I asked you if I could see you regularly."

"Before I could answer, what happened? I'll tell you. My phone rang and it was Juanita asking if you were there and reminding me that you were taking her home and spending the night."

"Markie, you knew what time I left here. By the time I picked her up from her father's and, took her to D.C., I was exhausted. That's why I stayed at her place. That night I did not sleep with her! Besides, I thought you wanted me to leave. After Juanita called, I thought for sure you were going to put me out. I just knew her call had reminded you of my many exploits. I saw the look on your face when you handed me the phone. I imagined 'I'm in trouble now.'

No way would you believe I was sincere when I asked for us to start dating regularly." Todd, shaking his head stated, "You mean I jumped to the wrong conclusion? I don't believe this." Then he asked, "Would you come here, please?" Todd held out his hands.

"No, I don't want you to hold me."

"Come here, please," Todd said coaxingly.

Marquetta ignored his requests and inquired, "Why Todd? I think it's time for you to leave."

Todd walked to where Marquetta was sitting and sat beside her. Determined to hold her hands, he refused to let her pull them away from him. He held her hands firmly as he looked into her eyes and asked, "If that night meant nothing, why would my sleeping with Juanita bother you so much? You knew I slept with her and other women—it never bothered you before, or did it?" The warmth from Todd's hands seemed to send a message to her heart. She knew she had to tell him the truth. Tears streamed from her eyes as that night seemed to come alive in her heart. She looked down at Todd's hands holding hers as she spoke. "It's not your sleeping with them that bothers me; it's because I almost became one of them." She looked squarely in his eyes as she continued, "I don't want that lifestyle anymore and I'm not going to be one of your women. I can't, I'm sorry, that's not me." She, took her hands from his and held them tightly as if for control.

He wiped her tears with his hands as he explained, "Markie, the only reason I suggested we have sex is because I want to marry you. I feel stupid marrying a woman I don't know in bed, but I do respect you. Sam wanted me to marry Juanita and have sex with you. You see, Sam knows it's you I want, not Juanita, or any other woman. He suggested if I were to break you in again, I could convince you to have an affair with me. That way I could have everything—the wealth, prestige, and you. But I couldn't do that to you or to me. I believe in the sanctity of marriage."

Collected, Marquetta commented, "Sam can be so vicious. Todd, I hear what you're saying, but for me no sex before marriage."

"I know," resolved Todd.

Marquetta queried, "Where is Sam? It's getting late, do you think you should check on him? It's 9:00 p.m.."

"May I use your phone?"

"Sure." Marquetta replied. She went into the bathroom to blow her nose and wipe her face with a damp cloth. She tried to freshen up her makeup, but when she looked in the mirror and saw puffy eyes and a pink nose, she thought the attempt would be futile. She rested the damp cloth on her eyes for a few minutes and then her nose, hoping to get rid of the pink look.

Todd called his townhouse and Juanita answered the phone. "Hello."

Todd said, "I'm sorry, I must have dialed the wrong number."

"No, you didn't, Todd. Where are you? I've been waiting over here for hours."

"Juanita, I didn't invite you to my townhouse. I want you to leave."

"I'm spending the night!"

"Well, I won't be home! Put Sam on the phone now!" Juanita, shocked at Todd's reaction, handed the phone to Sam. Sam looked at Juanita's surprised facial expression, laughed as he picked up the phone, and asked, "Did you do it?"

"No, Sam. I told you I wasn't going to try to have sex with her. Why is Juanita there?"

"I thought you would need a real woman after you finished with Miss Goody-two-shoes. I'm telling you now, you had your chance tonight. Tomorrow will be, too late. She will sleep with me!"

"Sam, don't touch her! She's off limits to you and I'm not coming home! I'll see you tomorrow." Todd slammed the phone down on the receiver.

Marquetta overheard some of the conversation, but didn't understand it, so she said, "Juanita's at your townhouse and Sam is trying to sleep with her? Why did you say you're not going home?"

"Markie, you don't understand. Sam wants you and he is determined to sleep with you tomorrow. Sam has been known to be somewhat forceful in getting what he wants."

"Do you think he'll rape me?"

"No, but he can become aggressive and persistent in convincing a woman to do things his way."

"Todd, I'm not worried about Sam. I told you I've been in

contact with his type before. Since Juanita's over your place tonight, I have a question for you." Marquetta always had a way of calming Todd down. He laughed and said, "What is it?"

"How do you feel knowing I know you not only sleep with Juanita, but other females as well?"

"I can't believe you asked me that question. I'm glad you're not an attorney. I wouldn't want you on the opposing side."

"Stop stalling; answer the question."

"Well, in the beginning it didn't bother me. You knew I was a man with physical needs and you made it clear the first time I let you know I was interested in seeing you, that you wouldn't have sex until you were married. I liked you and still wanted to see you on occasion, so I did what I felt I had to do. My plan was to sleep with other women until you became so jealous that you would change your views. On occasion, I deliberately waited until the last minute to break plans we made by saying I needed to be with a woman that could satisfy my physical needs. I wanted you to complain, but you wouldn't. In short, my plan backfired. You grew on me. You always look gorgeous. You dress modestly as if not to draw attention, but you do draw attention. I never told you this, but Earl Smith smiles when you walk into his business meetings. He even questioned me about being on every committee you're on. Then after I started dating Juanita he came to me one day and asked, 'Isn't one beautiful lady enough for you?' It was as if he were monitoring my behavior."

"Earl Smith said that? That's nice. You know, he always ask how my company is doing. He told me he thought I had a wonderful mission. He also told me he would do whatever he could to assist me."

Todd inquired, "Do you think he has the hots for you? That could explain why he's pressuring me to marry Juanita."

"No, I think it's because he's a nice man. He's nothing like Juanita. Todd, nice try, but don't change the subject. Answer my question. I'll fix us something to eat and then call Phillip to see if you can stay with him. Okay?"

Todd laughed and remarked, "Somehow I didn't think I would be staying in your guest room. That's good, I don't want to stay up all night trying to think of ways to persuade you to have sex with me."

Marquetta laughed and said, "Good, now answer the question. I can hear you in the kitchen."

"Do you remember when I started going out with Juanita?"

"Go on."

"Okay, it was the first time I slept with her. It bothered me."

"Juanita, why?"

"I don't know. I think it was how we met. Remember, she joined the committee you chaired."

"I didn't chair that committee—you did. I ended up doing a lot of work but Juanita gave us good publicity. Continue, I'll hold my questions and comments for later."

"Okay. Remember the night we all met at her condo, and after the meeting we went out for dinner. That's when Juanita asked me if I was seeing you. I asked her why and she told me she asked because we were on the same committees, arriving and leaving most of the time together. I told her we were good friends. Then, she boldly asked if that meant we were having sex but weren't committed to each other or we had sex and it didn't work out. I told her neither, we were just good friends. You don't have sex. That's when she informed me your loss was her gain. She suggested we get rid of the committee members and go back to her place. That's what happened. I guess I felt guilty because I deliberately joined the committees to win you over. Instead,

Juanita and I became an item. Now her father is watching my movements. After we almost made love two years ago, it really bothered me when you would see me with a woman, especially Juanita. I thought you would think they meant to me what you mean to me. Think about it. How many women have you seen me with in the last two years?"

"No comment—let's eat," Marquetta said as she came out of the kitchen carrying a tray with food on it.

After dinner, Marquetta put the dishes on both trays that were on the dining room table, and asked Todd to bring one tray to the kitchen while she carried the other. Marquetta forgot about the folder's being under the tray she chose to take to the kitchen. When she picked up the tray, the folder fell on the seat of the chair near the window and the papers spilled out of the folder and went under the table. The papers where now hidden by the table cloth and were out of sight. Marquetta put the dishes in the dishwasher and washed the pans. Todd assisted. Once they were finished, they walked into the living room and, took their respective seats. Todd sat in the chair and Marquetta sat on the sofa near the phone. Crossing her feet at her ankles, she slightly twisted her upper torso as she reached for the receiver to call Barbara. Phillip was getting ready to kiss Barbara good night at her door when her phone rang.

Barbara walked to her telephone table near the chair in her living room to answer the phone. Phillip followed. He decided to wait until Barbara got off the phone before he'd leave. He, took a seat in the chair near the phone table. "Hello," answered Barbara while standing near the table.

"Barbara, this is Marquetta."

Barbara queried, "Did Todd come over to your place this evening?"

"Yeah, he's here now. That's why I'm calling. Is Phillip still there?"

"He's just getting ready to leave. Hold on."

Barbara handed Phillip the phone, then, took a seat on her sofa across from the chair where Phillip was sitting. When Marquetta could tell Phillip, by the difference in breathing, was on the other end of the line she said, "Hi, Phillip, this is Marquetta. May Todd stay at your place tonight?"

Phillip laughed and said, "Sure. I don't need to ask any questions, because he's staying at my place tonight."

"Thank you, I'll share with Barbara, later."

Phillip said, "Tell him I'm on my way. He can leave his car at your place. I'll take him to it tomorrow. It'll give us more time to talk if he wants."

"Good thinking. Tell Barbara to call me. See ya soon. Good bye."

"Good bye."

As soon as Marquetta hung up the phone, she turned to look in Todd's direction and stated, "Todd, Phillip is coming to get you. He wants you to leave your car here. He'll bring you to it tomorrow."

Todd, determined to return to his last question, replied, "You didn't answer me. How many women have you seen me with since then?"

Marquetta responded, "Only Juanita. I thought it was because you two were serious. Remember, you considered both living with and marrying her. You're still trying to decide whether you should marry her."

Todd impishly responded, "Well that's true. I have slept with her, too."

"That's true, you have. That may make your decision a little easier," declared Marquetta, unruffled, with arms folded and feet planted firmly on the floor.

Before either of them could say another word, a knock came on the door. Marquetta rose from her seat on the sofa, deliberately bumping the hassock where Todd's feet were resting as she walked toward the door. Todd smiled and then removed his feet off the hassock. Marquetta peeped through the peephole, saw it was Phillip, then opened the door. As Phillip walked in, Marquetta offered him a seat. Phillip declined the offer and stood near the door. Marquetta wanted Phillip to know she was grateful for his assistance, "Thank you, Phillip. You and Barbara are so good to me."

Todd walked to the door and said, "Thanks, Man for putting me up for the night."

"No problem. I would say 'anytime,' but I'm getting married soon. On that note Todd opened the door and he and Phillip walked out. Todd and Phillip laughed as they went down the stairs and got into Phillip's car. Marquetta closed the door, then began turning lights off in her condo to prepare for bed. Todd, fastening his seatbelt, remembered he had not left Marquetta's place properly, said, "Phillip, wait a minute. I forgot to say good night to Markie." He got out of the car, went into Marquetta's building, walked up the stairs and knocked on her door. She turned on the light near the door; peeped out the peephole, saw it was Todd, and opened the door. As soon as she opened the door, Todd walked toward her, put his forefinger on her lips to quiet her, moved his head towards hers, lifted his finger off her lips, and kissed her lips gently. Then he looked in her eyes and said, "Good night, I'll see you tomorrow."

Marquetta responded in a tone a little above a whisper, "Good night." She closed the door, then closed her eyes as she leaned on the door and prayed, "Father God, what are you telling me? Is Todd going to be my husband? Whomever he weds, please give me the strength to accept your decision. In Jesus' name. Amen." Marquetta turned off the light near the door and walked into her bedroom, using the light from the bathroom as a guide. She flipped the switch on the wall as she entered her bedroom and the room lit up. She then moseyed over to the side of her bed near the night stand where the phone rested. Not wanting to read, too much into the events of the evening, she decided to speak with someone she believed had a level head about such matters and could give her Godly counsel. But first, she needed to get dressed for bed, because she thought it could be a long conversation and she would be, too exhausted to dress for bed later. She determined she would hurriedly take off her clothes and put on her pajamas, then call Barbara but she could only move at a snails pace. Her thoughts kept going back over the events of the evening. Scenes kept playing back over and over again in her mind. Trying not to analyze what had transpired on her own, she was battling her thoughts while getting dressed for bed. Finally ready for bed, she reached for the phone. But it rang. Startled, Marquetta paused, then answered "Hello."

"Marquetta, have Phillip and Todd left yet?" Barbara was a petite woman, 5'1" in stature and 100 pounds, dripping wet, that seemed to have a bottomless pit when it came to food. She was sitting on the end of her bed in front of a T.V. tray with a bowl of popcorn on it. The television was on, but she had stopped the sound by using the mute button before she called Marquetta.

"Yes, Barbara. You timed that perfectly. I was getting ready to call you."

"Phillip saw him pull up as we were leaving your complex. He was concerned, but he said you had to handle this on your own."

"He did, Barbara?"

"Yes, I was concerned, too. The two of you haven't been together this long in your condo except…."

Marquetta cut her off and said, "I know, two years ago. I prayed before I let him in, but I have to admit, I was the one who told him we needed to discuss what happened two years ago."

"So the two of you discussed that night, tonight!" After Barbara made that statement she began putting popcorn in her mouth, one kernel at a time as if she was listening to a good movie.

Marquetta heard the crunching noise and knew she was eating popcorn. She smiled to herself, but was, too concerned with the events of the evening to address the crunching noise in her ear. "Yeah, Barbara, I can't believe it. He saw me cry."

"What did he say to make you cry?" Barbara was waiting attentively for Marquetta's response while crunching on her popcorn.

"He asked me how I felt, knowing he slept with Juanita and other women."

Barbara almost choked on her popcorn. She starting gagging and coughing. She was surprised at the answer. Marquetta first asked if Barbara was all right. Once she found out she was, she laughed, then commented, "That serves you right. I told you whenever I call for advice to stop acting as if you're listening to a movie—as if you have to have popcorn at your side while I entertain you. This is my life I'm discussing with you." Both laughed.. Barbara apologized, then asked Marquetta to hold on. She, took the bowl of popcorn and put it on the kitchen counter; went to the bathroom to wash and dry her hands quickly, sat back down on the end of the bed, picked up the phone receiver, and queried, "He asked you that tonight? I guess it was a matter of time. You two talk about everything. But I thought he wouldn't be as direct on this subject. He has to know you care for him."

"That's why he asked the question. He wanted to know how that night affected me. He told me he didn't sleep with Juanita that night. He also told me he feels guilty when I see him with Juanita, and other women, after that night. He asked me if I had noticed how many women he had been with recently. Oh yeah, he asked me would I marry him."

"What? What did you say?"

"I told him I knew he was still seeing Juanita, but I hadn't seen him with anyone else."

Barbara said excitedly,"Not that, I mean about getting married."

"I said no. Barbara, he doesn't know whether he wants me or Juanita. When he first came into my condo he asked me how I would feel if he married Juanita."

"What did you say?"

"I prayed because I didn't want the expression on my face to change and then I told him he was fickle."

Barbara and Marquetta laughed loud and long. Finally, they gathered their composure and Barbara stated, "He told me that's one of the things that makes him love you so much. Even if it hurts, you can analyze the situation and tell him what he needs to hear."

"He did, when?"

"I'm sorry, I blew it."

"You promised you wouldn't tell me he said that? Why? He made comments like that before?"

"It wasn't the comment. It was where we were when he made it."

"Where?"

"I can't tell you, yet."

"Barbara, what do you know? No, forget it. I wouldn't want you to feel bad. I'll find out in good time, I guess."

"Yes, you will. So, what happened?"

"Barbara, he asked if we could have sex just before we get married. He even came up with the 'how would I know if it will fit' routine?'"

"That's an old trick," commented Barbara.

"But what was surprising was how he reacted when he called home to check on his brother, Sam, and discovered Juanita was at his townhouse. That's when he decided he wasn't going home tonight."

"Really? That tells you he didn't want to be with her tonight, but he wanted to be with you."

"Whenever Todd has a problem he calls me, you know that."

"I don't understand the two of you. You really date often. You just don't acknowledge it as dating. Think about this, every business committee you're on, he's on. You decide to ride together to most meetings, after which you go out to get a bite to eat. You treat him to lunch and he treats you to lunch, anytime. The two of you are alone even in your homes, but he only makes a pass when you tell him he can consider your being together a date. I don't care what you say, he loves you. He respects you, too much not to love you." Barbara was in her element. She picked up the phone and moved it with her as she walked to the head of her bed. She fluffed a couple of pillows and positioned them against the headboard then she sat on the bed with her back pressed against the pillows. Now she was comfortable and believed she could do an excellent job of advising her friend. She continued to talk. Determined to give her friend proper counsel, she knew she needed to leave no stone uncovered. Having one hand on the phone cord, twirling it around her finger and the other holding the phone firmly, she listened and talked. After she felt she had responded correctly on an issue, she moved to the next. "Getting back to the tears—I never thought you cared who he slept with as long as it wasn't you. At least, that's what you told me."

"That's right. But Barbara that night it almost was me, remember. The thought of being on his list of conquests was discomfiting for me."

"Oh, but honey, you didn't get on the list. He knows that, and that may have something to do with why he can't get you out of his mind."

"Barbara, tonight before he left, he went to the car with Phillip, he got out of the car, came back into my building, knocked on the door, and kissed me softly on my lips, said good night and he would see me tomorrow. What do you think?"

Ecstatic Barbara remarked, "That boy's in love! What about his brother? Did you meet him?"

"Yes, Sam. He wants Todd to marry Juanita. He's determined to have sex with me, to the extent that Todd is concerned. Todd told me Sam could be forceful but when I asked him would he rape me he said no but he could be persistent and aggressive in getting his way."

"We've had those types before. We'll pray about this date with Sam, right now." Barbara led, "Father God, we thank you for protecting Marquetta. In Jesus' name. Amen."

Did you pray about your date with Sam earlier?"

"Yes, I did."

"Well, it's done."

"Why does Todd feel so pressured to marry Juanita? Is it just because of Sam?"

"No, Earl Smith called him today and talked to him about

marrying her, too. He reminded him of his business connections, and I think Todd got the impression he would take some of his clients if he didn't."

"Marquetta, you always gave me the impression Earl Smith was a fair man. Do you think you read him wrong?"

"I don't think so. Nevertheless, it is his daughter Todd is sleeping with, and she is an only child. Todd told me Earl Smith has commented about seeing him with me, so he is watching his movements. But all in all, I don't think he would pull Todd's business. But I don't think Todd knows that. Barbara, this is a tough time for Todd. Todd is going to have to seek God for advice. The decision Todd makes will affect the rest of his life. All we can do is pray for him."

"Marquetta, you are absolutely right. Isn't it interesting all this is happening around the time you're staying on his mind? We have been praying for you to get married. Do you think Todd is your future husband?"

"I prayed about it, but I don't know for certain. I'm glad I leave for vacation on Saturday. I really need to get away to think."

"You feel comfortable leaving Todd here with Earl Smith, Juanita, and his brother Sam?"

"Barbara, you know just like I do, if Todd is for me, no one can prevent me from marrying him. Especially, since we prayed about it. Just like Todd needs to know if he can handle the pressure, so do I. If we marry, and if it's going to last, Todd has to get a better understanding of marriage from God's perspective, not man's."

"I still say he has a lot of respect for you. Have you ever talked to him about his thoughts on marriage?"

"No, I haven't. I found out today he believes in the sanctity of marriage. In the past, we talked so much about what I thought, I never asked what he thought about marriage. In fact, I never thought I needed to know his opinion."

"I don't believe you. Todd is such a good man and you'll admit it, except when it comes to being a good husband. Now, let me tell you something. Tonight, I became weak, but Phillip remained strong and determined to wait until we were married before we make love. He reminded me that we want God to bless our marriage. That's the same way I think Todd would be with you."

"Barbara, you don't get it. If I had become weak and said yes, Todd wouldn't have turned me down. It's more than having respect for my opinion—he must be willing to do what's best for me, even if it's at sacrifice to his own need. Phillip understood and acted accordingly. Todd doesn't understand. It's getting late, I need to get to bed. I'll see you tomorrow. Good night."

"Good night," said Barbara.

———————

Barbara read her Bible and said her prayers. She said, "Father God, thank you for the strength you gave Phillip and Marquetta tonight. Please lead and guide Marquetta and Todd. Thank you for this day. Please forgive me for my sins. In Jesus' name. Amen."

When Marquetta said her prayers, she said, "Father God, please let me see Todd the way you would have me see him. Please teach Earl Smith, Juanita, and Sam how to love. In Jesus' name. Amen."

———————

Sam was taken aback by Todd's behavior, but he believed he could change his mind later.

Sam suggested, " Juanita, you might as well go home. I'll talk to him when he gets here."

"No! I'm not leaving until he comes home."

Sam could tell Juanita was not going to go home unless he gave her cause. "Juanita, your being here upset Todd. He told me he's not coming home and to tell you to go home. He'll call you tomorrow. Remember, Todd does not like to be pushed into a corner. If you really want to marry him, you're going to have to give him space."

"Perhaps you're right. I'll stay at my father's house tonight. It's only 15 minutes from here. Tell Todd to call me as soon as possible." Juanita rose from her seat on the sofa near Sam, and walked toward the door. Sam, always playing the gentleman, rose from his seat when she did and walked ahead of her as if escorting her to the door. Juanita's assuredness interested Sam. As he opened the door to let her out, he commented, "Juanita, you amaze me. You mean you're not worried about him even if he stays at Marquetta's tonight?"

Juanita looked Sam in his eyes, placed her hand on her waist, and remarked, "No, because I know what I can do. Maybe if he sleeps with her, he'll realize it isn't worth the headache." Juanita slung her leather jacket over her shoulders and left. As she left, Sam smiled. He was swayed.

Sam, now fascinated by Juanita's confidence, thought, "Perhaps I need to check out Juanita. Girlfriend acts like she knows what she's doing. She may be a welcome challenge, attractive and loaded, not bad. Little Brother better get his act together or he may lose a honey."

---

That night Juanita's thoughts were focused on how she was going to win Todd over and destroy Marquetta.

---

The drive to Phillip's house was quiet. Todd was still trying to sort out his feelings. Phillip prayed silently, "Father God, please lead and guide me as I talk to Todd. I don't know how I can help, but you do. Thank you. In Jesus' name. Amen."

Todd finally spoke. "Man, how is your construction company doing? Markie told me you hire at least two of her clients every six months."

"Yeah, I do. The company is doing well and her clients are good workers. He turned off the main street, made a left at a side street and drove into a circular driveway, then announced, "We're here." Surprised, Todd stated as he unhooked his seatbelt and got out of the car: "I thought you had a townhouse." He then asked, "What do you want with all this space?"

Phillip laughed, then replied as he removed his seat belt and got out of the car, "Most people think I live in a townhouse or a condo because I'm a single man. But I'm a single man with a vision. I want a wife and children. I want my children to have a yard they can play in. That's why I bought some land and built my house. It sits on an acre of land. Some developed and some undeveloped with trees on it. By building it myself, I have the type of house I want and I didn't have to pay an arm and a leg for it." He then used his keyless entry to lock his car door.

Todd remarked as he nodded his head in approval, "That's all right." They walked in the house as Todd continued to speak. "Phillip, may I ask you a question?"

"Yes, but that doesn't mean I'm going to answer it." He smiled.

"I want to know if you and Barbara have had sex. I'm asking you this because the two of you are going to be married."

"No, we haven't, and we won't until we marry. That's why I want to be married quickly."

Todd queried, "Man, what year are you people living in?"

Phillip chuckled as he put the key in his locks to unlock the door to enter his house. He then said, "It's our choice based on our beliefs." Phillip looked at Todd and speculated, *I have a good idea where the brother is coming from, being a former womanizer myself. I'm a handsome, deep chocolate African-American, with deep dimples that are defined when I smile. I have dark brown eyes with long eye lashes and keep my hair cut close to accent my face. Most women take a second glance when I enter a room. Before I committed my life to God, I couldn't take being rejected by a honey, either. I think I know what he's going through right now. It seems like he may be willing to take some advice. Maybe I can help him if he asks.*

Todd broke Phillip's thoughts when he said, "I noticed you've made a circular driveway. It's perfect for this size house. You know, Earl Smith has a circular driveway, too. Who does your landscaping?"

"Lee's Landscaping Company."

"That name sounds familiar," remarked Todd.

"It's another company that does business with SCI. If I give them the business, it will provide more of Marquetta's clients with jobs. Besides, they do good work."

"That's nice, Man. The work is good, too. The yard looks beautiful. It looks better than Earl Smith's yard and I thought their work was noteworthy. I like the lights around your land, too."

"Thanks, Man. I use them to enhance the beauty of the yard at night and as a form of security. Anyone getting ideas about coming on this property at night know they will be seen." Phillip yawned then said, "I'm sleepy. If you don't mind, you can make yourself comfortable and I'm going to hit the sack."

Todd was so moved with the design of the house that he continued to walk through the house, asking questions which caused Phillip to follow. Todd inquired, "Who designed your house?"

"Man, if I tell you, you're not going to believe it."

"Why do you say that? Do I know the person who designed your house?"

"The persons," said Phillip. "Yes, Barbara and Marquetta designed my house."

The house appeared to be a colonial, but as Todd walked toward the back of the house, there were stairs that led to different levels. The game room was on a lower level and as Todd walked around admiring the layout, he found more stairs that led him to the back of the house, where he discovered an indoor pool. Todd, stunned at the sight of a pool, regrouped, then queried, "Your company is doing very well, isn't it?"

"Don't let the pool fool you. This house didn't cost as much as you think to build. However, my company is doing fine, but it's not the money per se, it's what you do with what you have. I try to use mine wisely. I didn't plan on giving you the tour tonight, but if you take the stairs near the laundry room they will take you directly to the bedrooms." Phillip led the way. Once upstairs, Phillip showed Todd the room he would be staying in and said, "Make yourself comfortable."

Phillip went to his room which was directly across from the room he gave Todd. As Todd became acclimated, he compared the size of the room to his master suite in his townhouse. He thought, "It's about the size of my bedroom. It's fully equipped with TV, radio, alarm clock and dressers. It even has a full bath. Not bad!" As Todd undressed, he remembered he didn't have his pajamas, so he decided to sleep in his shorts. Then Phillip knocked on the door and gave Todd a pair of pajamas and a change of clothes, which included shorts for the next day. He said, "I think you are about my size. You can have them."

"No, I'll give them back once I have them laundered."

"The pajamas maybe, not the new shorts."

Both laughed. Todd said, "Thanks. Good night, Phillip."

Phillip, now in his room, read his Bible, then prayed. In addition to his regular prayers, which included Barbara and Marquetta, he said, "Father God, please reveal to me if you want me to continue to help Todd. If so, how? In Jesus' name. Amen."

Phillip finished his prayers just as Todd knocked on the door and asked, "Phillip, I would like to bounce something off you if you don't mind?"

"Come in." Todd went into Phillip's bedroom and, took a seat on the window seat. Phillip moved from his bed to a cushioned leather chair with a foot rest attached. When both men were comfortable and positioned where they could see and hear each other clearly, Phillip continued to talk. "What's on your mind?"

"First, I would like to thank you for not asking me what happened tonight. Aren't you a little curious?"

"What's going on with you is not my business. If you want my help, then it becomes my business."

"I do want help. Can you help me?"

"What's the problem?"

"Well, I'm not really sure. Markie has been on my mind a lot lately. I think I know why, but I'm not certain. Now, I'm getting pressure to marry Juanita. I want to sort out my feelings with Markie before I make a decision to marry Juanita."

"That sounds reasonable. So, what's stopping you?"

"My brother. He thinks Markie has my nose wide open. He believes she's playing a game and I'm, too stupid to see it."

"What kind of game does your brother think she's playing?"

"Miss Goody-two-shoes until we get married, and then she's going to let me have it."

"What do you think?"

"The problem for me is, my brother in the past has been right when it comes to women, but I keep trying to tell him Markie is different. I told him she's not trying to play innocent. She told me she wasn't a virgin and she's not happy with some of her past behavior, especially when it came to male/female relationships. She changed her lifestyle when she rededicated her life to the Lord because she wanted to be pleasing to God. Phillip, I just don't want to get hurt."

"It sounds like Marquetta isn't the problem. May I ask you a question?"

"Sure, I'm listening."

"Have you been talking to God, recently?"

"I usually try to pray before I go to sleep. I guess that is something I learned as a child. Recently, I've prayed during the day."

Phillip asked Todd a question he didn't expect. He said, "Why do you pray?"

Todd exclaimed, "To talk to God!"

"Why do you want to talk to God?"

Todd, a little annoyed, responded, "Because I need answers to problems I can't solve."

"Do you believe God can solve your problems? Before you answer, think about the question." Phillip repeated the question because he wanted it to sink in. Do you believe God can solve your problems?"

There was a long pause as Todd began considering the question and reflecting on his life and his experiences. He finally stated, "Well, I know in the past, when I got into some tough situations, I prayed, and somehow they were worked out." As he spoke, Todd's thoughts drifted back to a particular instance where the future of his career seemed to be in the balance. He recalled not being able to see his way clear, he was trapped between two bad decisions and felt he had to choose one to survive, then he remembered to pray. He knew only God could fix the mess he had found himself in and so he began praying for God's intervention. As soon as he started praying, a peace came over him and he could see with clarity. New ideas popped into his head. He knew that day he had solved the problem God's way. Revived, he walked home like a new man. The weight had been lifted, he was at peace. At that second, he discovered every time he humbled himself and sought God's help, what seemed impossible and unsolvable became possible and solvable. He became enthusiastic as he continued, "So, I would have to say 'yes, I believe God can solve my problems.' He has in the past and He always will, in His way and in His time. All I have to do is ask Him." By this time, Todd had become firm in his belief. With a smile on his face he said, "I just realized something, that in the midst of all the wrong I did and do, when I call on God, he is there to help me. God loves me in spite of me. Phillip, are you listening to me! I only call on God when I'm going through something but now I want him to lead and guide me in everything I do. I want to please Him. I want Jesus Christ to become my personal Lord and Savior."

"All you had to do was ask," said Phillip.

"At that moment a weight was lifted. He once again saw with clarity. He inquired, "Phillip do you have a Bible? I would like to read it before I go to sleep."

Phillip smiled as he responded, "There is one on the dresser near your bed." As Todd left Phillip's room he said, "Thanks, Man, for letting God use you to let me see him."

Phillip thanked God for using him to help Todd and went to sleep.

Todd, now inspired, knew he wanted to know more about God and how he could please him. He talked to God for hours in prayer and read scripture after scripture. Finally he drifted off to sleep. As he went to sleep, he had a smile on his face. He knew his life would never be the same. He looked forward to the future.

---

Ring, ring. Suzette was sweeping off the balcony when she heard the phone ring, so she hurried to the nearest phone which was in the living room. She didn't want to wake Juanita. She didn't know Juanita slept over her father's house last night. "Hello, Miss Juanita Smith's residence, may I help you."

In a husky male voice the caller said, "May I speak with Ms. Smith. Tell her Horace is calling."

"May I have her call you back. She's asleep."

"It's very important. I need to speak with her today! Tell her to call Horace Greely on his private line. She has the number."

"Okay," replied Suzette. The line went dead.

Just as Suzette hung up the phone, Juanita walked into her condo and stated, "I stayed at Daddy's house last night. Who was that on the phone?" She thought it was Todd.

"It was a man by the name of Horace Greely. He wants you to call him on his private line. He said it was very important."

"Okay," Juanita said as if it was of no concern to her. Then she requested, "Suzette, could you prepare a honey dew melon with my toast and juice this morning?"

"Sure," answered Suzette. She went to the kitchen to prepare the food.

As soon as she was out of ear range, Juanita called Horace Greely.

"Hello, Horace Greely, may I help you?"

Juanita whispered in a harsh voice, "Why did you call my house this morning? I thought I told you never to call me at home except on Saturdays. If you need me, you can beep me. You have my pager number. Or call my office and leave a message with my secretary— she knows how to reach me."

"I called you because your plan is not working. The guy from Second Chance, Inc., did not scare as easily as you thought and the company is more on the ball than you anticipated. My brother told me they must have a procedure in place when clients are suspected of committing a crime while on the job, because Marquetta Logan responded immediately. She was on her way to his company with an attorney. He had to back down. We don't want that kind of trouble."

Juanita, took the phone with its long cord onto the balcony so she could talk freely. Once she sat in one of the patio chairs she asked, "What happened? Didn't you have him drive one of the tow trucks off the lot?"

"William told his son Robert to tell him to do it, but the boy never drove a tow truck before. So Robert, not knowing the plan, rode with him and had him park the truck on our other lot. William didn't know Robert rode with him at the time he confronted the young man. Apparently things began to go down hill after that. Tony insisted he'd be allowed to call SCI."

"How stupid! I guess it was hard to put a theft charge on him if the owner's son was in the truck and the truck was parked on your other lot. But we still can get him on something. Let me see—we just need to be more careful when giving him instructions. The next time you tell him to move the tow truck, have your brother put Robert on another assignment. Then Robert won't be with him. Then tell him to park it on the street near your lot. That way you'll be able to watch your truck, but you can say he stole it. There's no proof to the contrary. I know, pretend you lost the keys and have him hot wire the truck. He'll really look guilty then." Juanita smiled.

"Look, if he hot wires a truck, we're going to have to pay money to get it fixed."

"If the truck is stolen, the insurance company will fix it."

"I'm not dragging them in this. We could get in trouble for insurance fraud. Anyway, the insurance company we use is owned by your father. Who is Marquetta Logan to you and why don't you want her company to continue to operate? Your father seems to have respect for her and her company."

"You know Daddy is an old softy when it comes to helping people, but this time I think he's wrong. She cuts honest people out of jobs by convincing people to hire convicts."

"They are ex-convicts and they need jobs."

"If you ask me, that's their problem. Why should we make it ours? I don't think we should get involved. Now, are you going to tell William what I said or should I call my father and tell him about us."

"No, Honey child, I'll tell him. I'll see you tomorrow. Bye-bye."

Horace called Greely's Towing Service as soon as he got off the phone with Juanita, but there was no answer. The phone just rang and rang. Horace was not happy. He called every five minutes until someone answered. As soon as Robert picked up the phone from his end, Horace said "Who is this?"

"Uncle Horace, is that you? This is Robert. I just got in the office. Daddy won't be here until later. May I help you?"

"No, tell your father to call me. It's urgent."

"Okay, good bye Uncle Horace."

"Good bye."

---

Ring, ring. "Hello," answered Marquetta, waking from a deep sleep. Once she recognized the voice as Barbara's, she propped herself up in the bed while Barbara talked. She cushioned her back with two pillows turned vertically.

"Hi, Marquetta, it's Barbara. I've been thinking, we need to pray about the Davis/Greely situation. Too much is happening. You're going on vacation and Todd is trying to figure out his life. I don't want them to try to put something over on us. If we give the situation to God, he'll handle it." Marquetta knew Barbara's concern for the company and knew her suggestion was right.

Marquetta got the sleep out of her eyes with her finger as she agreed, "You're absolutely right." She led the prayer, "Father God, please forgive us for our sins and thank you for being our God. We know we can give all problems and concerns to you and you will handle them. Please take care of the Tony Davis and Greely's Towing Service situation. Please protect Second Chance, Inc., its clients, employees, volunteers, and me. Please give Barbara and me wisdom to make decisions pleasing to you. In Jesus' name. Amen."

"Now, we can relax," said Barbara.

"So true. I'll see you tonight, right?"

"Right, good bye."

"Good bye."

---

Todd woke up and looked at the clock on the dresser. It was 10:00 a.m. He picked up the phone and called his office. "Hello, Todd Parker and Associates, may I help you?"

"Hi, Myrna. It's Todd. I'll be in around 2:00 p.m.. Cancel all my appointments. Good bye."

Todd reasoned, *I hate being short with Myrna, but I know she would want to know where I am and I don't want her to reveal my whereabouts to Sam or Juanita.* He got on his knees and prayed. "Father God, thank you for this day. Please forgive me for my sins and let me do things that are pleasing to you. Give me the strength to make decisions that are in line with your purpose for my life. Please continue to protect me and my law firm. In Jesus' name. Amen."

He, took a shower, put on the clothes Phillip gave him and went downstairs. Todd could smell the food as he entered the kitchen. Upon entry, Phillip commented, "There is a quicker way to get to the kitchen from the bedrooms. However, you're here now."

Todd laughed, then replied, "I just came down the same way we went up last night."

Phillip prepared breakfast for both Todd and himself. He cooked a pound of bacon, a half dozen of eggs and twelve slices of bread. Each had a 12 oz. glass of orange juice to wash down the food. As they sat down at the table and commenced eating, Phillip stated, "If you have time this morning, after breakfast, I'll show you around my yard."

"That's great. Phillip, what do you think about Bill Clemmons?"

"Well, you know I like him. He's a good guy, plus he's a good corporate attorney. Although, he's only been out of school a few years. Are you considering him as an employee? Because, if you are, you should know, I was the one who told him to talk to you and he is my company's attorney."

"Yes, I am considering hiring him. I told him I would let him know today. But I don't have my phone book with me. Can you reach him? I would like you to be with me when I talk to him."

"That's fine with me. I took off today. Now, let's eat. I didn't cook breakfast for nothing." While eating, Todd said with a grateful heart, "Man, thanks for being there for me last night. I know everything is going to be all right. I'm going to try to read the Bible daily. I want to know more about God. He knows everything about us. I realized last night, if you really love God, you want to know about him. You know—know His character. Now I understand what Markie is talking about when she says she wants to please God. In order to be able to please God, I need to learn how, and I can only do that through reading his Word and being taught and led by his Holy Spirit. Man, I'm excited! It's a wonderful change that comes over you, isn't it? God is good."

Phillip replied, "Yes, it is. You're right, God is good."

———

Sam paced up and down the floor in Todd's outer office until he arrived. As Todd entered, Myrna pointed to Sam. Todd smiled and said, "Hi, Big Brother. What's up?"

Sam tried to stay composed as he asked, "May I speak with you in your office?"

Todd responded, "Sure." Then he looked at Myrna and said, "I'm expecting Mr. Clemmons and Mr. James. Buzz me when they arrive."

"Yes sir, I will."

Todd thought, *Big Brother looks tense*. He said as they entered his office, "Take a seat. Why do you look so uptight?"

"What do you mean, I look uptight?" Todd could hear the agitation in his tone.

"No need to get upset, but you look uptight. Are you? I'm just asking the question because that's the way you appear to me."

Todd's boldness made Sam hesitate briefly before he remarked, "I just don't want you to ruin your life."

"Thank you, Big Brother, for your concern, but tell me how I'm ruining my life."

Sam, baffled, replied, "If you don't know, I won't tell you."

"Please, you made a statement and I want you to finish it. How do you think I'm ruining my life?"

Sam didn't like Todd's insistence at this time. He wanted him to be less assured. Todd's confidence bothered him. He decided he would skirt around the question until it would be more appropriate to bring it into the conversation, so he said, "How did you sleep?"

Todd smiled and said, "I slept very well. In fact, I can't remember when I've slept better or been more at peace with myself. But let's stay focused. You were going to tell me how I was ruining my life. I'm waiting to hear your logic."

Sam, still trying to stall, asked, "How is Marquetta doing?"

Todd refused to be swayed. "What's going on with you? I asked you to explain how I was ruining my life and I want to hear your answer. I will not permit you to change the subject. You made a statement and I want you to clarify it. Now, tell me what you mean."

Sam squirmed a little in his seat, then stated hesitantly, "If you marry Juanita, you can get the benefits of her father's wealth not just for you, but for your children as well. Man, don't you understand? Your children won't need scholarships to go to college. You won't have to worry about your business failing. With his contacts, he'll keep you supplied with clients. With five words, you'll be on easy street. Just say, 'Juanita, will you marry me?' She'll say yes. This stuff about love and happiness isn't real."

Todd, in amazement, queried, "What happened to you? You know that isn't true. Look at our folks; Uncle Todd and Aunt Rita, they still love each other and are very happy. If they're unhappy, it's because of our not visiting them like we should. We're so busy trying to get ourselves established, we only call them on the holidays. We're sorry excuses for children, if you ask me!" While responding to Sam, Todd rose from his seat behind his desk and walked around to the front of his desk and leaned against it. He positioned himself closer to Sam because he believed the conversation warranted it. Looking in Sam's direction, he crossed his legs at his ankles and folded his arms. He was ready to parley.

Sam, now relaxed in his dialogue with Todd, crossed his leg by resting his ankle on his knee. Then he placed one hand on his ankle and one on his knee. Sam ignored the last statement, "Little Brother, I'm not talking about them. They come from the old school. I'm talking about today's couples."

"I didn't know how brainwashed you had become over money, Man. Man, you can have all the money in the world, but without God you don't have anything. Do you know what? I rededicated my life to God a few months ago and last night I got an understanding of what that meant. That empty void I had been trying to fill all these years is filled today. It's not because of money, women, or my business; it's because of God. I can truly say, today I'm satisfied with being his child. A child of God. Whatever blessings he has for me is in addition to knowing that I am his child. Sam, do you understand what I'm saying? I finally have an idea of God's love for us (mankind) and me as His child. Do you realize that everything I am and have is because of God? It's not because of Juanita and her father and it's not because of you, either. So don't tell me I have ruined my life, because today I know I am saved. The only advice I can give you right now, my brother, is to seek God for yourself. Now Sam, is there anything else you would like to say to me?"

Sam was flabbergasted. He just shook his head in a horizontal movement. Todd understood it to mean "No." Once composed, Sam said, "I'll see you at the banquet," and left.

---

Marquetta opened the door for Barbara and said, "I'm glad you and Phillip arrived before Sam. Where is Phillip?"

Barbara replied, "He's parking the car. You look beautiful—those colors accent your complexion wondrously. The earrings are perfect." Marquetta was wearing a white and gold satin gown with a full length matching coat.

Marquetta responded, "You picked them out. Thanks for going shopping with me. You're a knockout yourself. I know Phillip tried to push the wedding date up, after he saw you tonight." Barbara was attired in a blue satin gown with a matching evening jacket.

"You know him too well. He was comical. He said he's not letting me out of his sight. He'll even follow me to the bathroom. But he'll wait outside the door. I told him thanks for waiting outside." Both laughed.

Marquetta said, "He's, too much."

"Isn't he, though? Oh, by the way, have you talked to Todd today."

"No, I haven't."

"Well, you're in for a surprise."

"Oh, really?"

"All I'm going to say is God hears and answers prayers."

"Praise the Lord."

"Marquetta, since we have time, twist both sides of you hair and pin them back. That way more of your face can be exposed. Your facial features should be emphasized and your cheek bones highlighted."

"You do it. I'm not good at fixing my hair."

"Okay." Barbara pinned both sides of her hair back and the long cluster of curls fell into place with the others. The twisted sides formed a "V" shape which accented the curls beneath it. Marquetta's clusters fell midway her back Once completed Barbara said, "Now look."

Marquetta walked to her bathroom, looked in the mirror, and commented when she returned to the living room where Barbara was sitting. "Hey, why go to the beauty salon when I can use you? I need you to style my hair more often. I like it."

Barbara replied, "Good. Did you hear a knock?"

Marquetta remarked, "Yes, it's either Phillip or Sam. Either way, we're ready." Marquetta opened the door and to her surprise, it was Phillip and Sam. Marquetta commented, "Perfect timing, we're ready."

Barbara stood up with her evening bag in her hand and walked toward the door where Phillip and Sam stood. Marquetta walked into her living room to pick up her evening bag and her keys off her coffee table. Phillip, took the keys from her hand and locked the door while instructing Barbara and Marquetta to take the stairs to the parking lot. Seeing Marquetta in her evening gown made Sam more determined to have her. It was hard for him to keep his eyes off of her, but he knew he had to act like a gentleman until he could get her alone. Marquetta and Barbara stood at Phillip's car waiting for Sam and Phillip to arrive. As Sam and Phillip walked onto the parking lot toward Marquetta and Barbara, the wind started blowing, slightly lifting an isolated small piece of tissue in the air while simultaneously blowing Barbara's and Marquetta's hair. It was a warm night, so both Marquetta and Barbara welcomed the breeze and tilted their heads to receive the wind in their faces—both oblivious to the actions of those around them. The expression of pure pleasure on Barbara's face made Phillip put his arm around her and kiss her before opening the car door. When Sam saw the expression of joy that came over Marquetta's face, his thoughts were less pure. He knew he had to sleep with her. Phillip asked, "Why don't we take one car?"

"That's fine with me," replied Marquetta.

"Me, too," responded Barbara.

Hesitantly, Sam agreed, "That's fine. But I was hoping to take you dancing later, Marquetta."

Marquetta remarked, "Thank you, Sam, for the invitation but I have an early morning flight. So I plan to get home and to bed early."

Sam commented, "Oh yeah, that's right. I forgot you leave for vacation tomorrow."

As they entered the banquet hall, the hostess said to Marquetta, "Ms. Logan, you and your escort are to sit at the head table."

"Thank you," responded Marquetta.

Sam contemplated, "Good, I may be able to play with her under the table if I can position myself right." Sam became disappointed when they arrived at the head table because the head table faced all the others and was open. He pondered, "How am I going to get her alone?" His thoughts were interrupted by Todd's voice. "Hi, Big Brother. I hope you don't mind if I sit beside you." Before Todd took his seat, he leaned over Sam and said, "Hi,,Markie."

Marquetta, feeling confident Todd's conversation with her was sincere, wasn't disturbed by seeing Todd with Juanita. Besides, she knew she had given the situation to God. She replied, "Hi, Todd and Juanita. How are you both, this evening?"

Juanita refused to respond. Todd replied, "I'm fine."

Sam thought, "Um, he has Juanita with him. That's good to know."

The Master of Ceremonies came to the microphone, stated the purpose for the evening, then announced, "Now, to introduce our guest speaker is Mr. Todd Parker of Parker and Associates Law Firm."

Marquetta was surprised. She thought, "Todd didn't tell me he was responsible for the introduction."

She listened with interest to his introduction. Todd declared, "I have known the guest speaker for 10 years and it has been a wonderful experience. She is sincere, especially when it comes to helping the offender population. The interesting thing about our meeting was that I was a police detective at the time and I was gathering evidence to prosecute one of her clients. But, after speaking with her, she convinced me that her client was innocent and was willing to find evidence to prove it. Needless to say, she was correct. Today, that young man has his own company, and a wife and children that love and respect him—all because an organization was willing to give him a second chance. We know that organization was Second Chance, Inc., owned and operated by Ms. Marquetta Logan. Without further ado, I would like to present to you Ms. Logan."

Marquetta prayed as she walked to the podium, took a deep breath and began. She acknowledged all the people responsible for the banquet and commenced with her speech. Beginning with a Bible verse, taken from: John 8:7 (KJV). She read:

"John 8:7 (KJV)"

"'So when they continued asking him, he lifted up himself, and said unto them, He that is without sin among you, let him first cast a stone at her.'"

She paused after reading the scripture. She wanted the words to take root. Then, she continued.

"All too often in our lives, we have a tendency to justify our sins or believe our sins should be forgiven, but those sins committed by others should not be forgiven. Fortunately, that is not our choice to make. However, we do have a responsibility to love. In making this statement, I am in no way condoning crimes but, I am saying, after people have been released from the criminal justice system and have entered mainstream America, we must treat them as fellow human beings. This can be done by giving them jobs and training opportunities so they can provide for themselves and their families. Second Chance, Inc., provides that type of atmosphere for their clients. They're reeducated with a sense of purpose and with a new understanding of the place God should have in their lives. They learn to appreciate responsibility and respect authority. Those of you who have not decided to open your arms and extend forgiveness and love to the offender population, ask some of those around who have and see how rewarding it has been for them. They now have employees that are loyal to them and their organization. Most companies that are affiliated with Second Chance, Inc., have increased their business. You will be surprised by the amount of business one loyal employee can bring to a company. Not to mention the tax dollars you could save by not having to support so many offenders in correctional institutions." Marquetta continued on this vein, then finally said, "In closing, I would suggest that you can give back to society by hiring people from the offender population. You'll save money and maybe even your life. Because an offender who is employed and happy is no longer an offender. He (she) is a positive citizen in our community. Thank you." People all around the room stood up and applauded her. As Marquetta walked to her seat, she said silently, "Thank you, Father God, for being with me." Sam stood up as she, took her seat at the head table. Once seated, John Wordsler, the gentleman Todd referred to in his speech who was accused wrongfully of a crime and was acquitted, based on Marquetta's hard work, appeared at her chair with a plaque in one hand, and a microphone in the other. John said, "This award is being presented to you, Ms. Logan, on behalf of your past and present clients. We just want to say thank you for supporting the offender population." He handed Marquetta the award and kissed her on the cheek. Marquetta was overwhelmed. Tears streamed down her face as she responded through a crackling voice, "I can never tell you how much this really means to me. Thank you so very much. I thank God for the opportunity to serve." Marquetta hugged John and kissed him on the cheek. She whispered in his ear, "I want you and your family to come visit me."

John smiled and replied, "We will." John walked away with a smile on his face. Sam reasoned, *Brains and beauty. This one's mine, Little Brother.* Throughout the evening whenever Todd tried to hold a conversation with Marquetta, Sam or Juanita would interrupt. Finally, Phillip walked over to Sam and Marquetta and asked if they were ready to leave.

---

On the drive home, Marquetta felt relaxed, the anticipation of the evening was over and she had to admit she was truly blessed by the occasion. She prayed silently, "Thank you, Father God, for this night. I am blessed. Thank you for giving me the idea to develop this company, for blessing it and permitting it to bless others." After prayer she decided, *I can now get ready for the Caribbean.*

Her thoughts were interrupted by Sam. He inquired, "Marquetta, when we get to your place, how about I come in and we talk over a few drinks? I have a bottle of champagne in my car."

Phillip commented, "Oh, that's a good idea. I'm not ready to go home, either. How about you, Barbara?"

Barbara tried not to laugh, but a giggle slipped out when she queried, "If Marquetta doesn't mind us coming in for a short time? I know she has an early flight."

Marquetta responded, "No, I think one hour would be all right. Is that time frame all right with everyone?"

Sam remarked, "I guess so. You know, Phillip, I really haven't had a chance to be alone with Marquetta and I would like to get to know her better. Perhaps you and Barbara could see her when she gets back from vacation."

Marquetta replied, "Sam, thank you for your interest in me. However, I believe you can learn about me by seeing how I interact with my friends, for starters. Besides, I told you I'm certain I'm not your type. However, you are welcome to visit me tonight, as long as Phillip and Barbara are visiting, too. You see, I don't entertain men alone at my place until I feel more comfortable with them."

"Oh, I didn't know that. Didn't Todd sleep at your place last night?" Sam calculated, *This will expose the type of woman she is to Phillip. He'll see there is no need to try to protect her.*

Marquetta laughed. Sam reasoned, *She's trying to play it off. She's embarrassed. Let's see how funny it will be when I call her on it.* He asked, "Marquetta, what's so funny?"

Phillip replied, "He stayed at my place last night."

Sam, embarrassed, spoke in a lower tone, "He said he wasn't coming home. I knew he was at Marquetta's, and I assumed he was going to stay there."

"He stayed with me," repeated Phillip. Barbara positioned her head so Marquetta could see her face from the back seat, and smiled. They all understood Sam's game. As they walked into Marquetta's building, Sam walked to his car to get his bottle of champagne.

Phillip stated, "Marquetta, your rule is a good one to have. Now I see why you and Barbara use it. Boyfriend wants you sexually. You do understand that, don't you?"

"Yes, big time. Thanks for the help."

"When he leaves, Barbara and I are going to stay a few minutes longer. In case he decides to come back." Phillip, took Marquetta's door key; opened the door, handed her the key back, and all three walked into her condo, taking seats in the living room.

Once seated comfortably on her sofa, Marquetta commented, "Good thinking."

Phillip laughed. Barbara said, "What's so funny?"

"I can't believe I'm trying to stop a brother from getting some action. Boy, have I changed!"

"Thank God," said Barbara.

"You can say that again," said Marquetta. Marquetta rose to her feet and went into the kitchen.

When Sam knocked on the door, Phillip opened it and said, "Take a seat, Man."

Marquetta walked out of the kitchen carrying a tray with three crystal wine glasses and a flute for the champagne. Sam concluded, "She has some class and she drinks. That's good to know."

Phillip, took a glass of wine, tasted it, and stated, "I like this non-alcoholic wine. It's good."

"Thanks, I knew you would like it," said Marquetta.

"Now I can use those wine glasses I have at home. This is an excellent idea," declared Barbara.

Sam thought, *Non-alcoholic wine! These three are tripping me out. This isn't the 1920s—prohibition has ended.* Marquetta, took a seat by Sam on the sofa, after she hung up her coat and Barbara's jacket in the closet near the main entrance to her condo. Sam noticed the zipper in the back of Marquetta's dress. It, took every bit of strength he had not to pull the zipper down. Trying to take his mind off of the dress he inquired, "What do you do for fun around here?"

Phillip asked, "Are we boring you?"

"No, not really. Marquetta, could I talk to you privately for a moment." Sam wanted to be alone with Marquetta. Phillip and Barbara were cramping his style. He hated double dates.

Marquetta queried, "Sam, what do you need to say to me that Phillip and Barbara can't hear?"

Sam asked, "Are you afraid to be alone with me, Marquetta?"

"Sam, I'm not afraid of you. I just don't want to play games with you. Let's not try to waste each others time. Okay?"

"What if I told you I was leaving now and I wanted to give you a kiss, privately. Then could I see you alone."

Marquetta asked, "Sam, are you leaving now? If you are, I will escort you to the door, but that's it."

"No, I'll hang around a little longer," replied Sam.

Barbara decided it would be best to change the conversation. "Sam, you and Todd really resemble each other. Who do you look like?"

"Our father."

Phillip suggested, "Sam, if you would like to use the phone to call Todd, I'm sure Marquetta wouldn't mind. Perhaps he and Juanita are going to a night club."

Sam replied, "Thanks, Phillip, that's an idea." Sam called Todd's place and his answering machine picked up. He then called Juanita's home. Suzette answered and told him she wasn't in. He hung up the phone and conjectured, "They probably don't want to be disturbed—it is Friday night. He looked at Marquetta, admired her beauty and remarked, "Marquetta you look absolutely delicious in that dress. I think it's unfair that you would deliberately look this good and not let a man enjoy the pleasure of your company."

Marquetta queried, "What are you referring to Sam?"

"I should at least be able to hold your hand."

"So, you're saying because I wore an outfit I bought with my money, which you happen to like on me, I should permit you to hold my hand. Sam, you called me pretending to be someone else I might add, so you could have a date with me. I owe you nothing. As far as I'm concerned, you got what you wanted—a date. If you're disappointed, it's not my fault. It's getting late, perhaps you're ready to leave."

"No, I'm really enjoying your company." Sam grinned. He decided, *Barbara and Phillip will leave before I do tonight. I will get into that dress. I am not my brother.*

Phillip, determined, *He plans to out sit us, but I have a surprise for him.*

Barbara asked, "Marquetta, may I see you in your kitchen, please?"

Marquetta agreed, "Sure." She walked in the kitchen and Barbara followed.

Barbara queried, "He's persistent, isn't he? I'm so glad Phillip decided we double date. He plans to out sit us. You have figured that out, haven't you?"

"Yes, I have, however we already prayed about this date. It will be all right."

As they walked back into the living room, Sam stood up, and said, "Well, Marquetta, I'm leaving now. Nice to meet you, Barbara and Phillip. Marquetta, I haven't had a date like this since high school." Sam chuckled..

"Thanks for the comment. I like to make my dates memorable. Good bye, Sam."

After Sam left her condo, Marquetta, Barbara, and Phillip looked out the window to watch him drive off the parking lot. As they watched, the three of them laughed at Sam's behavior. "He was persistent. Todd said he would be, but I made it clear when you two went into the kitchen that Barbara and I would be here as long as he remained. I guess he thought about it and realized I was serious," said Phillip.

"I should have realized that Todd talked to you about Sam. I told him I could handle him," responded Marquetta.

"I think Todd knew a little more about what his brother was capable of than you did. Besides, I prayed about it, too. Now I see how Todd would lose girls to him. That boy is serious," said Phillip.

Marquetta thought about what Phillip said, then she stated, "Thanks Phillip, and when you see Todd, tell him I said 'thanks.'"

I thought Todd's introductory speech was very nice," remarked Barbara.

"Yeah, I did, too. Tell him thanks for the intro speech, too. Boy, this has been a long night."

Barbara inquired, "How are you getting to the airport tomorrow?"

"Thanks, Barbara, for asking me. I don't know. Would you take me? My flight leaves at 8:00 a.m."

"I'll pick up Barbara and we'll be here by 5:00 a.m. That should give you plenty of time," replied Phillip.

"I could drive myself. That way. I won't disturb your sleep," said Marquetta.

"No, I think we should do it. That way, I can help with your luggage," responded Phillip.

"Okay, thanks guys. Don't forget to pray about my trip."

Barbara replied, "I won't."

Phillip said, "Let's go, Barbara, we have to get up early and Sam should be long gone by now."

"Thanks for everything. See you tomorrow. Good night."

Barbara and Phillip, in unison, said, "Good night."

# CHAPTER 4

# RELATIONSHIPS

Marquetta dressed in jeans, t-shirt, and sneakers, smiled when she heard the door bell. She thought, "Barbara and Phillip are on time." She opened the door and asked, "It's a little early for you, isn't it?"

Todd smiled and said, "Not if you want a ride to the airport, it isn't."

Marquetta, dumbfounded, inquired, "You're taking me to the airport? What happened to Barbara and Phillip?"

"I convinced them to let me take you. I hope you don't mind."

"Not at all. You mean, you're willing to lose sleep over me," Marquetta remarked teasingly. I"m impressed."

"You get impressed, too easily," commented Todd. Both laughed.

"Well, help me with my luggage."

"I thought you'd never ask." Todd put her luggage in the trunk of his car and drove to the airport. Marquetta pleased with the turn of events, said, "Thank you for wanting to take me to the airport."

"Don't mention it. I figure the two of us have really been interfering with Barbara and Phillip's quiet time."

"You're right, we have been dumping our problems on them. Although they wouldn't complain, they do need a break."

"But that's not the only reason. I have a flight out today, too. I thought it would be nice to ride to the airport together. As he said the last statement, he glanced at Marquetta to see the expression on her face. It was one of wonderment. She queried, "Where are you going?"

"To the Caribbean with you."

"With me! How?"

"Barbara made reservations for me yesterday."

"You were able to still be booked?"

"Yeah, that's great, isn't it?"

Marquetta was excited and replied, "Yeah it is!" After ruminating, she asked, "Do you think it's okay?"

"I know what you're thinking. You're happy I'm going, but you are concerned about us being together in a relaxed, romantic atmosphere. Just be happy and don't worry. Markie, if this is going to work, I need to be able to respect your wishes, and you need to respect mine. You have shown me that you can respect mine. I need to show you that I can respect yours, okay?"

"You're serious, aren't you?"

"Yes, but I'll tell you this, this is going to be a new experience for me."

"You can say that again."

Both laughed. When they arrived at the airport, Todd parked the car and, took Marquetta's hand and said, "Let's pray."

Marquetta replied, "Okay!"

Todd led, "Father God, we thank you for this day. We ask you to let us have a safe and enjoyable trip. A vacation that would please You. In Jesus' name. Amen."

On the flight over, they held hands as they talked. Both of them knew their relationship was about to change and were looking forward to the future.

As they went through customs, they laughed, because passengers were standing in line dancing to the calypso music. Once through customs, Todd said, "I'm, too tired to dance. I'll get a cab."

Marquetta stated, "Good. Get the cab and I'll watch our luggage. The drive seemed extremely long, because they both were exhausted. At last, they arrived at their hotel. Todd stated, "I'm sleepy. I'll tell you what, let's get some rest and meet at the beach at 2:00 p.m. To the hotel clerk he said, "I believe we have adjoining rooms. The names are Marquetta Logan and Todd Parker."

The hotel clerk responded, "No, sir, the rooms are not adjoining, there is a suite between your suites."

Todd laughed then remarked to Marquetta, "I guess Barbara felt I didn't need to be that close to you."

Both laughed and got on the elevator. Todd tipped both bell boys, looked at Marquetta and commented as they got off of the elevator and began searching for their rooms. "Markie, don't forget to meet me at 2:00 p.m. on the beach."

"Okay, I won't. Have a good nap."

---

"Hi, Mom. I'm just calling to let you know I arrived safely. Tell Dad, Grandpa Tom and Grandma Kate that I'm fine and I love them. I love you, too, Mom."

"I know dear. I think this vacation will be good for you."

"I know it's going to be interesting. Good bye, Mom."

"Good bye, Dear."

Marquetta thought, *Mom doesn't need to know Todd is here. I'll probably tell her later.* She called Barbara. Barbara was waiting by the phone for her call. As soon as the phone rang, Barbara picked up. "Hello."

"Hi, Barbara, it's Marquetta. We arrived safely."

"How did you like our surprise?"

"It was a surprise. He's changed, Barbara. He let the Lord into his life. It's a wonderful change. We held hands during the entire flight, except when we ate. We decided we'll meet on the beach at 2:00 p.m.."

"Wear the yellow bathing suit. I think he'll be pleasantly surprised."

"Barbara, you're, too much," Marquetta laughed.

"Don't get married in the Caribbean! That wouldn't be fair to the rest of us. We want to see you walk down the aisle."

"Wouldn't that be something?" Marquetta yawned then stated, "Barbara, I'm tired. I'll talk to you later. Good bye."

---

Sam was in Todd's room, sitting on the corner end of his bed, reading the note Todd left him when the phone rang. He was so distraught he couldn't answer the phone. Juanita left this message. "Todd, call me. I need to talk to you about last night. Bye-bye."

———————

"Hello, Todd Parker and Associates."

"Let me speak to Todd. This is Juanita Smith." Juanita was walking in her bedroom, with the phone in one hand and the other hand held the receiver up to her mouth and ear so she could talk and hear clearly.

"Ma'am, our office is closed today. It is Saturday."

"Well, if it's closed, why did you answer the phone, Missy?"

"I thought you were Mr. Parker. He's the only one who knew we would be here today, I thought."

"He's not there? Where is he? I called his home. Since I didn't get an answer I assumed he was at his office."

"Ma'am, he's on vacation. He'll be in the office in a week. Would you like to leave a message?"

"What do you mean he's on vacation? Who's handling his clients?"

"Mr. Clemmons."

"Who?"

"Mr. Bill Clemmons."

"I don't know him. When did he come on board?"

"Effective Friday."

Juanita was outraged. Not because he had left someone she didn't know to run the business but because he went on vacation without her. Although she acted as if that was the reason she had an attitude. "You mean yesterday! He brought someone in one day before he left for vacation and made him responsible for the businesses he represents. What kind of business is he running? This is ludicrous! I want an explanation! Do you have a number where I can reach him? If so, I want it now!"

Myrna, initially not pleased with the position Mr. Parker placed her in with Ms. Smith, had to admit to herself, *I'm enjoying Ms. Smith's outrage. She's so arrogant. It's about time she realized the world doesn't revolve around her. But by the tone of her voice, I don't think she's getting the message.* She replied, "Ma'am, I don't have his number. However, I can transfer this call to Mr. Clemmons."

"You idiot. This is not a business call. Oh, tell me, is Todd's brother Sam still in town?"

"Ma'am, I don't know."

"What do you know? You're the most incompetent secretary I've ever met. When Todd gets back, I'm going to suggest he ask for your resignation." Juanita slammed the phone down on its receiver; Myrna heard its effect in her ear. Myrna reasoned, *Ms. Smith makes it difficult to keep a professional attitude. That woman has serious problems!*

Juanita placed the phone on the night stand near her bed. She walked to the window and peered out. She had a beautiful view of the city. She was nineteen flights up. Whenever she felt down in the dumps, she looked out the window and watched the poor people catching buses and running to catch the subway. It reminded her how important she was and how many people would kill to have her station in life. The window did the trick for her again. She noticed a young girl running for the bus and tripped. She laughed. That was all the reality she needed. She was herself again. She deserved Todd and she was going to get him. She speculated, *Maybe Sam is at Todd's but was asleep when I called earlier. I'll try again.*

She pushed the button that dialed Todd's house.

"Hello," answered Sam.

Juanita, excited someone answered the phone, replied, "Sam, it's you. What's going on with your brother? Has he lost his mind!"

"Calm down, Juanita, you're shouting in my ear."

In a calmer tone, Juanita queried, "Sam, where is he?"

"I don't know. I woke up this morning and walked to his room, determined to knock some sense into him, if I had, too—only to discover a note."

"A note. You mean he left you a note! You're here visiting him and he left you a note. I'm telling you, he's lost it!"

"Juanita, stay calm and tell me what happened last night. The two of you seemed fine at the banquet. What happened after you left?"

"Let me think, let me think, let me think," Juanita repeated swiftly. Then she replied, "Oh yeah, Todd suggested we go to the tidal basin to sit and talk. I thought that would be romantic, so I agreed to go. Todd didn't say anything as he drove us to the tidal basin, but when we arrived, Todd asked me a strange question."

Sam inquired, "What was the question?"

"Something like, where did I see myself five years from now?"

"What did you say?"

"I said making money and more money. Then he said, not from a business perspective, but with your life in general."

"Then, what did you say?"

"I told him I never really think of my life apart from business. I guess business is my life."

"What did Todd say then?"

"I don't remember. Let me see. He suggested we get out of the car and walk around the basin. He talked about how clear the night sky was and how bright the stars were. He even told me he enjoyed the warm gentle breeze from the night air as he felt it on his skin. He seemed to be more in tune with nature than me. So, I suggested that we go to my condo and make love 'til the sun comes up. We could come up for air by drinking champagne and listening to his favorite jazz CDs. Shortly after that, we walked back to the car and drove to my condo. I handed him my keys as I usually do when he brings me home, to open my door and that's what he did. He opened the door, reached inside for the light switch, turned it on and then said another strange thing."

"What did he say, Juanita?"

"He told me, he wasn't for me. He would hold me back. We wanted different things. He kissed me on the cheek and left. I thought, 'I know he didn't just break up with me. He's not that stupid. I'll call him tomorrow.' That's what I did. I called here, left a message, and then I talked to his idiot of a secretary. I thought perhaps you were still in town, so I called back. Hey, wait a minute! Did you just get home from last night?"

"No, why?"

"I called earlier and there was no answer. I thought perhaps you slept with Marquetta."

"No, I didn't. I didn't answer the phone because I had just

finished reading Todd's note. I was stunned." Sam, at that instant, remembered Marquetta was to go on vacation, starting today. "That's it! I hate to tell you this, but Todd is probably with Marquetta. She was going on vacation today. Her flight left early this morning. She went to the Caribbean."

Livid, Juanita said, "I don't believe it. No way did he decide to pick that woman over me."

"I didn't say he picked her over you. I just said he decided to go on vacation with her. That alone may tell us something. He may be knocking your door down when he comes back. Think about it. There's no way she's going to withhold sex in the atmosphere that is provided for vacationers in the Caribbean. If she can, she's a better woman than I thought. That environment promotes relaxation and fun. The warm, sometimes hot days in conjunction with the beach and the music—think about it. Party, Baby, party! That's the message I get and so will my brother. He's no dummy. He'll convince her to sleep with him. If you are as good in the sack as you say you are, Todd will come to his senses. He just needs to find out that she's no different than any other woman. Who knows, she may be a little worse. Once he acknowledges that, he'll come back and marry you. Let's face it, there is only so much any woman can do. No harm meant. But, you have a little more that comes with your package." Sam decided, *Juanita doesn't need to know about Todd's new-found relationship with God. After all, I believe in God,, too, but there are times I have to do things my way. When it comes to women and money you only call on God when you need help.*

Juanita queried, "So, you don't think I need to go over there?"

"That would only make matters worse."

"Perhaps you're right. This would be an opportunity for him to see right through her. Well, Sam, what are you going to do, go home or hang around here until your vacation is over?"

"I haven't given it much consideration. I guess I'll stay a few days more and then go see what's happening elsewhere."

"If that's the case, why don't you hang out with me? I know a real nice spot we can go to, if you like jazz. It's a supper club. You can eat and dance the night away, if you like. They make pretty good drinks, too."

"Sounds like a winner. I still have my car rental from last night. I'll get an extension and meet you at your place at 7:30 p.m."

"We need to be at the supper club no later than 8:00 p.m., 7:30 p.m. would be fine. See ya then. Bye-bye."

As son as Juanita hung up with Sam she remembered she wanted to talk to Horace. Juanita called Horace Greely's private line. There was no answer.

---

The drive to the church to meet Pastor Green to discuss their impending marriage was filled with anticipation. Phillip put a praise tape in the tape player he had in his car to help calm them. Phillip knew when Barbara was excited, because she couldn't stop talking. She had been talking since he picked her up. After he put the tape in the player, both commenced singing with the music and the ride became enjoyable. To their surprise, when they arrived at Pastor Green's study, he was there alone. When Pastor Green heard the knock on the door, he opened it and greeted them. "Hi, Barbara and Phillip. Come in and take a seat. Pastor Green's study was an 8x10 room. His favorite thing in the study was his built in book case with shelves. It housed his collection of religious books, books of history and different versions of the Bible. His degree from a seminary was in a picture frame and placed on the wall near his desk. The desk was made of maple wood. His chair was made of firm leather. It was a high back cushioned chair that was trimmed in maple wood. His desk faced the door and was adjacent to the book case. Two high back firm leather chairs trimmed in maple wood rested on the wall near the door. A small oval shaped coffee table made out of maple wood was between the two chairs. Barbara took the chair closest to the door and Phillip took the other one. Pastor Green proceeded to his desk and took a seat. Once everyone was seated, Pastor Green inquired, "Now, tell me why you wanted to meet with me?"

Phillip responded, "As Barbara mentioned to your secretary on the phone, I asked her to marry me and she accepted. We understand that in order for you to marry us, we need to come to you for counseling."

"You both have been involved in the singles group at this church, and I designed that group specifically to teach single males and females what is expected in marriage and how to conduct themselves while single. I have spoken to both of you at different times since you've been members here, so I have an understanding of your foundation in Christianity. That's why I will only make suggestions and ask or answer questions at this point. I will begin my questions with you, Phillip. Do you love Barbara?"

"Yes, sir, I do."

"How do you know she is the person you want as your wife?"

Phillip tried to gather his words as he rubbed his hands back and forth. He replied, "I have been praying for a wife, and after meeting and dating Barbara, I found her to be everything I want in a wife. She's beautiful, funny and smart. She's got everything I ever wanted in a woman, and more."

Pastor Green commented, "Phillip, I want you to remember the physical part will change. Now, think about these questions before you answer them. Can you love her fat? With missing teeth? Sick? Unable to work? Not able to have children? Would you care for her like you care for yourself? Would you be willing to sacrifice what you want to make her happy?"

Phillip answered, "Yes, sir. I've given it a lot of thought. I realize things can change from day-to-day and no matter what is going on in our lives, I must think of me and Barbara as one. I also understand that it is much easier said than done, but with God's help, we'll be all right. I also know that God's help won't eliminate some of the suffering we may go through as a couple, but it does mean we can and will get through it. Barbara is a warm human being that loves to help others, and I believe she will be a faithful wife and loving mother."

"You want children. What happens if she can't have any?"

"We talked about it and decided we would adopt."

"Well, Barbara you heard the questions I raised to Phillip. I'm sure you thought about them as I asked them. Do you have anything to say or to add?"

"I do love Phillip and I know, only through God, will we be able to last."

Pastor Green stated, "Phillip and Barbara, stand and let's hold hands. I'm going to pray for you and your decision to marry. Father God, first we come to you thanking you for being God and for being our Father. Two of your children, Barbara and Phillip, want to be married. We ask you to bless, lead and guide them on their decision to marry. In Jesus' name. Amen."

"Now, we prayed together for God's blessing on you and your decision to marry. When you go home, make a list of every possible concern you may have about the other and your pending marriage. Go in prayer giving the list of concerns to God. Because you need to understand your lives and your marriage are in His hands."

Both replied, "Yes, sir."

Then Phillip queried, "Thank you, Pastor Green. May we marry in two weeks?"

"Call my secretary and put the date on my calendar. If you have any questions, call me or come see me. Good bye."

"Good bye," Barbara and Phillip responded in unison.

As they walked to the car, Phillip remarked, "Look at me. I don't think I've ever been this nervous. I'm sweating. I had no idea what he was going to say." He took off his suit jacket and the back of his white shirt was wet with perspiration. "I'm glad this part is over and we can be married in two weeks."

Barbara was not surprised at Phillip's shirt because she knew whenever he was nervous he had a tendency to perspire. So she just nodded her head confirming his statement, then she said, "Let's not forget to write down our concerns and pray about them," commented Barbara.

"Do you have concerns? I don't. I figure we do the best we can for each other and it will work out."

"I want to give it some consideration, and see if I have any concerns, and if so, write them down. I think you should give it some thought, too."

"Okay," Phillip replied, a little disappointed.

"Look, it can't hurt anything. If we ask God to help us through our concerns, he will and we will be a better couple for it."

"You know that's true," responded Phillip. He smiled because his disappointment was lifted. As they got in the car, Phillip asked,

"How would you like to hear some jazz tonight?"

"At the supper club downtown?"

"Yeah."

"Sounds good to me. Phillip, we also need to discuss how much money we want to spend on this wedding."

"Okay," agreed Phillip.

---

"Where is he?" Marquetta thought as she walked the beach looking for Todd. "It's 2:00 p.m. exactly." She had on a yellow one piece bathing suit with a white and yellow pair of sandals and a pair of sun shades. In her hand was her swim cap. As she walked on the beach, the sand began to collect on her sandals and made her feet hot. She considered, *I should jump in the water and let Todd look for me.*

Finally, she heard Todd's voice. She turned and saw him waving his hand as he yelled, "Markie, I'm over here." He was seated at a table with an umbrella on it close to the beach. Once Marquetta arrived at the table, she commented, "Good thinking, the sun rays are hot. How long have you been sitting here?"

"About 30 minutes. I wanted to find a nice location for us. That way when you arrived, you could just sit and enjoy the view."

"Thank you for being so considerate. It's beautiful here, isn't it?"

"Yes, it is. I have been sitting here enjoying the view. It is magnificent! The water is absolutely superb in color. It's a beautiful shade of green and it's so clear. Speaking of water, would you like something to drink?"

"A ginger ale would be nice."

Todd flagged the waiter and ordered two ginger ales—after which he commented, "You look absolutely breathtaking. You know I think this is the most I've seen of your body since I met you."

Marquetta felt a little uncomfortable because of the way Todd looked at her as he admired her in her bathing suit. She inquired, "Are we going to swim or what?"

"Okay, let's swim," responded Todd. As they were leaving the table Marquetta spotted the waiter coming with their drinks and stated, "No, not yet, I changed my mind. I want to drink my soda first." As they walked back to their table, the waiter arrived with their drinks. Todd paid the bill and tipped him. As they sipped their drinks, Todd asked, "Why haven't we done this before? It's so peaceful here."

Marquetta was curious about Todd's decision to go on vacation with her, so she asked, "Todd, what made you decide to come on vacation with me?"

"I knew I wanted to get away from Sam and Juanita and I wanted to be with you. So I asked Myrna to call your office and asked Barbara to make reservations for me."

"Before I forget, thanks for the introduction last night. I told Barbara to tell you thanks because I didn't want to forget to tell you. Oh yeah, thanks for talking to Phillip about Sam, too. Barbara and Phillip wouldn't leave until he left. Then, Phillip waited a few minutes longer before he would consider leaving, because he wanted to make certain Sam wouldn't come back."

Todd laughed and remarked, "So my brother was disappointed, big time."

"Yes, he was, to say the least. I don't think he's going to rate me high on his list of choices of women."

"That's good. You don't need his ratings. Let's hit the water."

Once in the water, Todd queried, "Do you swim or am I going to have to watch you carefully to make sure you're all right."

Marquetta, now relaxed, replied with a smile. "I swim, but you can still watch me."

Todd responded, "I will." They swam and frolicked in the water for hours. Todd showed Marquetta games he and Sam played in the water as children. Todd stated, "You know, Markie, Sam and I would play in the water for hours just like we're doing now, but I'm having much more fun with you."

Marquetta laughed, then stated, "I'm glad you enjoy my company more than Sam's. Look out! Here comes a frisbee. See if you can catch it."

Todd caught it and threw it back to the couple that was playing with it. Nancy caught it and said, "Thanks, do you two want to play?" Nancy was in her late-thirties. Her red hair peeked from under her swim cap. She was a petite woman in height and size. She had big blue eyes that seemed to twinkle whenever she looked at Walter.

"Yeah, we'll play," responded Todd. As they played they talked.

Nancy stated, "I'm Nancy, and this is my husband Walter. We just got married and received a trip to the Caribbean as a wedding present." Walter was apparently her senior. He was in his late forties. His salt and pepper hair was uncovered. He was 6 feet tall and very slim. His green eyes danced every time he looked at Nancy. It was apparent they were in love.

"How wonderful! I'm Marquetta, and this is Todd."

Walter asked, "How long have you two been married?"

"We're not married. We're good friends," replied Marquetta.

"Oh, you're not married! I thought you were, but it's not my business," remarked Walter.

"We just, took our vacation at the same time," responded Todd. "We're good friends."

"Walter and I used to be good friends before we got married. That's a good way to develop a relationship—as long as you know what you're doing."

Todd stated, "I don't understand."

"I mean, as friends, you don't want to get, too intimate. That's when the friendship can become difficult," stated Nancy.

"We've been friends for 10 years and it hasn't gotten difficult yet," remarked Todd.

Marquetta smiled and said, "I understand what you mean. Thanks for the advice."

Walter stated, "Nancy, I'm starving, we have to go."

Nancy said, "Maybe we'll see you again in the water. We're going to dinner now. Bye-bye."

"Good bye," Marquetta and Todd replied in unison.

Todd inquired, "What was that all about?"

"She was telling me not to have sex with you."

"I don't believe it. It's a good thing I don't want to have sex with you or I would be upset. I mean, I want to but I have resolved to wait. I'm hungry. Let's get out of the water, too."

Marquetta requested, "Let's swim for another 30 minutes, please."

An hour later Todd announced, "I'm starving!"

"Okay, let's get something to eat. I'll meet you in the lobby in half an hour," replied Marquetta.

"Can't we order in my room and look at TV? I'm tired. I haven't played in the water this long for years."

"No, I want to go to a restaurant. But, if you go to the restaurant with me, I'll come to your room and watch television with you later. Okay?"

Todd responded, "Sounds like a winner."

---

Phillip and Barbara arrived at the supper club to find it was crowded. Barbara was starving and was looking forward to having her favorite meal at the club. Finally, they were permitted to enter and the waitress asked, "Are you willing to share a table for four with another couple?"

"Sure, if we can be seated," replied Barbara.

The waitress announced, "Fine, follow me."

As soon as they were seated, they ordered. Barbara commented, "The other couple must be dancing. I hope you don't mind sharing? I didn't think to check with you before answering. I'm sorry."

"If I wanted to object I would have. This is fine. I'm hungry, too," responded Phillip.

As Juanita and Sam walked toward their table, Juanita noticed Barbara and Phillip sitting there. Displeased, she cornered her waitress and stated, "There are people sitting at our table. I want them moved."

The waitress replied, "I told you if you wanted to sit at a table for four, you would have to share if we became crowded. You told me that was fine. Ma'am, we're crowded. Now, do you want to share?"

"Are there any more tables for four available that we can be moved to?"

"No, at least not now. Do you want your old seats, because if you don't, I can give them to someone else."

"We'll keep our present arrangement. Thank you," stated Juanita.

As they came closer to their table, Barbara noticed them and commented, "Phillip, look who's here. Do you think we're sitting at their table?"

Phillip was unable to get a clear view before they reached the table. He looked toward Barbara when she queried, "Hi, we're sharing a table with you?"

"Looks that way," Juanita responded, showing little emotion.

Phillip adjusted his chair so Juanita and Sam could get to their seats, and remarked, "Sam, I see you're enjoying the night life."

"Yeah, Juanita decided to show me a night on the town. I'm surprised to see you here."

Barbara asked, "Why?" After she asked that question, she realized she needed to pray. She prayed silently. "Father God, Phillip and I need your help. You know why we're here tonight. Use us, please. Thank you.

In Jesus' name. Amen." After she prayed, she listened intently to the conversation.

"I didn't know you listened to jazz," responded Sam.

"I like jazz and so does Phillip. In fact, this is one of our favorite places if we decide to come to the city for an evening out."

Sam remarked, "That's interesting."

"I hope we didn't give you the impression that we don't enjoy ourselves, because we do," stated Barbara.

"I know that's right. Like your friend Marquetta, a single woman, going to the Caribbean with a single man. One minute she's trying to portray Miss Innocence and the next thing you know she's trying to get my man. But you can tell her no one can please him like I can. So this is the biggest mistake she has ever made. She's playing my game now and she's going to lose. Once he has sex with her, he's coming back to me."

"Juanita, I think you're jumping to conclusions. However, whatever Marquetta and Todd does is their business. Phillip and I came here to enjoy ourselves and the two of you probably came for the same reason. I don't know about you, but that's what I'm going to do."

Phillip chimed in, "Me, too."

"I'm in agreement. Barbara, may I have this dance?" asked Sam.

Barbara responded, "Certainly." They left the table.

Phillip said a quick prayer. "Help me, Lord." He wanted to be certain he interacted with Juanita in a way that would be pleasing to God. The waitress brought the food Phillip and Barbara ordered.

Phillip stated, "Excuse me, could you bring us two ginger ales? Thank you." After the waitress left, Juanita commented, "You guys kill me!"

Phillip exclaimed, "Excuse me!"

"You heard me right. Ya'll try to be so 'holy'! Give me a break. You're not perfect. You sin just like I do. I bet if I wanted to, I could find all kinds of dirt on you."

Phillip replied, "I'm here to enjoy myself. I thought that was why you came here, too—to enjoy yourself. Just because I don't enjoy myself the way you believe I should does not mean that I'm wrong, and definitely should not cause reason for me to be investigated. I don't drink, so I ordered a ginger ale. That doesn't stop me from having fun. It may make me feel a little more comfortable when driving home later tonight. It also helps me keep a clear head so I can make better decisions. I've discovered whatever you do, you're making a choice. I want to make the best possible choice for me. I used to drink, and I found out when I did, I didn't make the best choice for me."

"I never thought about drinking that way before. That gives me food for thought. By the way, how did you know I was referring to the ginger ales?"

"Easy! I saw your eyes."

Juanita laughed and said, "A dead giveaway, huh."

"Would you like to share some of my food?"

"No, thanks."

The music stopped and Sam and Barbara came back to the table. Phillip stated, "I ordered our drinks."

Barbara replied, "Thanks, I'm thirsty."

Phillip, took Barbara's hand and prayed over their food. Sam and Juanita looked at them and then each other in distaste. When Sam noticed they were finished praying, he remarked, "Barbara tells me you two are engaged. Congratulations, Phillip."

Juanita commented, "Oh, I didn't know wedding bells were ringing for you two. How nice! Is that why the big night on the town?"

Phillip smiled and replied, "We do go out occasionally."

"I suppose 'no sex before marriage' for you two," Juanita

remarked pryingly.

Barbara changed the subject. "Juanita, what do you want in a husband?"

Juanita thought, *Since she asked, I'm going to give her an earful.* She replied, "I want a man that can make me holler. You know, Girlfriend, one who knows how to do the do, and can and will do the nasty all night long. That's the only thing that would make me want to come home at night."

Barbara turned to Sam and inquired, "Sam, what do you want in a wife?"

Sam was awaiting Barbara's comment to Juanita's response and was not prepared to answer the question himself. He stuttered a little while he gathered his thoughts. He responded, "I really never thought about it. I guess I know what I don't want."

Barbara queried, "I hope you don't think me, too curious if I ask, what don't you want?"

Sam replied, " Not at all. I'm tired of these honeys who think they can play a game on you. You know, act like they're wonderful until they get you or they think they have you. Then you see their true colors." He smiled and continued. "I know what I want. I want a real woman. One that loves me and one I can love. One in which I can share my inner thoughts, without fearing an attack on my person. Some of these chicks, you tell them a little about you, and they can't wait for an opportunity to throw it up in your face or try to hold it over your head. I guess, bottom line, I want someone I can trust."

Phillip jumped in the conversation, "I know what you mean. I must admit when I was out there hitting on women, I would say if asked, 'I don't want to get married.' But now I realize I was really screening each one for the position of wife. They all failed the test."

Sam stated, "Now, Man, you got me wondering. Do you mind if I get personal?"

"No, Man, go ahead," responded Phillip.

"Knowing what you know about the women of today, what made you decide to get married? He looked at Barbara, then queried, "No offense, but what makes you so sure that she isn't like any of those women you screened out?"

"Since you asked, I'm going to tell you using one word—prayer.

I finally decided my selection process was the pits. I went through the stages of breaking hearts and having my heart broken, so I decided to try to pad my heart by not feeling anything. I had sex just to satisfy my physical need, but my inner being was not being fulfilled. Nothing seemed right. I just felt more and more dissatisfied. So I decided to try God. I told Him, 'I've done it my way, now I want to do it Your way.' That's when I rededicated my life to God and my life started changing for the better. Finally, one day I met Barbara. We talked, and found out we thought a lot alike. We compliment each other, too. I know she's the right one for me."

"I hear ya man. That's nice," commented Sam.

Barbara interrupted, "Excuse me, Phillip, but it's 11:00 p.m.. You have to drop me off and go home. We should be leaving now."

Phillip replied, "Okay." He flagged the waitress, paid the bill with tip, and remarked, "I enjoyed the conversation." He looked directly at Sam when he said, "If you want to talk, here's my card."

Phillip gave his card to Sam. Just before he and Barbara left the table they said, "Good bye."

Juanita didn't say anything. Sam responded, "Good bye."

Juanita looked at Sam, then remarked, "I'm glad they're gone. Now, what would you like to do?"

Sam gave her a sexy grin, then queried, "What would you like to do is the question?"

Juanita looked at her watch, remembered she had a previous engagement, and replied, "You can drop me off. I'm ready for bed. Maybe we can go for brunch tomorrow."

"Brunch tomorrow—that's fine with me." Sam flagged the waitress, paid the bill with tip, and gave her a card with his name and Todd's phone number on it. The waitress returned the card without a comment.

———————

Todd and Marquetta arrived back at the hotel late evening. Todd stated, "Remember, you're going to my room to look at television."

"I know I said I would, but my feet are tired. I need to get off them."

Todd responded, "That's not a problem."

"The only bed I'm sleeping in tonight is the one in the hotel room I paid for."

"I could make a comment, but I won't. I ordered room service for us. I told them to have it set up by

10:00 p.m. That's why I want you to come to my room."

"Okay, I'll go, but my feet hurt. I haven't been dancing in a while. I'm tired. We've been out most of the day and night. I'm not used to this much activity. I'm glad we took a nap."

Once in Todd's room, he requested, "Markie, sit on the couch and take your shoes off, then put your feet up on the coffee table."

"That's a good idea. Thanks."

Todd handed her a glass and stated, "Take a sip." She did and thought, "Boy, I'm really starting to trust him. I, took a sip before I asked if it was non alcoholic." She smiled and replied, "This is good and tangy." In the room was a basket of fruit with a chilled bottle of non-alcoholic wine and a pitcher of fruit juice. Marquetta put the fruit basket on the sofa to search through it. Later, when she wanted to kiss Todd on the cheek, she discovered it was in her way and moved it. She kissed Todd on the cheek and stated, "You're wonderful. I really enjoyed the entire day."

"Good, now shhh. I want to hear the news."

She thought, *He's all right.* She started watching the news, too.

An unexpected kiss brought her attention back to Todd. He then inquired, "Are you really enjoying yourself?"

"Are you kidding? I haven't had a vacation in years. This is exactly what I needed."

Todd wanted to make certain she was completely happy so he requested, "Put your feet on the couch." Once again, she complied to his request. When she did, he proceeded to massage them.

Marquetta sighed, then stated, "This feels great. My feet feel revitalized."

Todd thought, *I'm glad she likes the way I massage her feet. She's something else.*

Marquetta found herself dozing off. She said, "Todd, I have to go, I'm falling asleep."

"Why don't you?" he caught himself then stated, "I'll walk you to your room." He did.

---

Marquetta was so tired she hurriedly got out of her clothes; said a quick prayer; got into bed and went to sleep.

---

Ring, ring. "Hello," answered Marquetta sleepily. The phone woke her.

"Hi, Markie, I found a church on the Island. I'll pick you up in an hour. Good bye."

"Good bye," replied Marquetta. Marquetta jumped out of bed, said her prayers, read some scriptures and dressed for church.

Todd was punctual. He knocked on the door and Marquetta answered it, wearing a beautiful red and white polka dot dress with a white belt, which emphasized her figure splendidly. Though the dress was modest, it made her look stunning. Todd had on a light-weight dark gray suit with a greenish blue shirt and a grey and greenish-blue tie. Todd made arrangements for their trip to and from the church with the hotel clerk. Todd stated, "You look stunning. Our taxi awaits."

"You look handsome, too. I'm ready, let's go."

As they left church, Todd remarked, "Here lately, every time I go to church, the Pastor seems to be talking to me. You know what I mean? I can really understand and appreciate the sermons."

"I know exactly what you mean. That's why I don't like to miss service." The cab driver was sitting in his cab near the church, waiting for the completion of service. He waited until the crowd fanned out, then blew for them. Both Marquetta and Todd looked in the direction of the sound of the horn. They noticed the cab and the driver, walked toward the cab, then got in. While riding back to the hotel, Todd reached for Marquetta's hand and held it. They rode in silence, both enjoying the warmth from their hands touching. Upon arrival at the hotel Todd knew the time had come. He exclaimed, "Hey, I have an idea. Let's have the hotel pack us a lunch and go to a more secluded part of the beach."

"Okay, that sounds like a good idea." They walked up the stairs to the hotel entrance and went directly to the concierge. He told them of a private beach that wasn't far from the hotel. They went to their rooms to change.

While changing, Marquetta thought, *Am I letting my guard down with Todd. No, I don't think so. I can tell, he's changed. If he asks me to marry him now, I'll say 'yes.'"* She smiled at that thought.

———

Ring, ring. "Hello," answered Marquetta.

"Marquetta, it's Barbara. How are you doing?" Barbara was pacing up and back in her bedroom, holding her cordless phone.

"I'm fine. How about you? Is everything all right?" Marquetta heard worry in her voice.

"Yeah, I'm just calling to check on you." Barbara, took a deep breath, sat down on the side of her bed and began to relax.

"Thanks, Mother Barbara. Todd has been a perfect gentleman. We're going to search out a more secluded beach. I thought it was Todd when you called."

"A secluded beach! Why? Don't let him throw you!"

"Barbara, he hasn't approached me in that way. I really feel comfortable with him. If he kisses me, that's it. No exploring!"

"That's great. Oh, you can tell Todd, Sam and Juanita knows he's with you."

"I knew it was a matter of time. But I'm surprised. I thought Juanita would be on the next plane."

Marquetta sat on the corner of the bed near the phone. She listened as Barbara laughed, and said, "She probably would have been, but she figures you'll mess up on your own."

"I'll mess up by doing what?"

"You know what! Having sex with Todd. She figures once you do, he'll come running back to her."

"Well, I'm sorry she's in for a surprise. She wants to be the world's greatest lover. I want to be a wife. Doesn't she know that's not what men look for in a wife?"

"I tried to let her hear what men want but I don't think she got the message."

"It's simple enough—the same thing women want, some one they can love and trust. But we know what we want now, after we rededicated our lives to God. She's not there, yet."

Barbara decided, "We need to pray for her." Barbara led, "Father God, thank you for this day. Please help Juanita. She needs to learn the truth about real love. Please forgive us for our sins. In Jesus' name. Amen."

"Thanks for the call, Barbara."

"Talk to you later, Marquetta. Good bye."

---

Todd knocked on the door and shouted through it, "Markie, are you ready? I'm getting hungry."

Marquetta put on her robe then opened the door. She directed, " Have a seat in the living room." Marquetta returned to the bedroom to finish dressing. Todd shouted to her, "Thanks for the fruit."

"What fruit? She finished dressing, went in the living room area and discovered a basket of fruit with a card in it. She looked at Todd, smiled and read the card aloud. "Markie, I hope you enjoy the fruit. Love, Todd.." She forgot Todd was eating. She went to were he was seated and kissed him. She got some of his fruit in her mouth, ate it, and said, "Thanks."

Todd laughed, then remarked, "You have never been this affectionate with me. I don't get it. Why now?"

"I guess it's because I'm starting to trust you."

"Markie, we've known each other for 10 years. You're telling me you are just starting to trust me!"

"Todd, I trust you in certain areas. How could I trust you in male/female relationships when our views for so long were different? Now, I feel you would do what's best for me, because you know it would be best for both of us in the long run. It makes me feel good and secure."

Todd replied, "I have to admit what you're saying is true. I do feel different about us." He grabbed her hands, pulled her off the sofa, and stated, "Let's go to the beach and eat our picnic lunch. Don't forget your bathing suit and towel."

Marquetta responded, "I won't."

---

Sam drove to Juanita's condo to pick her up for brunch, only to discover she had company. As he searched for a parking space, he noticed an older black man leaving her building. He decided to watch to see where he was parked. He thought, I may be able to get his space. *Oh no! He's walking back toward the building. He must have left something, because a woman is calling him. His name must be Horace because that's the name she's yelling.* Sam laughed, then said, "Horace, hurry up, I want your space." He noticed the woman who was handing him his briefcase and inquired as if someone was in the car with him, "Is that Juanita? I know she's not giving sex to that old man. Let me move in closer. I need a clearer view." Sam moved in closer, but stationed himself behind another car so he couldn't be noticed. He looked at the woman again, and then exclaimed, "It's her! I need to check this out. Sam felt in his inside jacket pocket for his note pad, found it, pulled it out and wrote in it. He wrote the man's name, his description and his license plate. Then Sam stated, "That's exactly what I'm talking about. Women! Dressed in a negligee, handing this man his brief case. He probably tricked his wife into thinking he had a meeting downtown. He had a meeting all right. Juanita was crying her eyes out for my brother. Right! Juanita was playing a game. She turned down my invitation for sex last night for this old man. Oh, I'm getting some of that. Girlfriend's a trip, but now that I know her number, I'm going to dial it a few times myself." He laughed, then ruminated, "There's more to this than sex. I'll wait a few minutes before I go in. I don't want her wondering if I saw them. Fifteen minutes should do it. She'll think he was long gone before I arrived." Exactly fifteen minutes later, Sam parked his car close to Juanita's building, got out of the car, and walked into her building. He caught the elevator to her floor, got off the elevator directly in front of her condo, and knocked on her door. To his surprise, Juanita answered. He asked, "Where is Suzette?"

"Oh, she stays at Daddy's house on Saturdays to go to church with them. You know her sister is my father's housekeeper."

"No I didn't."

"Well, I guess you wouldn't. Todd had no reason to mention it to you."

Sam commented, "You look fabulous. I'm hungry, but not for food."

Sam, let me brush my hair. I'll be with you shortly. Juanita kept her hair cut close to accentuate her cheek bones. She had on a jean outfit. Sam thought, *She's wearing that outfit. I want it off. I want to see what she can do.*

Juanita returned and suggested, "Let me take you to my favorite restaurant in Maryland. I'll drive."

"Okay," replied Sam.

On the road, Sam remarked, "I probably should have driven because it's hard for me to keep my hands off you as good as you look. I'm trying to keep my little brother from being upset with me."

Juanita smiled and thought, *I knew it was just a matter of time before he came out with it. He hinted last night but I couldn't take him up on it. I needed to be certain Horace would carry out my request. Having sex with Horace last night was to cement the deal. He'll be, too afraid to cross me now. Besides, I don't want to give up on Todd yet. I still could become Mrs. Todd Parker. However, I would like to try out his brother. But first I need to make sure he's not the kind to kiss and tell. I'll start by letting him know I'm inter-ested.* She stated, "One Parker at a time, baby. Right now it's Todd's turn. She, took one hand off the wheel and placed it on Sam's thigh, then said, "Sorry about that."

Sam shook his head with a grin on his face, looking toward Juanita, when he commented, "If you're trying to soothe me, it's not working." He grabbed her hand and kissed each of her fingers softly. Then he declared, "With exception of my brother, I would fight any man for you. You are all woman. I'm surprised you're not married. Why are you putting up with my brother's crap?"

Juanita grinned from ear-to-ear as she thought, *Good, he's still sympathetic to my cause. Which means he could understand my frustration and weakened state. I may be able to pull this off. Having sex with Sam could be beneficial later.* She said, "I have to admit I'm getting tired of this game he's playing. I may be willing to change partners soon."

Sam thought, *Typical! She thinks she's every man's heartthrob. I'm glad my brother wised up. He knew exactly what he was doing.*

They arrived at the restaurant.

---

Todd stated, "I'm glad I asked about a secluded beach. This place is really private. We could do anything we want here." When Marquetta and Todd arrived no one else was on the beach. The stretch of green water and some trees dominated the scenery. The trees were full with leaves and the trunks were thick The sand leading to the water was mixed with dirt and was cool from the shade trees.

"On that note, I think we need to get out of the water and go back to the hotel," replied Marquetta.

"Did I lose your trust? That's not fair. I can joke can't I? You have to admit I've been good all day and it's tough. You look fantastic in a bathing suit. That's part of the reason I wanted us to come to this area of the beach. You draw quite a bit of attention when you come on a beach."

"You've been good, I'll admit it. Let's go. We can sit in your room and watch television. Okay?" Marquetta stated as she got out of the water and reached for her towel. Todd followed her to the shore.

Todd responded, "That's a good idea. He thought, *I'm glad I gained her trust, and I don't want to lose it, because I'm having the time of my life with her. She's fun to be around, without sex.* They walked from the secluded beach to their hotel. While walking Marquetta commented on how strange it looked watching the cars on what she considered the wrong side of the street. At once, tires begin screeching to avoid a moped rider driving down the wrong side of the street. Fortunately, no one was injured and the moped driver turned onto a side street to get his bearings straight. Todd commented, "Tourist, I'm glad we opted to walk. When they entered the hotel, Todd stated, "Wait, Markie, I want to return the basket and tip the clerk."

"Okay," responded Marquetta.

As they approached Marquetta's room, she remarked, "Todd, I want to take a shower. It may wake me up. I'm tired. We've been in the water for hours. I'll meet you in your room in 30 minutes."

"Sounds good," replied Todd.

She, took a shower, changed clothes, lay across the bed, and went to sleep. The phone rang and woke her. "Hello," responded Marquetta groggily.

Todd queried, "Are you coming over here or do you want me to come to your room?"

"Come to my room. Good bye," stated Marquetta. She jumped off the bed, walked into the foyer area near the living room and opened the door. Todd was pleased to see her head peering from the door as he approached. He walked in the door, grabbed her firmly, and kissed her ardently.

Marquetta could feel Todd's body pressing against hers as they kissed, because her back was against the door. She squirmed until she could loosen his grip. Once loosened she moved her mouth from his and asked, "What got into you?"

"I'm sorry. You looked scrumptious. I had to kiss and hold you."

"You've been holding me off and on all day, but not like that. There was a little, too much body action in that one."

"Marquetta, I don't want to have sex with you, because I want to respect you. I really respect what we have, but I had to be close to you. I didn't use my hands. They were around you."

"I know you're being very careful, but I could feel your body against mine and for me right now, that's not good."

"I understand," replied Todd.

"Anyway, let's have a seat on the couch. I need to tell you something."

"Markie, no work talk. We agreed."

"I know. This isn't about work, but it may be important to you, and I don't want to keep it from you, so listen."

"Okay, what is it?"

"Sam and Juanita know we're together."

"That's fine. I told Juanita I wasn't the one for her before I left. Sam's my brother. He'll have to work through his concerns. Markie, I want us to really make a go of it."

"Make a go of it. What do you mean?"

"I want us to be together. Let me start all over. Todd stood up, then stated, "Markie, please stay seated and listen. I need to tell you what's on my mind. I've been thinking about us as a couple since I met you, but that night two years ago confirmed my true feelings. But I didn't know how or when to approach you about the way I felt, until recently. The night I spent over Phillip's was an eye opener for me. Now I understand what it means to rededicate your life to God. About 6 months ago I rededicated my life to God, but didn't fully understand what it meant. I just knew I wanted to do things God's way, still not sure how. While at Phillip's that night, it all came together. I could understand what God was telling me. It's like everything started falling in place. I know for sure you're the woman for me." Marquetta started to speak, but Todd put his hand up to stop her, "Let me finish. I realize we both have small businesses and we may never be rich, but I will be happy being with you. I will do everything I can to make you happy, too. I understand that God has to be the head of our household and that I will learn more about being the husband and father God wants me to be through his guidance and leadership. Markie, I believe we'll have a wonderful life together, if you're willing to give me a try. Todd then walked over to the sofa where Marquetta was seated, got on bended knee, and asked, "Marquetta Marie Logan, will you marry me?"

Marquetta's eyes were filled with tears as she answered, "Yes, I'll marry you, Todd Patrick Parker." Todd rose from the floor and sat beside Marquetta on the sofa, reached for her, and they kissed. After the kiss, Todd held her hand and announced, "Markie, I want to start this engagement and marriage off right. I want us to pray together." Todd led the prayer. "Father God, we thank you for being God all by yourself. Please forgive us for our sins. Father God, please bless this engagement period, our marriage, our lives, and our families. In Jesus' name. Amen." After they prayed, Todd kissed Marquetta softly on her lips and put the engagement ring he had in his pocket on her finger.

Marquetta inquired, "Did you plan to ask me to marry you when you decided to come on vacation with me?" Todd replied, "Two years ago when my love for you was confirmed, I bought this ring. However, I knew I wasn't ready to be your husband until Friday."

"I don't understand. Then why did you ask me how would I feel if you married Juanita?"

"I knew it was you, but I wanted you to bring it up. You wouldn't. Juanita was willing to bring up marriage, I couldn't understand why you wouldn't. Not only did you refuse to bring it up, you rejected me when I asked, initially. When you turned me down, I thought you didn't love me, and I would have to marry Juanita, not because I loved her, but because I knew she wouldn't turn me down. I felt so vulnerable, I thought, 'I can't feel like this, I need to go somewhere and think.' That's why I agreed to stay over Phillip's that night. In spite of your response, I thoroughly enjoyed the evening with you and was determined to win you over. That's why I made it a point to come back to your condo and kiss you good night. I wanted you to know I could do things your way and I wasn't giving up. Now, I understand why you rejected me. You wanted to make sure God would be the head of my life before I became your head. I realize the position of the husband is to serve and I will serve you."

Marquetta was in awe at the wisdom Todd had acquired about marriage. She knew it could have only come from the Lord. She stated, "You'll be a wonderful husband. Now kiss me."

Todd kissed her, then confessed, "I really planned to propose on the beach but I couldn't get my nerve up. But I knew when I saw you waiting at the door for me, this was it. You looked so welcoming. I never thought getting married would give me this much excitement. I wasn't this excited when I passed the bar. Now, I see why Phillip seems so satisfied. It's a beautiful experience when you find the right person for you." Todd, now seated on the couch with Marquetta, pulled her close to him and held her firmly in his arms. Marquetta, happy and relaxed, dozed off as they viewed the night sky and the beach through the balcony doors.. Todd searched the sky for stars and laughed as he watched people still playing on the beach. He then looked at Marquetta and himself. He quoted to himself a scripture from the Bible.

"Psalm 139:14 (KJV):"

"'I will praise thee; for I am fearfully and wonderfully made: marvellous are thy works; and that my soul knoweth right well.'"

He pondered that scripture as he thought about his life. At that moment, he realized how true and powerful that scripture was. He became more aware of why he should reverence God. He felt even more secure about the God he served and his life being in God's hands. He kissed Marquetta on the cheek to wake her. When she opened her eyes, he said, " I'm going to my suite so you can get some rest. I'll see you tomorrow." He kissed her gently on the cheek and left.

# CHAPTER 5

# VALUES ARE IMPORTANT

"Where is he, where is he? He better pick up that phone or I will go to his office. Oh no, I can't. It wouldn't look good for anyone to see me," commented Loretta. Loretta was sitting in the chair in her hotel suite with her feet propped on the coffee table, biting her nails on one hand and, holding the phone with the other.

"Hello, Horace Greely, may I help you?" The minute Horace heard the phone ring, he left his outer office and walked into his inner office and closed the door. He sat down, took a deep breath, then picked up the receiver. The ring came from his private line and he thought it was Juanita or Loretta. He hadn't heard from either that day, and knew it was just a matter of time before they gave him further instructions or threatened him again.

"It's me. Did you sell Juanita on the salon idea?"

"Loretta, take it easy, don't push me. Your daughter is no dummy." His mouth was so close to the receiver you would have thought he was trying to eat it. He had his other hand covering his mouth as if someone were in the room with him and could hear his conversation. As he stated, "I've been trying to wait for her to ask me about it, but she hasn't."

"Perhaps you're not the man you think you are if you can't get her to open up to you." Loretta stopped biting her nails, remembering the leverage she was using over him was working. She could hear fear in his voice.

"I told her I was interested in a new investment. I asked if she had any ideas. She told me she'd get back to me. Right now she's busy working on another project."

"Your job is to get her on my project, if you don't want my ex-husband to know you've been playing house with his daughter! He may not like me, but if I tell him that one of his business partners who's old enough to be her father, is between the sheets with his only child, I'm sure he would listen. Maybe I shouldn't be talking to you at all? Earl may be willing to pay me for this information. What do you think, Horace?"

Horace was nervous and started sweating as he remarked, "No need to panic. I'll convince her to give you the money. But I need more time."

"Sorry, Horace, I can only give you a week. I'm tired of living in this dump."

"I'll do my best. I only see her on Saturdays and she told me she may not be available this Saturday. She told me she would call and let me know."

"Horace honey, it seems like she's working you. Take charge and get my money! I'll call you the same time next Monday. Answer the phone quicker. Bye-bye."

Horace leaned back in his chair, with his hands clasped together under his chin, in his office as he pondered, *These women are trying to drive me crazy. To get Juanita off my back, I need to get William to get something on Tony Davis, and to get Loretta off my back, I have to convince Juanita to give her $50,000. Well I can start by calling William and telling him how Juanita suggested he should handle the set-up.* Horace picked up the telephone receiver and dialed Greely's Towing Service. The phone rang and rang and finally, just as Horace was about to hang up, William answered it. "Greely's Towing Service, what can I do for you?"

"Where have you been, Bill? This is Horace. I told Robert to tell you to call me."

"What is it?"

"It's about that Davis boy. We need to get something on him fast."

William commented as he wiped his hands with his handkerchief,

"He's a good boy and he's a hard worker, too. I think we should leave him alone. He's trying, Horace."

Horace panicked. He thought, *If Earl Smith finds out I'm sleeping with his little girl, I won't have a business and neither will William for that matter. I knew I should've paid him the money I owed him instead of letting him have a percentage of my company. It seemed like a good idea at the time, because I wanted to expand. The money I got from him was being used as part of my reserve. After all, he owns a percentage of just about every African-American company in this area. I never heard any complaints from any of the other owners. But they haven't been sleeping with his daughter, either. At least I don't think so. As a member of Earl Smith's consortium, we all do quite well, so I don't think the other members would back me if Earl suggested I be kicked out of the consortium. William and I both would be ruined, not to mention the impact it would have on our families. I'll have to tell William what's going on.* He queried, "William, do you like owning your own business?

"Sure, I do. I know you lent me money, but I've never missed a payment. So why did you bring that up? I thought you were talking to me about Tony Davis?"

"That's what I'm trying to tell you. Do you know who wants him framed? Earl Smith's daughter. We don't want Earl upset with us, so I think it would be smart to please his daughter. Remember, Earl has ownership in your company, too. Is this Tony Davis worth losing your company? I say, of course not, let's frame him."

"I know if it weren't for the money you and Earl lent me, I wouldn't have acquired the fleet of tow trucks I have now, but I just don't feel good about this. I think we ought to talk to Earl personally before we get involved with framing this kid who's trying to get his life together. I happen to know Earl doesn't endorse everything his daughter does. You know she's a lot like her mother—bad news!"

"You're probably right about Earl, but I can't go to him with this."

"Why not?"

"I can't talk about it on the phone. Meet me at our favorite place in an hour."

"Okay, bye Man."

———————

Juanita walked into her advertising firm, looked at her secretary, Lucille, and inquired, "Do I have any calls?"

Lucille responded, "No, Ma'am. Just then the phone rang. It was Earl Smith. Lucille asked, "Ms. Smith, would you like to take a call from your father?"

Juanita walked to her office, made certain she was comfy, and answered the phone. "Hi, Daddy. How are you doing today?"

"Fine, Honey. I want you to come over for dinner tonight. Bring that Todd character with you. He cancelled an appointment with me and I want to know why."

Juanita, not wanting her father to know he went on vacation without her, replied, "He had to go to the Caribbean but he'll be back next week. His brother is still in town. May I invite him to dinner?"

"Fine, I'll see you later. Good bye." Earl hung up the phone but continued to look at it, shaking his head. At last he remarked, "Something is happening but I'll get to the bottom of it."

Scheming, Juanita contemplated, *Sam is a better catch than Todd. He has that killer instinct. Todd cares about people a little, too much for me. He's, too honest. Sometimes I wonder how he succeeds as an attorney. It's a good thing he's into corporation law. Sam, on the other hand, realizes if we're to be in the big leagues, we need to act like sharks; if we smell blood—attack.* Juanita laughed, then continued, *He can be ruthless and vicious. I like that in a man. With Daddy's money and our know-how, we can go places. I'm getting excited just thinking about it. I'm going to call Sam.*

"Hello," said Sam sleepily. Sam reached for the phone with one hand, while still lying on his stomach gripping a pillow with the other hand.

"Hi, Sam. Did I wake you?"

"No, what's up?" Sam turned on his back and sat up.

In a sexy voice Juanita responded, "I don't know—you tell me!"

"Nothings up that you can't handle. I won't tell if you won't," remarked Sam.

"Tell who, what?" Juanita had her feet on top of her desk with her shoes off, looking at her polished red toenails, as she talked to Sam.

Sam asked, "Why don't you come over here and visit me? I would love to feel you next to me."

"Well, I do need to take a lunch. How about I give you a lunch we will both remember?"

"Sounds good to me, as long as you're included on the menu."

"I would have it no other way. I'll see you at noon. Bye-bye."

Sam jumped out of bed and into the shower. He dressed, went to the liquor store, bought a bottle of his favorite champagne, and then to the florist where he purchased a dozen of long stem red roses. He pondered, *Girlfriend, you don't know who you're messing with. It's time you met your match. Oh, I'm giving her, too much credit because she is no match for me. She'll find that out soon enough.* Sam grinned.

Lucille buzzed Juanita and stated, "Ms. Smith, you have a 10:30 a.m. with W and Z Realty."

Juanita replied, "Thank you." She was so excited about her rendezvous she had forgotten about her 10:30 a.m. appointment with W and Z Realty and to call Horace. She decided, *I'll call Horace now. That way, I won't forget later. I need to make certain he's still worried, so he'll call William and make sure my plan is being carried out. I want Marquetta Logan and her company destroyed.* She pushed the button that would connect her to Horace's private line."

"Hello," Horace responded, hurriedly.

"I meet with Daddy tonight. I don't want to tell him but if I haven't heard anything from you by this evening he will know that you forced me into having sex with you. Let's see how my father likes that bit of information." Juanita hung up the phone and smiled.

Lucille knocked on Juanita's office door, then turned the knob and walked in. Once in the office, she put the folder which had W and Z Realty information in it on Juanita's desk and announced, "Mr. Wilson and Mr. Zooks of W and Z Realty are waiting in the conference room. Juanita picked up the folder and walked into the conference room, shook their hands, and sat down. They followed suit. She said, "Gentleman, generally I prepare a preliminary layout with jingles based on the clients line of business. However, in this case I decided it would be more feasible if you tell me the area in which you want to be advertised. You gave no indication other then you were in real estate."

"A wise decision," commented Mr. Wilson. You see we're involved in land acquisition and sales. Our board has determined that one of our areas of expansion would be in this area. With research, we discovered a large minority population, which is one of the reasons your firm was contacted. We deal primarily with the purchase and sale of residential land masses. It could be advantageous to the buyer if he were to buy the land then build to suit his needs. It could save the purchaser a great deal of money. Because most purchasers are novice in this area, in addition to buying land from us, we are willing to offer our services and expertise in preparing blueprints and suggesting designs. Of course—for a nominal fee."

"I understand. I could provide the type of advertisement needed to attract the minority market for this endeavor. May I ask, how did you hear about my company?"

"Your company's name came up in a business meeting. However, we have been looking at other companies that could give us similar service. We will give you one week to submit your advertising package to us. You will receive our decision by the end of that week," stated Mr. Zooks. Mr. Zooks handed Juanita a paper with the amount their company would be paying the agency that is selected. Juanita smiled. Mr. Zooks commented, after he saw her response, "Thank you for your time. Good day."

"Good day to you, too," replied Juanita.

As they left, Juanita thought, *I need to check out this company.* Juanita buzzed Lucille and said, "Have Ron and Dave come to my office. Ron Waltons and David Mc Daniels were Juanita's top advertising executives. Both came in quickly and, took seats in chairs directly across from hers. Juanita stated, "Ron, Dave, this is the deal. Do all the research you need to find out the type of package W& Z Realty are accustomed to receiving; find out the names of our competition; compare their advertising packages with ours and then make our package twice as good. If we land this account, both of you will get a $500 bonus. I want the package on my desk by Wednesday. I'll review it and we'll do a test market on Thursday. It should be ready for delivery by Friday. Work as late as you have to. Am I making myself clear?"

Both replied, "Yes," in unison. She grabbed her briefcase and walked out of her office. Once in the outer office, she said, "Lucille, I'll be gone the rest of the day. If an emergency comes up, page me. Good bye."

---

As she drove to Todd's townhouse, Juanita plotted, *Boyfriend doesn't know who he's playing with. I have plans for him. First I'm going to break up the attachment he has with his brother and then use him and his talents to work for me. I can do that by sleeping with him. Once Todd finds out that his brother has slept with his girlfriend in his house, that should do it. Todd would see Sam has no respect for him. But, in order to get Sam to see things my way, I'll have to first act as if Todd will never know what happened—like it will be our little secret. Then, when the time is right, I'll hold the sex over his head. He'll be forced to do things my way. If things go well, I won't have to tell Todd, because Sam and I will get married and Todd can guess the rest. But if he tries to play hard ball, I'll have to let him know who's the boss. Either way, Todd will know eventually, and once he finds out, that should destroy the bond. Todd will be convinced that Sam betrayed him to get to me so he could have access to the good life. Who knows? Todd could come to his senses and marry me. But I don't think I want him if I can have Sam. Todd can be, too soft at times. However, Sam is ruthless. At first, I thought marrying Todd had an upside because he was such an honest person, he could draw businesses to us. Once he drew them, I could work it so they would have to depend on us to survive. With Todd's legal knowledge and my business sense it could work. But the problem would be convincing Todd to see things my way. His brother, on the other hand, already thinks like I do. We could run this town. Daddy can't run his businesses forever. When he turns them over to me, Sam and I could put this small township on the map.* As Juanita arrived at Todd's townhouse, Sam was watching for her. She parked her car and walked toward the townhouse. Sam stood in the doorway waiting to greet her with a dozen of long stem red roses in his hand. As she entered the entryway of the door, Sam handed her the roses and kissed her on the cheek. Both thought, *It's on.*

---

The park was virtually empty of people when the brothers arrived. William said, "Let's sit close to the duck pond."

"Okay," replied Horace.

William turned to his brother and inquired, "Now, tell me what happened to get you in this mess?"

"Well, let me see. It started a few months ago. I was at Earl Smith's house for a business meeting when he announced that he had been looking at some companies he thought would be interested in becoming a part of and good for the consortium. Then, he asked us if we know any companies that we would like to join the consortium. Different ones gave suggestions, but the two I remembered were the two names Earl mentioned. They were Parker and Associates Law Firm and Second Chance, Inc. We voted to do our usual investigation of these businesses and would discuss the preliminary outcome at our next meeting, which is this week. After that meeting, Juanita asked me if I would be available to come to her condo on Saturday around 11:00 p.m. I thought she was sending a double message, so I was determined to see what it was. I met her at her place to find she was the only one home. The housekeeper wasn't there. She poured me a drink and talked to me about advertising until I was relaxed. She told me ways I could increase my business through marketing, what the fee would be, and gave me a contract to look over. While I was reading the contract, every time my glass was empty she refilled it. Before I knew it, I had consumed quite a bit of liquor. I was tipsy. Man, she knew exactly what she was doing. She knew when it happened, because shortly after that she told me to continue to read the contract, and if I had questions, she'd answer them when she returned. When she came back she had on a white gown that you could see right through and she wasn't wearing anything under it. She straddled herself on my lap and started kissing me. That girl is wild. Man, oh, man." Horace scratched his head, then continued. "You wouldn't believe the things that girl does. I'm telling you, I think she's a 'pro'. Now she's threatening me. She makes me meet her every Saturday, unless she cancels. One week her mother caught me leaving her house."

"Horace, why did you continue to have sex with her?"

"She told me she would tell her father I raped her if I stopped. Man, I'm so confused. Now Loretta is threatening to tell on me, too."

William queried, "She wants Tony Davis framed, too? What did Marquetta Logan and Second Chance, Inc., do to them?"

"I don't think Loretta knows anything about this situation with Tony Davis. Loretta wants me to convince Juanita to give her $50,000 to start a business. She wants me to convince Juanita it's a good investment. That way, Earl won't have to find out about it."

"Man, Earl has to know Juanita sleeps around. I heard Todd Parker of Parker and Associates was one of the men she's sleeping with."

"Yeah, but she's supposed to be marrying him."

"That's not the point. The point is she sleeps around. I think we need to go to Earl on this. What could it hurt?"

"It could cost us our businesses. William, let me explain. Earl owns a large portion of your business now. You see, when I decided to expand, I gave Earl a large percentage of my portion of your company. If he wants to force your hand, he could. You still owe mortgage on your portion."

"Why would you give him such a large percentage? I thought we agreed to keep him under 20 per cent."

"I needed the money. It seemed harmless enough at the time. Besides, he got more than that in my company now, too. Plus, a note that hasn't been satisfied."

"When did all this happen?"

"About six months ago, when I upgraded my equipment and opened up two more offices. I didn't realize how much control Earl had in both of our companies until now. I'm sorry, Man."

"I still don't get it. Why Second Chance, Inc.? I think they turn out good employees. Did she have a problem with one?"

Horace answered, "No, she told me the offender population doesn't deserve a second chance. If you ask me, what makes her think she's any better than the people at Second Chance, Inc?"

"That girls a trip. We need to figure out what we can do without hurting ourselves and anybody else. I'm going to call my wife. She's good at handling crises."

"What does she do?"

"First, she prays, and then the next thing I know, it seems to work out."

"That's what we'll do. Let's pray," said Horace.

"I haven't prayed in years," replied William.

"You said it works for your wife. Let's pray. I'll start—I'm desperate. "Dear God, I'm asking you to forgive me. I have committed adultery and because of this, my business and my family could be destroyed. I agreed to help destroy someone else's business, hoping it would keep me and my family from being disgraced. I'm sorry, Lord. Help me be a better person, husband and brother. Teach me to live in a way that is pleasing to you. In Jesus' name. Amen."

William began, "Father God, thank you for permitting me and Horace to talk to you. We haven't prayed together in a long, long time but you brought us together today to pray. Forgive me for trying to destroy Marquetta Logan's business. She has never done anything to me. Keep her business running, please. The company's name is Second Chance, Inc. Now Lord, we ask you to show us how to solve this problem. You know about Earl Smith, his daughter Juanita, and his ex-wife Loretta. We pray that they would come to understand your love and desire to please you. Please let Horace and me understand more about your love and desire to please you. Save our businesses and our families from destruction and disgrace, we pray. In Jesus' name. Amen." After the prayer, the two men embraced. They held each other in silence as tears streamed from their eyes. A peace came over them and they knew everything would be all right.

---

Juanita, pleased with Sam's prowess in the sack, asked, "Don't you think we ought to give this one more try?," as she placed her breast on his chest.

Sam reasoned, "Why not? I got all day." He replied, "I couldn't think of a better idea." They had sex throughout the afternoon and into early evening. They finally drifted off to sleep. Juanita woke up as her hands searched for Sam's body. She couldn't feel him next to her. She jumped up in a panic as she called out his name. She hurriedly dressed and went downstairs. Sam was dressed and watching TV. She inquired, "Did you hear me calling you?"

Sam smiled, then remarked, "Yeah, I knew you would eventually come downstairs." Juanita, now embarrassed, thought, *With that outburst, I wonder what he thinks of me. I look stupid. Why did I panic? Why did I feel so alone? What's come over me? I don't need anybody. Certainly not Sam Parker. If anything, he needs me. In fact, what does he do, anyway? I wonder what time it is?* She looked at her watch and it was 6:15 p.m. She decided, *I have time to shower and dress before I invite Sam to my father's house for dinner. That way, it will look as if it was an after thought.*

After she dressed, she sat by Sam on the sofa and said casually, "Sam, I have a meeting with my father at

7:00 p.m. and he'll serve dinner at 8:00 p.m. Would you like to have dinner with us?"

Sam grinned, kissed her on the forehead, and replied, "Sure, give me the address. Is it going to be hard to find? Remember I don't live around here."

"No, it shouldn't be, but if you want my father to send a car for you, he will."

"That sounds more like it. Have a car sent for me."

Juanita succumbed to his request, "Okay." She pondered, *What's wrong with me? He needs me. Why don't I act like I know it? Get a grip. Todd needs to know this happened. Sam is, too arrogant. I'll have to figure out another way to control him. But first he needs to be rejected by his younger brother. That should put his attitude in check. I know, I'll put my watch under a pillow in Todd's room.* She did.

When Juanita went back upstairs, Sam concluded, *Oh, Girlfriend wants to play the game of leaving something behind, does she? There's no other reason for her to go back upstairs. After she leaves, I'm going to check the rooms to see what she left.* As soon as Juanita left, Sam went upstairs. *I wasn't born yesterday. Apparently she doesn't know who she's playing with.* Sam checked both rooms thoroughly, and finally in Todd's room, he lifted up a pillow and exclaimed, "Gotcha!" He picked up the watch and declared, "No, Girlfriend, I'm not the one being exposed, you are!" He smiled and dressed for dinner.

---

Barbara stated, "I've been checking Tony's journal daily. So far, everything seems okay. I keep praying that I'm not overlooking anything. I must admit, I have such a peace about this situation. The only thing I can say is God is working it out."

"Well, you prayed. Now, trust God," replied Phillip.

Barbara queried, "How is Bill doing?"

"So far, so good. I check on him daily, too, and talk with Myrna. Both of them say the same thing, everything is going fine. Bill told me, all the files were up-to-date. Todd noted possible problems with possible solutions. But nothing has happened to cause alarm on any of the cases."

"Marquetta told me Todd was very thorough. It seems his thoroughness has paid off."

"Enough about the two of them. How about you and me and a date to be married?"

"I've been thinking, we've done everything Pastor Green required. Let's select a date within the next two weeks from the calendar. I prefer a Saturday, but it doesn't have to be."

"Great, I'll get a calendar."

Barbara commented, "I can tell you're really excited about this. So am I."

"I need a date. We're coming down to the wire and it's getting tougher to be strong. The date is like reaching a goal."

"I understand. Just think, in two weeks, we'll be legal. We can make love any time we want and we'll feel a sense of accomplishment because we have repented of the sin of fornication, trusted God for a spouse, and have received His blessings. We can wait."

As she drove to her father's house, she couldn't get Sam out of her mind and what happened at Todd's townhouse. Normally, on the way to her father's house, she would look for new homes that were being built to see how they compared to her father's mansion.. But today the only thing that was going through her mind was her time spent with Sam. She thought, *He's not Todd. Although Todd is no wimp. One thing the brothers have in common is they know what to do with a woman in the sack. The difference is, Todd may be aloof, but Sam seems mechanical. How can anybody be that good and not have himself in it? I don't get these brothers. Todd's aloofness always turned me on, because I knew he knew I was good, even if he refused to admit it. That's why I know, Girlfriend can't take him from me. One thing I can do is rule in the bedroom. I can show some emotion with Todd, but I knew better than to show any with Sam. He probably saw it as a sign of weakness. I don't know why I did that. Why did I feel alone? I don't ever remember feeling that way before, except when Mother left. At least I didn't have the nightmare where I yell for her to come back. Sam would have had a field day with that. Maybe I need to talk to Daddy about this. He usually knows how to make me feel better. I promised myself I would never let anybody get that close to me again, that it would hurt when they left. This is crazy. I don't know Sam that well and Todd won't leave me. He's just afraid of getting married. I'll tell Daddy to ease up on him when he gets back. Now that I think about it, Todd is better for me than Sam. Both of us shouldn't be ruthless—only me. Sam frightens me a little. I don't think I'll have as much control with him as I would Todd. I need to get that watch back, because Todd can be a prude at times. He may not like it if he finds out I slept with Sam. But if he finds out, I'll tell him Sam forced me. That should work. What was I thinking? No need to panic, Sam wouldn't want him to know either. The way Todd admires him. My secret is safe with Sam. He nor I want Todd to know, at least not now. I'll tell him after we're married. But I'll say Sam forced me. Todd believes in the sanctity of marriage, so he won't divorce me. However, it should put an end to that buddy-buddy relationship of theirs. My original plan can still work—break the strong bond between Todd and Sam. You know, now that I think about it, I think I love Todd, after all.* Juanita parked her car and went into the mansion.

Violet greeted Juanita as soon as she walked into the center hallway. "Hi, Miss Juanita. Your father wants to see you in the library. He'll be with you shortly." Juanita walked into the library and saw a woman that had to be her mother. She looked like her but older. Juanita walked to the chair where she was seated and asked, "Mother, is that you?"

"Yes, Juanita. Let me look at you. I must say, you're gorgeous. You look like me." Juanita acted as though she was a model. She pranced around her mother, then stopped in front of her, as she commented, "It is amazing how much we resemble each other. Even to my build. Well, Mother, I guess I have to thank you for something."

"Enough! Juanita, I'm ashamed to say, you act like her, too. I thought we were going to have one of our father/daughter talks tonight on one issue. Instead, I had to call this gathering of you and your mother because of some other issues that have been brought to my attention today. I am not happy. Juanita, take a seat near your mother and I do not want either of you to interrupt me. Is that clear!" Earl said sternly, as he left the entryway of the library and took a seat in his favorite chair.

Juanita responded, "Yes sir."

Loretta replied, "Sure, Earl."

Earl continued, "It has come to my attention that the two of you have been trying to extort one of my business partners. I'm not pleased! Juanita, the reason you're able to live in the comfort you find yourself has a lot to do with my business partners. I respect them and they respect me. I have been in business with some of these men since you were very young and before Loretta left. I plan to remain in business with them. We support each other. Horace supported me tonight by agreeing not to press charges against either of you. That's the way we operate. We support and trust each other. Sure, if I wanted to, I could have chosen to threaten him with the loss of his company or additional income, but we don't work like that. You should be glad I don't. I want you to learn this, if you treat people fair they will respect you. That can take you a lot further than your way of wheeling and dealing, which almost got you behind bars. Things work better when you can genuinely trust and support your business associates. Loretta, you are aware of the help I was given when I started my insurance business, and, Juanita, I told you over and over again how I got started. Do you remember?"

"Yes, Daddy, it was through the help of others."

"That's right. Through the help of others. A business isn't just for you to acquire wealth, but for you to help others acquire wealth as well. Because of your selfishness and greed, you almost caused a consortium I have worked very hard to put together, to be weakened. But I'm here to tell you, with God's help, it will continue to blossom. Now, Loretta, if you wanted a loan for a beauty salon why didn't you come directly to me? I'm not holding a grudge after all these years. How could I and raise our daughter who looks just like you? I love Juanita, so I can't hate her mother. Just because we didn't work out as a couple doesn't mean I wouldn't help you, within reason. I heard you were in town and I instructed my employees to put your call through or to let you in the mansion to see me, if you desired. You never called or came by. Instead, you decided to blackmail Horace Greely into convincing Juanita to lend you money. That shows how much you know about your own daughter. Juanita thrives on controlling people, especially men, so your attempt was fruitless. Loretta, that was always your problem, you never, took time to think before you acted. It's time to grow up. Now, if I decide to invest money in this salon, my people will work closely with you and report to me every business transaction you're involved in. You will remain the junior partner until you can afford to buy me out. Think about it. Now, Juanita, what is wrong with you and Marquetta Logan, the owner of Second Chance, Inc.? I think her work is commendable and needed. Why are you trying to destroy her business? Do you realize the impact that would have on this community? There would be a lot more crime in this area if she didn't have businesses who wanted to hire her clients. Do you realize how many ex-offenders live in this community? All people need a second chance. Aren't you happy that I'm willing to give your mother a helping hand?" Earl didn't wait for a response. He continued, "Perhaps you haven't considered this, but the reason this community is so viable is because of businesses in my consortium willing to work together for a common cause, specifically to help one another. I will not let you or your mother destroy it. I have an idea, Juanita, why you targeted Second Chance Inc., but I want you to tell me now, in front of your mother."

Juanita, embarrassed, stated, "Daddy, I want to discuss it with you alone. She doesn't know me."

"Unfortunately, I think she knows you better than you think. Spill it!"

Juanita refused to look at her mother. She looked directly at her father as she spoke. "She and Todd are friends. She's with him, in the Caribbean, on vacation."

Earl remarked, "I knew it had to do with Todd Parker. When Todd cancelled his appointment with me, I knew something was wrong. That's why I called you today. I wanted you to come home so I could help you sort out your feelings—after which you could decide what's best for you. After all, that's one of the reasons we have our gatherings. I heard you were hanging with his brother and I knew it was true when you invited him for dinner tonight. If you want Todd, do not sleep with his brother. Do you understand sleeping with a man will not guarantee you a husband?" Earl stated, "I'm no expert on men, but I am a man and nothing disappoints me more than an easy lay. My darling baby, I love you, but you are just like your mother. You are an easy lay. No amount of money or class is going to make you desirable to a decent man, if you have no values. Values are important. You tell me times have changed, but no man who loves and adores his wife wants one he can't trust. In my opinion, when you're an easy lay, you can't be trusted. You may not believe this, but a decent man has values. Let's think about Todd's character. Does he have standards?"

"Yes, he does," Juanita replied softly.

Earl said, "Now, think about your standards. I thought I raised you to use your mind, not your body, to get what you want in life. Think! How many men do you want jumping in and out of your bed? What standards are you measuring them by or do they need standards? Do you want to be married? If so, why? If not, why not?"

Juanita stared at her father and thought, *He's acting like I'm a prostitute or something. I just like to have fun. What's the big deal about marriage? He's doing fine without a wife. I don't get it.*

Earl looked at Juanita and queried, "What do you have to say?"

Juanita fought his questions by refusing to answer them. "Daddy, I have a question for you. What's the big deal about marriage? I mean, you're doing fine without a wife.

"Juanita, are you trying to tell me you never saw the sadness in my eyes sometimes when I held the picture of your mother in my hand, when you were younger. I was devastated when I found out your mother was cheating on me. Let me explain to you a little about that time in my life. I had just become a millionaire. It, took hard work and planning, but I reached my goal. I had such plans for the family. I figured…well, never mind…you wouldn't understand. Let's just say I wanted to see my family. I thought I could then. I decided Warren was going to be the first person I would set up in business. I was going to buy him out, then help him establish his own company by giving him my small accounts. This would be done in gratitude for the favors he performed for me, like running errands and helping out with my household responsibilities. I knew people called him my errand boy, but I wanted to show him I appreciated his help. I had my attorney draw up the documents and as soon as they arrived at my office, I rushed home to surprise Warren. I knew he was there helping Loretta with one of her projects; or so I thought. Only to discover Loretta and Warren, my wife and my best friend, on the garage floor having sex." Earl looked at Loretta and commented, "I don't know why I was so surprised. I forgot, Loretta, how eager you were to take off your clothes—the place never mattered. Loretta, I know it was God that kept me from hitting you with my car." He then looked at Juanita, "Juanita, I want you to know that same evening I asked your mother to leave and told her she couldn't take you. I did tell her I would help her get established some place else if she didn't contest the divorce. She agreed because she told me she couldn't live with me anymore, and she didn't want her parents to know what happened. I gave her $50,000 cash. I'm telling you this now, in front of your mother, so you will know this is the truth. Now, if Todd decides not to marry you, I will not hold it against him. My darling, I wouldn't want anyone to go through what I went through with your mother. I haven't remarried because, for a long time, I was afraid to trust another woman. Instead, I put all my energy into my insurance business and the consortium. Juanita, I will not let your mother's or your lack of morals destroy this consortium. Have I made myself clear!"

"Yes, Daddy," replied Juanita.

"Yes, Earl. When can I call you abut the beauty salon?"

"Call me tomorrow at my office. I will assist you with the salon under the conditions mentioned earlier. Loretta, I wanted you to know how you have impacted our lives, even in your absence. If you are interested in getting your life together, you need to pray. Good night, Loretta. Violet will see you out." He pushed a button made into his desk to buzz Violet Within seconds, Violet appeared at the library door. Loretta rose to her feet and left.

Earl looked at Juanita and remarked, "I want you to think about what I said." He walked to where she was sitting and stood by her chair. Juanita rose to her feet and Earl hugged her, then said, "I love you. You know that, don't you?"

"Yeah, Daddy, I know." Juanita felt like a child again whenever Earl hugged her. She was happy to be his daughter.

"Now, are you ready for dinner? By the way, I heard we had to send a car for your date."

Juanita grinned shyly.

Earl commented, "I hope you heard what I said. Do not sleep with Todd's brother!"

As Juanita and Earl walked toward the dining room, they met up with Sam and Violet. Violet was escorting Sam to the dining room. When Sam saw Juanita and Earl, he walked toward them. When he reached them, he grabbed Juanita's arm. Earl noticed the look that passed between them and he thought, *It's, too late. She slept with Todd's brother."*

# CHAPTER 6

# PROBLEM SOLVED

For Marquetta and Todd the fun was over and now they had to take care of more pressing matters. "One more stop, and then to Maryland," said Todd.

As Marquetta sensed Todd nearing his parents' home, she felt like butterflies were gathering in her stomach. She decided to pray silently. "Father God, I need your peace. Thank you."

Todd pulled into the driveway and announced, "This is it." As they were walking up the grey wooden stairs leading to the modestly built Cape Cod, the door opened and an older version of Todd and Sam appeared and stood on the landing. Marquetta noticed him first and commented, "Your father's come to greet us."

When they reached the top of the steps before the landing Todd extended his hand to his father to greet him. Sam Sr. extended his hand to him in like fashion. They shook hands. Once Todd was on the landing with his father, Sam Sr., Sam Sr. patted him on his back. He then opened the door with one hand and held the other out as a courtesy telling them to enter before him. Before entering the house, Todd turned to look at his father to ask him to excuse his manners. "Dad, I'm sorry about the short notice that we were coming to visit, but I have something to tell you.

Sam Sr. queried, "When have you had to explain a visit to me and your Mom? We haven't heard from you in a while. I hope everything is all right. Come in the house and have a seat, you and your lady friend." Marquetta followed Todd into the house. She watched the way Todd interacted with his father, and she could tell they had a good relationship.

As they entered from the front door Todd's mother came in through the back. Todd saw her and said, "Hi, Mom."

Wilma responded, "Come here, Boy." Todd reached for Marquetta's hand as he walked toward his mother. She pinched his cheeks; squeezed his face and kissed him. Then she gave him a big hug. Marquetta released her grip so that Todd could return the hug. She smiled as she looked on. Wilma stood back to look at Todd, then asked, "How is my baby boy doing? You look good. A little thin, but you still look good." Wilma looked at Marquetta standing a few inches way from Todd, and stated, "Honey, you can take a seat on the sofa. We're glad to have you here.

Todd replied, "Mom, this one's for keeps." Wilma said, "Well, then, let me hug her, too." Wilma reached for Marquetta and gave her a bear hug, the same type she gave Todd. Wilma Parker was an attractive, pudgy woman with a lot of love in her heart, and kept an apron around her waist. She stood 5'5" in her stocking feet. Her light brown eyes made the beauty of her caramel colored skin unmistakable. She agreed Todd and Sam both looked like their father, but Todd had her eyes.

Sam Sr. responded, "Well, then, both of you come here and give me a hug. Todd and Marquetta gave Sam Sr. a hug. After Todd hugged his father he stated, "I miss you two a lot. In fact, I miss the entire family. How are Aunt Rita and Uncle Todd doing?"

"Fine. When you called from the airport I told them you were coming. They'll be over shortly to see you. Now, introduce us to the young lady you brought with you," stated Sam. Sr.

Todd announced, "Mom, Dad, this is Miss Marquetta Logan, my fiancee. Marquetta this is my mother, Wilma Parker and my father, Samuel Parker, Sr. Mom, Dad, I call her 'Markie'."

Marquetta smiled and said, "I'm pleased to meet you both."

Wilma stated, "Honey, welcome to the family. Would you like to see our family album? After all, you and your children will be in it some day." Wilma reached under the coffee table and handed Marquetta the album.

Marquetta giggled and replied, "Yes ma'am, that would be nice." As she, took the album from her hands, Marquetta opened up the album and begin glancing through it.

Sam Sr. said, "Welcome to the family. You're quite a looker, you know. That's one thing about the Parker men, we have an eye for beauty and class."

Marquetta responded, "Thank you, sir." Marquetta continued to glance through the album. Todd sat beside her on the sofa and began to look with her.

Wilma commented, "See, Sam, I told you we raised those boys proper. They would get married eventually."

Sam Sr. touted, "Son, I must say, you are making me feel good. You understand all you need is one woman to love and treat good. You got yourself a handsome woman; that's for sure. Now, can she cook? If not, teach her. I taught your mother."

"No sucha thing. Stop telling your tales, Sam," responded Wilma.

Marquetta and Todd were listening to Todd's parents as they glanced through the album, but when Sam Sr. made his remark and Wilma responded with hers, they stopped looking through the album and began laughing. The room filled with laughter. Finally, Wilma regained her composure and inquired, "Hungry, Honey?"

Marquetta replied, "No ma'am, we ate on the plane."

"See what you've done. You got the child scared to eat my food," remarked Wilma.

Sam Sr. retorted, "No sucha thing. Now Honey, you'll eat something won't you?"

Marquetta looked at Todd for a response. Then she agreed, "Fine, as long as you don't have to cook. I don't want to put you to work."

"Honey, cooking isn't work. I enjoy it. I'll be right back. Todd, I'll fix you a plate, too."

"Thanks Mom."

Sam Sr. queried, "How long will you be here?"

Todd responded. "Until tomorrow; in fact, we have an early morning flight. We need to get to bed early. Dad, is it all right if we stay here or do you think it would be better for us to stay in a hotel?"

"Boy, you know better than that. Your and Sammy's rooms are free. We might as well get some use out of 'em. Todd, did you explain to her we're old fashioned folks?"

"Dad, she is, too."

Sam Sr. gave a big smile and remarked, "You've done good, son, real good."

Wilma announced, "The food is ready; come and eat. What you can't finish, I'll pack for you to take home. Okay?"

"Thanks, Ma, that's fine."

"Thank you," replied Marquetta. They went to the dining room and ate some of the food Mrs. Parker prepared for them. Marquetta smiled as she ate because she felt very relaxed in Todd's family home. She never imagined Todd's parents to be comedic. In their normal conversations she could hear joy and laughter. The home was filled with love. She was glad to become a part of this family.

The doorbell rang and Sam Sr. declared, "I'll get it. I know it's Rita and Todd."

Marquetta looked at Todd and asked, "Did he say Todd?"

Yeah, I'm named after my mother's brother. Around here, I'm called Little Todd. But I'm much taller than my uncle."

Marquetta smiled, then commented, "There's another Todd. I'm looking forward to meeting him."

They had eaten all they could and left the rest on the table per Mrs. Parker's instructions. Todd walked around the table to where Marquetta was sitting to assist her in getting up. Just before they were to enter into the living room Todd turned to Marquetta and kissed her softly and quickly on her lips, but Todd's mother caught him. "Todd Parker, what's going on in there?"

Todd answered as he walked into the living room from the dining room. He was still holding Marquetta's hand as he led her to a seat beside him on the sofa. "Mom, we're going to be married in two weeks. I think I can at least kiss her."

Wilma, tickled, responded, "I guess that's right." Then she queried, "In two weeks, why so soon?"

"Mom, to you it may seem soon, but to me, not soon enough! We have known each other for 10 years. Have gone out together on occasion and almost...."

Marquetta hunched him. Todd continued with, "It's time, Mom."

"It sounds like it," replied Wilma.

Sam Sr. reentered the room with Todd's Uncle Todd and his Aunt Rita. Sam Sr. announced, "Marquetta, this is Todd's Uncle Todd and his Aunt Rita."

Rita responded, "Honey, call me Auntie, and we call my Todd 'Big Todd.' She laughed.

Big Todd remarked, "It's not funny. I may not be as tall as him but I probably weigh more than him. Honey, you have your work cut out for you. That boy needs to gain some weight. He won't be but so much use to you in the winter, with all those bones."

"Don't pay him any mind, Child. Todd will be all right," replied Wilma. She looked at Big Todd and remarked, "Don't scare the child."

Everyone laughed. After which Big Todd asked, "Marquetta, did Todd tell you the family history?

"No sir."

"I'll tell you. You see, I married Rita, Sam's sister, and Sam had to copy me and marry Wilma, my sister."

"Stop telling your tales. I asked Wilma to marry me first," responded Sam Sr.

"I told you I was going to ask Rita to marry me first," replied Big Todd.

"Anyway, we're married," stated Rita.

Wilma remarked, "Too long to talk about!"

Marquetta laughed, then inquired, "Mr. Todd, how did you meet?"

"Call me Uncle Todd, honey. I know you're marrying Todd. Sam Sr. told us when we came in."

"Uncle Todd." responded Marquetta.

"Well, Honey, we lived next door to each other, it seems, all our lives. We played with each other as children and went to school together. We've been together most of our lives, except when Sam and I did our stint in the military. Sam Sr. and I were so close, when I decided I wanted to marry Rita, I told him. That's when he told me he wanted to marry Wilma, too. So that's what we did."

Rita queried, "Honey, do you feel like you can talk to Little

Todd about everything?"

Marquetta smiled and replied without hesitation, "Yes ma'am."

"Good," commented Rita.

Wilma asked, "Are you and Todd friends?"

Todd and Marquetta looked at each other and then Todd answered, "Yes, we are friends, but now I'm ready to be her husband."

Sam Sr. smiled and blurted, "That's my boy! You feel like you're bursting at the seams, right, Son? I know that's how I felt before I married your mom. That's good."

Todd grinned like a Cheshire cat and stated, "You know exactly how I'm feeling." Everyone laughed again. They talked for hours. After they finished, Marquetta felt she knew all she needed to know about the Pickens and Parker families."

Todd looked at the clock and queried, "Is that clock right?"

Big Todd checked his watch and replied, "Yep."

"May we be excused, Dad? We have an early flight."

"Sure, Son, you told me that earlier. Wilma shows them the rooms and let them decide where to sleep."

As they arrived upstairs Wilma looked at Todd and stated, "I thought Marquetta could sleep in your old room and you could sleep in Sammy's. Wilma turned to look at Marquetta and remarked, "Todd is fussy about whom I let sleep in his old room. Although, he seldom visits. He gets upset if I tell him a relative or friend slept in his old room."

Marquetta snickered. Todd replied, "Thanks a lot, Mom. Marquetta can sleep in my old room."

Marquetta looked at Todd and said, "Thank you." When Marquetta entered Todd's old room, and opened the closet door, it still had his old baseball bat and glove in it. They were leaning against the wall. She put the suitcase on the corner of the bed near the closet and began to unpack it. As she unpacked her suitcase, she took out what she planned to wear to the airport the next day. She hung her jeans and T-shirt on hangers and sprayed them with the wrinkle free spray. She, then, closed the closet door and sat on Todd's old bed. She looked around the room trying to picture Todd as a child sleeping there. She could tell the room had recently been painted. The pictures on the wall were of sail boats. Each sail boat was in an 8x10 inch frame. The pictures were used like a border around the room except they were hung lower–about twelve inches away from the ceiling. Todd's bed was a full size bed and had a nightstand and lamp on each side of it. Across the room was a window and from it you looked into the park. As Marquetta looked out the window toward the swings, she saw a man and woman from the distance. The woman sat down in one of the swings and the man stood near her leaning on the pole. Marquetta decided to pull down the shade before she dressed for bed. As she dressed for bed, she imagined how hard it was, at times, for Todd to go to sleep without peering out of the window. After she put on her pajamas, she pulled her Bible out of the suitcase, read it, then said her prayers, got in the bed and went to sleep.

The next morning before they left Sam Sr. stated, "Todd before you and Marquetta leave, we need to have a family prayer."

Todd responded, "Yes sir."

They gathered together and Sam Sr. led the prayer. "Father God, we thank you for this day. We thank you for your grace and your mercy. We thank you for continuing to bless us. Thank you for letting our son visit us with his future wife. We thank you for the new addition to our family. Please continue to keep us safe. Please continue to be with Todd and Marquetta as they return to their respective homes from vacation. Please bless their marriage and our families. Please unite the families with your love. Thank you for hearing and answering our prayers. In Jesus' name. Amen." After the prayer, they hugged and kissed each other. Marquetta knew she was accepted into the Parker family.

---

"Well, Markie, we're back home. Todd said as he stood in the airport parking lot, near his car. He put their luggage in the trunk of his car. After he closed the trunk he asked, "Where do you want to go first, your place or mine?"

"Yours. You need to see if Sam is still there. Then we can go to my place, so I can drop off my luggage and call my parents."

"That's right. I need to ask your father for your hand in

marriage. How do you think he's going to respond?"

"You'll be fine," Marquetta smiled, and remarked.

Todd commented, "That's easy for you to say. I'll tell you how I feel afterwards. Our first stop will be to my house." The ride from the airport was joyous. Todd placed a praise CD in the CD player and they sang with the songs on the CD. Throughout the ride Marquetta would stop singing to make a comment about their wedding plans or praise God for his beautiful landscape. The trees were full with leaves and the vegetation was luxuriant. The traffic was lighter than Todd anticipated. He was going away from the city, at the time, when most cars were coming into the city. He looked at his watch as he pulled into one of the parking spaces designated for his townhouse. He saved a half-hour in drive time. He smiled in disbelief and thought, *I need to make a note of this for future reference.* After Todd parked the car, he walked to Marquetta's side and opened the door. Once both of them were out of the car, he went to his trunk and took out his luggage.

Todd walked into his townhouse with his luggage and Marquetta nearby.

Marquetta stated, "Todd, I think I saw Juanita's car on the parking lot."

"You did. I think, Big Brother, fell in love while I was gone."

"Are you all right?"

"Remember, I told you Sam loved to play sex games with women I dated. That's between the two of them. It has nothing to do with us. I love you. This doesn't change anything, it just confirms my decision." He leaned over and kissed Marquetta on the cheek.

Marquetta queried, "Should we let them know we're downstairs or should we go up to greet them?

"Go up that way they won't have to make up a lie later," replied Todd.

"I'll follow you," stated Marquetta.

Sam and Juanita were so involved in sexual activity, they didn't hear the bedroom door when it opened. They were in Todd's bed. Todd, not pleased about that, inquired, "Hey, couldn't you guys have done this in the guest room. On instinct, Sam and Juanita reached for cover. Once covered, Sam gathered his thoughts and asked, "Little Brother, what did you do, change your flight again? Myrna told me you changed your itinerary and you were scheduled to be in late this evening, not late morning or early afternoon."

Todd replied, "Yeah well, we're here. We changed our itinerary because we had to make another stop."

Sam inquired, "Where?"

"To see Mom and Dad. Get dressed, Man, I want to talk to you."

"Okay," responded Sam.

As Marquetta and Todd walked downstairs, they heard Sam as he shouted, "Move, Juanita! So I can get up." Marquetta and Todd laughed. Marquetta and Todd walked directly into Todd's kitchen and sat at the table. "I don't know what's in the refrigerator, so I don't know what to offer you," said Todd.

"We still have the food your mother packed in my suitcase, remember? I'm fine. How are you, Todd? I know you love me, but for Sam to be sleeping with Juanita in your bed can be a hard pill to swallow." Todd was sitting across from her at the kitchen table. She moved her right hand, which was resting on the table, over to Todd and placed her hand on top of his hand that was resting on the table for comfort. Her left hand was resting in her lap.

"Sam knows how I am about my bedroom. My Mom even told you how I am about my bedroom at her house. Sam has no respect for my things. As a child my only argument with Daddy was about Sam's never getting corrected for messing with my things, no matter how many times he did it. When I couldn't take it any more, I would punch him. Then I would get into trouble for starting the fight. But after I fought him, he stayed away from my things, for a little while. But I might as well face it—Sam doesn't get it. I don't care about the girls he slept with that I liked and dated because I have come to realize he thought he was protecting me. You know— expose them for the type of women they really were. Anyway, now you have a better understanding of your future brother-in-law."

"You know Sam better than I do, but maybe he likes to do things to irritate you, when you're happy and he's not. On second thought, let's not concern ourselves with what Sam thinks. All I know is, if we pray for him, he's bound to come around sooner or later."

"Good point. You know, Markie, I really missed my family. I

didn't realize how much until we visited them. I think I want to visit them at least once a year."

"That's fine with me. I like going to the beach with you. You can show me where you and Sam would swim as boys."

"Hey that's a good idea." They heard both of the showers go off. Todd commented, "They'll be coming downstairs soon. Let's sit on the sofa in the living room, but first let me hold you." Marquetta walked toward Todd and he held her in his arms tightly. Then they walked into the living room and sat on the couch.

Sam entered the living room and, took a seat on the love seat, then inquired, "Man, did you put on a pot of coffee?"

"No, but you can," replied Todd.

"So, what's up? I thought we agreed to go visit the folks together." Sam leaned his back against the love seat and crossed his legs by placing one foot on its side on the other knee.

"Man, if I waited for you, I still wouldn't have seen them. How long have you been saying, 'let's go see them together?' I wait for you to adjust your schedule but you never get around to it, so we never go. Anyway, where is Juanita? I want to talk to you together."

"Here I am," answered Juanita, as she jumped off the last step onto the floor.

Todd stated, "Good, please have a seat."

Sam asked, "Does anyone want coffee?"

"I do," responded Juanita.

"Okay," said Sam.

Juanita looked at Marquetta and queried, "How long have you been back?"

"We just got back. This is our first stop," replied Marquetta.

"Oh, really! I would have thought a gentleman would drop off a lady and her luggage first."

Marquetta thought Juanita's aim was to attack Todd. So she said, "I suggested we come here first because we wanted to see if Sam was still in town."

Juanita exclaimed, "Excuse me!"

Marquetta then recognized that this gathering could get out of hand, so she prayed silently. "Help us Lord."

Sam entered the living room with two cups of coffee and

inquired, again, "What's up? What do you want with us?" He handed Juanita her coffee and the two of them sat down on the love seat. Todd put his arm around Marquetta then announced, "Markie and I are getting married—hopefully in two weeks."

"Little Brother, a little sudden, isn't it? I mean you've only been hitting it for a few days. No matter how good you think it is, it's not worth committing yourself like that. Marriage is a big step. Did you tell the folks?"

"Yes I did. That's why we stopped by the house. We received their blessings! You are so busy living wild that you assume all people live that way. I don't have to tell you anything about my vacation. But I will say this, you have never met a girl like Markie, so you can't appreciate one. I hope, Big Brother, one day you will."

Sam looked at Marquetta and remarked, "No offense, Marquetta. If my brother chose you as his wife, you will get the utmost respect from me." Then he apologized, "Todd, I'm sorry, Man, I didn't mean any harm. I love you and want what's best for you. Sam walked over to where Todd and Marquetta were sitting and offered his hand to Todd. Todd and Marquetta stood up. Todd shook his hand and then Sam kissed Marquetta on the cheek and said, "Congratulations."

Then all three hugged. Juanita looked at the display of emotion and felt unwelcomed. She grabbed her purse and walked toward the door. Sam saw her and said, "Juanita, I would like to treat everybody to breakfast. If you don't mind, afterward, I'll visit you and leave for the airport from your place."

Juanita smiled and said, "That's fine."

Todd said, "Thank you for the offer, but we're exhausted. This was our first stop. I need to take Markie home and she needs to call her parents. Call me when you get home. I'll be here or at Markie's. I'll see you at the wedding. Good bye."

———

As Todd drove, Marquetta went to sleep. He woke her when they arrived at her condo. They carried in her luggage and Marquetta said, "Todd, I have to take a nap. I'll take the love seat and you can take the sofa. If you're not sleepy, you can serve yourself.

Remember we have food in my suitcase, too. The television won't bother me if you turn it on."

"Are you kidding? I'm taking the sofa. I'm tired, too." They went to sleep.

Marquetta woke up and noticed Todd was still asleep on the sofa. She thought, "I'll warm up the food his mother gave us, then wake him. As she heated the food, she called her company.

"Hello, Second Chance, Inc. May I help you?"

"Hi, Barbara, this is Marquetta. How are things going?"

"Welcome home. I missed you! But there were no problems. Thank God! Tony Davis has been checking in regularly and we have no complaints from Greely's Towing Service."

"God is good."

"Yes, He is. Tell me, has Todd changed or what?"

"He has, Barbara. I had a wonderful time. Todd has given his life to the Lord. Barbara, I liked being around him before, but now I can't explain it. I feel so secure with him. I trust him. You wouldn't believe how many times I have slept around him or in his arms since we've been gone, with no worries. He respects me and he wants what's best for us. I like that. He asked me to marry him, again. This time I said, yes."

"Great! I'm so excited! Ooh, I want to jump up and down and scream!"

"So do I, but I'll wake Todd. Will you and Phillip have dinner with us tonight?"

"I better check with Phillip before I answer."

"That's right, we're going to see my parents later on today."

"To tell them you're getting married?"

"Yeah, I'm so happy. Let's try for Saturday."

"Sounds good. That way, if we have any plans we can change them. Good bye."

As Marquetta hung up the phone, she felt Todd's hands around her waist. He kissed her on her neck in a very sensitive area for her. She turned to him and kissed him fervently. Todd, astonished by her response, said, "Oh I have a feeling I'm going to enjoy being married to you." Both laughed.

She calmed down and said, "Have a seat at the table. I warmed up your mother's food. She's a great cook, isn't she?"

"Yeah, and so is my dad. I guess that's why I enjoy cooking, too. As kids they would let us help them make desserts. It was a lot of fun."

"That sounds like it would be. Speaking of parents, let's go see mine after we eat?"

"That's a good idea. Let's get this part over with."

---

As they were nearing Marquetta's parents' home, Marquetta said, "Todd, here's the scoop on my parents. When I was growing up, they were government employees. But now they have a business—three laundries. My dad is tall and slim. He has a thin mustache and salt and pepper hair. I look like my mom, including my build, so don't be surprised when you see her."

"Are you saying your Mom is voluptuous, too? I don't think so, Markie."

"You'll see. She told me when she was growing up, I looked just like her. She taught me how to ignore the whistles and the stares."

"Is that why you dress modestly?"

"No, not really. I dress the way I do because I work around a lot of men. I want them to keep their minds on business and not me. Although, I have to admit, it doesn't take much for some men to be distracted."

Todd laughed and said, "Wait a minute. Are you trying to tell me we may have a daughter that looks like you?"

"Todd, I thought men wanted their children to look like their wives. You don't like the way I look?"

"Yeah, I do, but I know other men do, too. If we have a girl, that means I'll have to watch her closely. What did your parents do?"

Marquetta laughed and said, "Watched me closely."

"You probably drove your father crazy."

"Todd, stop it. Let me continue. Everybody knows everybody here. So don't be surprised when I start waving at people once we enter into the neighborhood. Okay, now make this turn."

Todd said, "You want me to make this right?"

"Yes," said Marquetta.

Todd said, "Now, are we in your old neighborhood?" As Todd asked the question he glanced at Marquetta and noticed her waving to people as they drove by. Finally, she said, "Todd, you can park now. This is the house. You can park on the street or in the drive-way." Todd parked his car in front of the Logan's home.

As they got out of the car, Miss Peabody was standing by her fence. When she noticed Marquetta and Todd, she said, "Hi, Marquetta. Who is the young man with you?"

"Hi, Miss Peabody. His name is Todd Parker."

"I would like to meet him, Marquetta."

"Yes Ma'am, but my parents are expecting us. Maybe another time."

"Sure, but if you have any news for the paper, you need to give it to me by tomorrow."

"Yes Ma'am, I'll remember. Good bye."

Todd whispered to Marquetta, "Miss Peabody is nosy, isn't she?"

"Well, she owns the town's newspaper."

"This small town has a newspaper?"

"Yes, and a very good one. Remember, that's how I got my initial funding for SCI."

"That's right, you told me. This small town must have serious connections." As Margaret opened the door, Todd said to Marquetta, "These people don't miss a thing."

Margaret answered, "It keeps us on our toes. No one wants to make the paper unwillingly. If you get my drift. Come in and have a seat." Marquetta and Todd took seats in the Logan's living room. They sat in the center of the sofa. Mark was sitting on his cushioned cloth chair, adjacent to the sofa.

Marquetta said, "Hi, Mom."

"Hello, let me look at you." Marquetta rose from her seat and stood near her dad, who was sitting near a window. As the sunlight shone through the window, Margaret could get a good view of her daughter's present condition. She looked her daughter over as if inspecting her before going to school. After she was finished inspecting her, she said, "You look like you got quite a bit of sun.

You must have been at the beach everyday." Margaret prided herself on knowing if and when Marquetta did something she should not have in her absence. Although Marquetta looked fine, there was something about her appearance that made Margaret feel she had a secret. But Margaret decided not to pry. She knew Marquetta well enough, that if, she asked the right questions it would surface. "Yes, ma'am, I was. I had a good time."

"You look good. Did you just get in?"

"A little while ago." Marquetta knew her mother well. She knew if she kept asking her questions, she would have to tell her Todd was with her while she was in the Caribbean. She wasn't ready to explain Todd's presence with her at the Caribbean so she decided to change the subject. "Well, Mother, you haven't asked me who the young man is that I brought to meet you."

Todd looked at Margaret Logan and thought, "This woman looks good for her age. How did she keep that shape? Marquetta is right, she looks like her mom. When she stands near her dad, you can see him in her but she looks like her mom."

Margaret said, "I'm sorry, Marquetta looked so refreshed that I had to ask her about her vacation. I wouldn't normally be so rude. Please, forgive me."

Todd remarked, "I understand. She looks absolutely beautiful."

Marquetta smiled, then stated, "Ma, Dad, I would like to introduce to you Todd Parker. My..."

Todd hunched her, then interrupted her when he stated, "Mr. and Mrs. Logan, I am here to ask for your daughter's hand in marriage."

Margaret smiled, and Mark said, "Son, let's talk privately for a moment. Margaret and Marquetta, please excuse us for a moment." Todd followed Mark. Marquetta thought, *Daddy probably, took Todd to the rec room. That's his favorite place to talk.* She asked, "Mom, what do you think of Todd? Do you think Daddy will approve our getting married. I really do love Todd. I know, before, whenever I mentioned his name, I told you we were just friends but I think I've loved him for a while now. I just didn't realize it."

"That's probably the case. I thought he meant a lot to you."

"You did, Mom? Why do you say that?"

"It's something in your voice that changes whenever you

mention his name."

"Really, Mom! Why didn't you tell me you thought I liked Todd as more than a friend?"

"I knew you would discover your feelings for him in time."

"What did you think when I told you I was coming to see you, and bringing Todd with me?"

"Marquetta, I thought you were bringing home a young man you wanted me and your daddy to meet. Probably because you were contemplating marriage."

"Did you tell Daddy that?"

"You know I did! I'm glad you decided to bring him over, because your father was concerned after disapproving your last prospect for a husband, that you wouldn't bring any more young men home."

"I wouldn't do that. I want Daddy to approve of my choice of husband. I love and respect his and your opinions."

"I know, Dear, but your father wasn't as sure as I was that you wanted his approval. He has often thought that he would never see a young man you were serious about again, until after you married him. After all, you stormed out of here in such a huff, yelling that he'd never meet another important man in your life, until after you married him."

"Oh, Ma. That guy wasn't right for me. In fact, I broke up with him that same night. Besides, that was 11 years ago. A lot has changed since then. I've changed. I look for different things in men now. I would like to think I have matured."

"I think you have, Baby. Since you have obviously prayed for your mate, I'm going to tell you something else. Now that you have him, don't stop praying for him, especially when he becomes your husband. That's when you really need to pray for him. Remember, you're trusting him to do the right thing for you and your family. He can't do that by himself. He needs God's leadership and guidance, and so do you. As husband and wife, you should work together as one. It's no longer 'you or him,' it's 'we.' That's the way you can last. But God must be the head of the household."

"Yes ma'am. Thank you for your advice and continued support. I love you. I know you're right about continuing to pray for Todd and I plan to do just that. Now, Mother, what do you think Daddy will say?"

"Here they come. Let's here what your father has to say." Mark and Todd both walked into the room with smiles on their faces. Mark sat down by Margaret and grabbed her hand. Todd stood beside him. He said, "This young man, Todd Patrick Parker, asked for our baby's hand in marriage, and after a lengthy conversation, I have come to realize he has a realistic understanding of what marriage entails, and he knows our daughter very well. He has been chasing her for 10 years. Now as her mother, Margaret, what do you say?"

"As her mother, I say yes."

"Well then, it's unanimous. Congratulations, Baby," said Mark. He went to Marquetta and hugged her. Margaret stood up; walked to Todd, hugged him and stated, "Welcome to the family."

Todd replied, "Thank you very much for approving my request to marry Markie."

Mark remarked, "I know your mouth is dry, because mine was when I asked Margaret's parents for her hand in marriage."

Margaret announced, "I have just the thing. Lemonade. Marquetta, that's what Grandma Kate gave your daddy after your Grandpa approved our marriage. Let's make it a family tradition." Margaret went to get their drinks. The room that once was filled with anticipation was now filled with happiness. As they talked, they shared some family history. Not wanting sadness to enter in on their joy they skimmed over any conversation concerning Marquetta's uncles. Before they left, Mark said, "Marquetta, Todd told me that his father prayed for your marriage. So, I'm just going to say to you both, whatever you go through, God is with you. Both of you have businesses but you must always remember that family comes first. Don't let anyone make you compete against each other. You must always work as a team—even when dealing with your children."

Todd responded, "Thank you so much for your hospitality and your advice."

"Daddy, Momma, thank you for your advice and thank you again for approving our marriage. But we have to leave. I'll call you tomorrow. I love you. Good night." Todd and Marquetta got into

Todd's car and drove off.

———————

Sam unpacked and checked his messages. Sam lived in a one bedroom condominium in Los Angeles, CA. He kept his living room sparsely furnished so he could direct his dates to his bedroom. His bedroom was a master suite, complete with Jacuzzi and bar. His entertainment system was equipped with the latest sound system, TV and DVD. He had a king size brass bed and a love seat in the room. The love seat faced the entertainment center and the bed faced the balcony. He sat on the love seat as he listened to the messages. He thought, *Tom is checking in with me already? I wouldn't put it past him to investigate me. How did he know what time I was scheduled to arrive home? Well, I guess when you work for a private investigator as good as Tom, you can expect this. The guy is brilliant. The company's concept is excellent, and the way we are able to operate is fantastic. I'm glad I work for Investigations Unlimited. We only have to report to the office when necessary, and we can check into the office from any place in the United States, to be assigned. I was able to visit my brother, while investigating Earl Smith's consortium, at company expense. Not to mention, I received a free lay from Earl's daughter and no one was the wiser. I like the idea of not revealing we're private investigators until we have to. He's right, a lot of information falls into your lap, if you position yourself properly and I do that well. I better call Tom and update him.* Tom was in his den, sitting in a chair with his foot propped up on an ottoman, looking at a recorded baseball game he taped some time earlier, and just got around to look at it. As soon as his team scored, the phone rang. He immediately stopped the tape before he answered the phone, not wanting to miss anything. "Hi, Tom, it's Sam."

"How was the trip? Get a little rest and recreation while you were there?"

"You know me. I must. It wouldn't be me if I didn't."

"Is there anything wrong with Earl Smith's consortium?"

"No, nothing I could find. However, I think I have something. Was the woman's name Mattie Greely that hired us to investigate the company?"

"I think so. I'll look at the files tomorrow at the office to double check. Wait, I put that information in my note pad. Tom pulled his note pad out of his pants pocket, looked through it and said, "Yeah, that's her!"

"I think Mr. Greely may have used the consortium as an excuse to spend the night out with Earl Smith's daughter."

"I've been working with Earl for years. I thought he was clean. His daughter is a character, though."

"I know. I had the pleasure of her company and I plan to again. I have a wedding to go to in two weeks. My brother is getting married."

Tom smiled and said, "Oh, really. One of my investigators told me he was dating Earl's daughter."

Sam admitted, "I did, but that's over. Tom man, I go up there to check on the consortium and it's legitimacy with thoughts that if it was legitimate, I was going to convince my brother to marry Juanita. That's Earl's daughter's name. I thought he was passing up a chance of a lifetime. Boy, was I wrong! Juanita is so hot in the pants, I don't think she knows what the word 'faithful' means. She picked me up from the airport and started spilling her guts. She told me how much she loved Todd, that she knew his goals, and wanted to help him reach them. She believed she could be an excellent business asset for him if he would forget about Marquetta and marry her. I believed her. What she said made a lot of sense, and I knew she could help Todd because of her father's connections. I'm telling you, she was very convincing. Based on her information, I tried to show my brother that the other woman was no good for him."

"Did you?"

"No way. He was right. She's the best thing that happened to him. He's so happy. I can't believe it and the girl is a knockout. Don't get me wrong, Juanita's attractive, too, but his fiancée has class. Man, she stood her ground with me. In fact, I don't think she likes me."

"Did she say that?"

"No, but it's like she sends me messages in her words like…'I don't play games. So bug off.'"

"What's her name? Does she have a business? If she does, she may be one of our clients."

"She may. Her name is Marquetta Logan."

"Ooh yeah, we have her company listed as one of our clients. Second Chance, Inc.—that is the name of her company, right?"

Sam said, "Yeah, that's it. I know because I was her escort at a banquet. She was the guest speaker. Man, she looked gorgeous. But she only has eyes for my brother. He was at the banquet, too. He brought Juanita. He introduced Marquetta, so he had to sit at the head table with us. I saw the look that passed between them. It was something. It reminded me of the look that passes between my mom and dad. I knew then what they had was special. Even though, I still tried to interfere. Marquetta dresses modestly, too. Not that her clothes are dowdy but that she sends messages even in her dress. Like, 'yes I know I'm all woman but my goodies don't come easily. If you want my goodies, you have to buy the complete package. Love, marriage, family–the whole nine yards.' However, my girl Juanita dresses so you can get a nice view of what she has to offer. She looked good, too. I stared at her breast off and on all night. It wouldn't be me if I couldn't look down some woman's dress."

Tom commented, "Sounds like you had an interesting trip and still got the job done. Prepare a preliminary report on your findings, and when you go back in two weeks, you can double check your findings and finalize the report. I'll send her a copy of the preliminary, pending final report in two weeks. That way she'll know we're working."

"Great. I'm going to get some sleep. See ya later. Bye-bye."

"Good bye." Tom said as he hung up the phone. Tom thought, *I opened the door, let's see if he's going to walk in.*

---

Juanita lay across her bed, as she thought about her time spent with Sam. A large grin came on her face as if stretching from ear to ear, then almost as quickly as it came, it left, and a saddened look appeared. She remembered Todd's pending marriage. The idea of Todd's marrying Marquetta made her want to scream. She couldn't resist temptation any longer—she let one out. After she screamed as loud as she could, she jumped off the bed and began searching through her closet frantically. She searched and searched until she pulled out a very seductive looking red dress. She held it up to her and stated, "It's Friday night, Sam's gone, and I feel all alone. I'm gonna get me a man. I don't want to be by myself tonight and I won't. First, I'll call Horace. She tried his private line but there was no answer. She contemplated, "He doesn't know how I'm going to handle his telling my father on me. He's probably scared. I'm not going to hurt him. I just want sex right now. Juanita felt sex was a panacea. She paced the floor as she decided what to do. I have it! I can go to a club. I'm bound to meet somebody there," reasoned Juanita.

---

Bill Clemmons thought, *I like Myrna. She's in her 20s, just like me. She's attractive and intelligent, too. I wonder if she'll go out with me? Well, it's Friday. It is a good time to find out.* Bill left his office and walked to where Myrna was working. First, he made a statement, then he inquired, "Myrna, it's getting late. Do you have any plans for this evening?" Bill, took the seat by her desk, waiting for her response.

Myrna was surprised at Bill's request. She didn't respond right away but she did stop typing and look at him. "No, but I have never dated a co-worker. I don't know how Mr. Parker would feel about that?"

Bill asked, "Do you think you could reach him, because I would like to take you out this evening?"

"Okay, I'll try to locate him. If I can't, I'll put it on his answering service. If he has a problem, he can tell me on Monday."

"Tell us on Monday. Remember, I work for him, too."

Myrna called Todd's house and got his answering service. She decided to leave a message. "I'm going out with your new associate, Bill Clemmons. If you think it would cause a problem in the office, please call me. Thank you, Myrna." After Myrna hung up, she buzzed Bill's office.

"Yes, Myrna," responded Bill.

"I left a message on Mr. Parker's answering service regarding our date. Do you still want to go?"

"More than ever." Bill thought, *This girl understands loyalty and work ethics.* He inquired, "Myrna, do you like to dance?"

Myrna replied, "Yes, I do."

Bill said, "Well then, let's go to a restaurant that provides dancing, too."

"That's a great idea."

"Do I need to follow you home so you can take your car?"

"No, it's in the shop," answered Myrna.

Bill stated, "Let's close up the office so we can go."

They closed the office for the evening and drove to the restaurant. Once seated in the restaurant, Myrna glanced around and noticed a woman who seemed familiar sitting at one of the game tables. Bill commenced talking to Myrna, which turned her attention to him before she could put a name with the face. Bill queried, "Tell me about Mr. Parker, as an employer. Is he hard to get along with?"

"No, he's very nice. He's a good employer. He's very fair. As long as you know and do your job, you won't have a problem with him. You saw his case folders. That's how thorough he is, and expects you to be, too. Can you handle that? If so, you won't have a problem."

Lights began flicking off and on in the direction of the dance floor, then the music began playing. People started leaving their seats and going toward the dance floor. Bill noticed the floor getting crowded, when he said, "Thanks for the advice. Then he asked, "Myrna would you like to dance?"

Myrna smiled and replied, "I thought you'd never ask." As soon as they reached the dance floor, Myrna was in her own world. She loved to dance. It was as if the music just, took over her body. Her moves were very natural and rhythmic.

Bill remarked, "You dance well."

"I like to dance. It relaxes me, but since I've been in school I don't go out much. I must admit, I don't go out with just anybody, either. People tell me I act old for my age, but I like to have a nice time with no hassles."

"I completely understand. Do you think you'll go out with me again?"

"If you ask, probably and if it's all right with Mr. Parker."
Suddenly there was a loud commotion which caused Myrna and
Bill to look in the direction of the disturbance. When they did,
Myrna saw the familiar face again. She was causing the distur-
bance. Myrna recognized the face and said to Bill, "That's Ms.
Smith, Juanita Smith, Mr. Parker's friend. Did she flip that chair
over on its side? Was that the loud noise we heard? Why is she
arguing with that old man?"

Bill's response had questions in it, too: "She's a friend of Mr.
Parker's? She looks like she's drunk. Is that possible? Do you think
we should help her?"

"I don't know. She isn't a nice lady. Besides, she may not want
our help, especially mine."

Bill asked, "Why do you say that?"

"Do you remember a conversation I had with you regarding one
of Mr. Parker's lady friends? I told you she was angry he was on
vacation and said she was going to tell him to fire me when he
returned."

"Yeah."

"That was her."

"She's, too drunk to remember that now. So, what do you
think?"

Myrna resolved, "Let's help her. I don't want her to get hurt
trying to drive home. It looked like she was by herself earlier when
I saw her."

"You saw her earlier?"

"I saw her face. I couldn't remember her name until now. We
better go to her." As they walked to Juanita, Myrna saw the face of
the older gentleman and gasped. When collected, she explained,
"Bill, the man she's arguing with is a client of Mr. Parker's. By the
way, so is Ms. Smith. Look, there's an older lady at the table. Do
you think she's his wife?"

"If so, she looks calm for a woman whose husband is being
chewed out by a younger woman in a very seductive red dress,"
replied Bill. Myrna looked at the dress and commented, "Wow, that
dress has openings just about everywhere. Although it's made cute,
if you like that much exposure. The dress had a deep V shape cut in

the back, where the belt buckle was facing, to bring emphasis to the derriere. In front of the dress was a smaller version of the V shape cut— just enough to expose a little bit of breast, for the purpose of enticing the onlooker. The mini-dress, also, offered slits on both its sides to not leave out the man who likes legs. She had black silk stockings, with Italian leather sling-back shoes to complete the ensemble. I say she was definitely out to catch a man this evening." Bill opted not to comment. As they waded through the small group that surrounded the table where Horace was sitting, and Juanita was standing, they heard Horace speak in a controlled voice, "Juanita, please go home. You're drunk and making a scene. I'm sure your father doesn't want to hear about this tomorrow."

Juanita retorted, "That's right, you'll tell him, won't you? You tell him everything. What did you tell my father about me? He thinks I'm a prostitute. You old goat." Juanita was now leaning against the wooden rail near the table where Horace sat, to keep her balance while yelling at him.

Horace queried, "Perhaps we can talk about this later, when you sober up?" He then turned to his wife, put his hand over hers in a soothing manner and apologized, "I'm sorry, Honey. I didn't know she would be here or I would have taken you somewhere else."

"Horace honey, you're handling this just fine. We've finished eating. So, I'm going to the ladies room. You pay the bill and I'll meet you at the car." Mattie kissed Horace on the cheek, then left. As Mattie walked to the ladies room she thought, *That poor child needs prayer. Her mother deserted her at such a young age, and a man cannot raise a daughter the way a woman can. I know this is my opinion, but I have always felt sorry for that child. Instead of me reaching out to help her, the Lord used her to help me. Ha,ha,ha, in a round about way. Because of her shenanigans, my husband had to call on the Lord for help. He is a praying man, now. And that's a good thing.* Mattie nodded her head in agreement, as if she had been talking to someone other than herself. Then she pushed on the door, and went into the ladies room.

Myrna thought, *She's a tough lady. Juanita didn't upset her at all. Talking about confidence, I haven't seen confidence like that in a long time.* When Juanita quieted down, Myrna went to her and asked, "Ms. Smith, I'm Myrna, Mr. Parker's secretary. Would you like a ride home?"

Juanita, inebriated, responded, "Who?" Then she proceeded to follow Horace out the door as he was going to his car. Staggering as she walked, Bill and Myrna followed closely behind in an effort to hide her condition from bystanders, and to try to make certain she arrived at her destination safely.

"My name is Myrna. Would you like a ride home? I don't think you're in any condition to drive."

"I can drive, thank you."

Bill asked, "May we drive you home?"

Juanita looked at Bill and thought, *Not bad.* She walked over to him, grabbed his arm and said, "Sure, Honey, you can take me home."

Myrna glanced at Bill, smiled, and stated, "Let's go."

Horace looked at Myrna and Bill, and in a low soft voice said, "Thank you."

Bill and Myrna acknowledged him with a nod. Bill stated, "I'll drive her, but I need you to follow me in my car. Oh yeah, do you know her car?"

Myrna showed him Juanita's car. Her name was on the tag. She helped Bill put Juanita in the passenger's seat of the lipstick red jaguar. The minute Bill asked Juanita for her keys, she handed them to him without making a fuss.

Myrna waited for Bill to pull out of the parking space, then she followed him. While driving, Myrna thought, then prayed, *I'm learning a serious lesson tonight.* God, please forgive me for what I said about Juanita needing to know that the world doesn't revolve around her. I should have prayed for You to help her. Please help her, Father God. She needs you. In Jesus' name. Amen."

As Bill turned into the parking lot where Juanita's condo was located, Myrna followed. Once she parked Bill's car by Juanita's, she, took a deep breath then announced, "We're here, good."

Juanita told Bill where she lived and invited him to spend the night, but he wouldn't respond. He, took her to her condo and asked her which key on her key ring opened her door. She replied, "Ring the bell, Baby. I have a live in."

Bill rang the bell. Suzette opened the door and helped Juanita into her condo. Bill handed Suzette Juanita's keys, then left. Bill smiled as he walked to his car. He thought, *Mr. Parker needs to pick a different type of lady friend. If I wanted to, I could have slept with her tonight. That's not good. But, I have to give her the benefit of the doubt—she was drunk. Unfortunately, some men would take advantage of that. She must've had a bad day.*

As Bill got into his car, he inquired, "How did you like driving my car?" He put his car in gear and drove off of the parking lot and onto the street as he waited for Myrna's response.

Myrna hesitated before she responded, because she didn't understand the question. To her a stick was a stick and either you liked driving a stick or you didn't. She liked driving sticks, so she responded, "It's okay."

"I'm glad you drive stick. I didn't think to ask."

"I'm glad I do, too, and I'm glad Ms. Smith got home safely."

"She was a very intoxicated lady. But enough about her, Myrna. I really like you. I think we have more in common than the ability to drive manual transmissions." Bill smiled. Then he asked, "Do you know what that was all about tonight?"

"No, but both do business with Mr. Parker. I hope we're not going to see a fight in the office if the two of them are there at the same time."

"I don't think they would fight in the office. At least not for us to see. I think she responded like this tonight because she had something on her mind."

"Well, she has been boisterous with me at times when she was upset."

"Really, she's impudent. But you said she is also a friend of Mr. Parker's. Why?"

"There's something you should know. Our boss loves women. All kinds."

"Is that right? I didn't get that impression when I met him."

"I will say, he has changed, but Ms. Smith is still around. Now, do you like women?"

"I see you don't bite your tongue."

"We work together. I just want to know the truth."

"I'm guilty. I have been one who likes a lot of women, too. However, I'm changing my ways. Anyway, I'm in between women right now, meaning I'm not dating anyone seriously."

"Me, too. I mean I'm not dating anyone seriously." They laughed. Then Bill said, "That's good. I like you, Myrna."

Myrna forgot he didn't know where she lived and was about to pass by her apartment complex. She said, "Stop here. This is it, my apartment building." Myrna, took her keys out of her pocket book and put them in her hand as she got out of the car. Then she said, "Thanks, Bill, I had fun. It's late, please don't get out, I can see myself to my apartment. We're parked right in front of my building and I'm on the second floor. Myrna pointed to her window. "I'll turn the light off and on so you'll know I'm in safely. I had a good time."

"Me, too. See ya Monday." Bill watched the building until he saw a light flicking off and on in the window Myrna pointed at; then he drove off.

As Myrna dressed for bed, she thought, *I need to make a note to tell Mr. Parker about the incident at the restaurant.* She wrote a note about the incident, using a note pad and pen from her night-stand, then went to bed.

---

After Bill arrived home, he thought, *I better tell Phillip what happened at the restaurant. He'll know if Todd needs to know this information. I would hate for a problem to arise in the office from this incident.* Bill made a note to call Phillip and then switched his thoughts to Myrna. *I like the way she thinks. She's all right. I want to get to know her better.*

---

Marquetta got up early on Saturday and decided to clean her condo thoroughly. When she pulled out the chair near the window to vacuum, the folder in the chair fell on the floor. She bent down to pick up the folder, and under it was the paper that had fallen out of it some time ago. She picked up the folder and the paper, placed the paper inside the folder, then, put the folder on the table. She continued to vacuum. When she finished, she went back to the table and sat down in one of the chairs, to open up the folder and read the paper that was in it. It was information on the owners of Greely's Towing Service. Surprised, Marquetta read the information with interest. After she finished reading the paper work, she placed the folder in the file cabinet in her den. She said, "I thought William Greely was the sole owner but he's not. Horace Greely and Earl Smith are partners in Greely's Towing Service. This needs to be looked into further. I need to talk to Barbara when she comes here tonight." She finished cleaning, then prepared dinner and dressed for her evening with Todd and friends. After she dressed, she remembered, *I haven't heard from Todd today. I'll call him.* Just then the door bell rang. She thought, *It's Todd.*

She opened the door and Todd began talking. "Hey, Baby, you want to hear something funny?" Todd said as he continued to walk into her condo.

Marquetta smiled because Todd always did that to her. Patiently, she waited for the pause and then answered him. "Yeah."

Todd kissed her on the lips, took a seat on the couch in her living room, and continued, "Myrna left a message on my answering service asking if it was all right for her to go out with Bill, my new employee. She didn't want to cause an unnecessary problem in the office. That girl is something else. She takes her job seriously. She is dedicated to my firm. But asking me about dating, Markie? As long as they can separate business from pleasure, it won't bother me."

"I like her. She's smart. She realizes office relationships can get crazy and she doesn't know how you feel about your employees dating. She's also making a statement. Her dating him will not interfere with the working relationship the two of you have developed. By the way, who is Bill?"

"So much has happened, I forgot to tell you. When I decided I wanted to be with you in the Caribbean, I knew I needed an attorney I could trust to assist Myrna in my absence. So, I thought about the young guy not long out of school that asked me if he could work for me. Later, I found out Phillip suggested he talk to me. Phillip told me he referred Bill to me when I asked his opinion of him. Phillip also told me he was his attorney and he liked him. After talking with Phillip, I made an appointment for Phillip and me to meet with Bill. I prayed about it and then hired him. I instructed Bill to alert Phillip if any problems came up, no matter how minor. I gave Phillip my number in the Caribbean."

"What's his complete name?"

"Bill Clemmons. You probably know him, because he told me he's active in the singles' group at the church."

"I do know him. Bill and I are usually partners when we go bowling as a group."

"You dated him?"

Marquetta laughed and said, "No, Todd, be for real. We both like to bowl."

"So, do you think he'll be good for Myrna."

"I think so. Myrna seems like she can handle him if he gets out of line. But generally speaking, I think he's a nice guy."

"What about loyal in relationships? I guess now that I've changed, I don't want to see a woman burnt. Myrna is a tough cookie. You're right—she'll be able to hold her own. Come here my future wife, and kiss me."

Marquetta laughed, walked over to where Todd was sitting on the couch, and kissed him. Todd asked, "Markie, can we get married today?"

"No! We have to be counseled first. Hopefully, we can be married in two weeks, but we may have to wait longer."

"I hope not. Anyway—no reception."

"No reception? Todd, why not?"

"We have a marriage to consummate."

"Maybe we can have a reception but we'll leave early. What do you think?"

"I can't say right now. I know one thing—I'm looking forward to the marriage. I'm just like my father said."

"What?"

"Bursting at the seams!"

Both laughed long and hard. Finally, Todd said, "Seriously, Markie, I always wondered what people did on their honeymoons, when they have been having sex all along. Even though it gets rough at times, I like the anticipation period. I didn't realize how special this time is for two people getting ready to be married. You know, being comfortable with and trusting each other to stay within certain boundaries. Trust is a good thing, isn't it?"

"Yeah, if the trust is based on your foundation in God."

"Markie, why did your mother look like she was going to cry when I asked her if she had any sisters or brothers, and why did your father change the subject?"

"Because it's a topic we don't discuss with her or Grandma Kate."

"Why?"

"Because all they do is cry. So, Grandpa Tom, Daddy, and I never discuss her siblings. It's a sad story and I want to think about nice things. Let's get back to us. Todd, I never thanked you for the fun we had in the Caribbean. I'm very glad you decided to come. I can't remember ever being this happy. But it's a different kind of happy than I'm accustomed, too. I guess it's because I've never felt this type of closeness with a man, even when I was having sex." As she talked, she was facing Todd on the sofa, holding his hands in hers as she spoke.

"I know what you mean. It's hard to explain, you just know its right. It feels so natural. May I put on one of your praise tapes?" She let his hands go gently and moved to a more comfortable spot on the sofa where her back could rest against the back of the sofa.

"Sure, you can check the CDs, too."

"Good idea, thanks for reminding me."

---

Bill called Phillip and told him what happened at the restaurant. Then he inquired, "Phillip, do you think Todd would be interested in this information?"

Phillip replied, "Get a date and meet me at Marquetta's condo for dinner. It may be nothing, but I think it should be shared. Do you know where Marquetta lives?"

"Yeah, I should. I've been there a few times with you when you dropped her off after we went bowling together."

"Good. If you get lost, beep me. I'll let Marquetta know to prepare for two more mouths." Urgency was in Phillip's voice as he spoke to Bill.

"Wait, Phillip, what time should I be there?"

"Sorry about that. Make it 7:30 p.m. sharp."

"Good bye," said Bill.

Phillip hung up the phone and called Marquetta's condo.

"Hi, Marquetta, how are you?"

Marquetta sensed urgency in his voice as she said, "Hi, Phillip, I'm fine. Is anything wrong? You're coming tonight, aren't you?"

"Sure, I'm looking for Todd. Is he there?"

"Yeah, you want to speak with him?"

Hearing the concern in Marquetta's questions, he then acknowledged the tone in his voice was rushed; so he slowed down, laughed and said, "Yes, please." Marquetta heard the laughter, then felt the smile through the phone and felt more at ease.

She responded, "Okay, hold on." Marquetta called Todd to the phone.

Todd, took the receiver from her and said, "Hello."

"Hi, Todd. This is Phillip. Bill has some information I think you should hear concerning Juanita Smith and Horace Greely. I told him to get a date and meet us at Marquetta's at 7:30 p.m. sharp, to discuss it. Of course, I offered him dinner. I forgot to tell Marquetta. Do you think she'll mind?"

"No, I don't think so, but remember I'm going to be the one who gets it if she does mind. Hold on, I'm going to ask her."

"Boy, you're learning fast."

Both laughed, then Todd repeated his initial statement, "Hold on." Todd then covered the phone with one hand and said, "Markie, your bowling partner Bill is coming over at 7:30 p.m. with some information for me. Is it all right for him to bring a date and eat with us?"

"Sure, no problem."

"Good, thanks, Babe," replied Todd.

Todd removed his hand from the receiver and said, "Phillip, it's fine. What time are you and Barbara getting here?"

"How about 7:00 p.m.? I want to see your vacation pictures."

"Make it 6:45 p.m. but I'm not going to show you all of them."

"I've seen Marquetta in a bathing suit before. I belong to the singles group at the church, remember? We've all gone swimming together. Now you see what you've missed. But now that I think about it, you weren't ready then."

Both laughed. Todd responded, "I don't care what you say, you won't see those pictures tonight. Man, not because of you, but because of me. I know now that it was only because of God I was able to restrain while we were in the Caribbean. I looked at some of those pictures the other night and I knew I couldn't look at them again until we were married."

"I know what you mean. I still have pictures of Barbara in her bathing suit, buried in a drawer covered with clothes, in a guest room. They laughed again. Then Phillip said, "I'll see ya later, Man. Good bye."

Todd, took a seat beside Marquetta on the couch with a smile still on his face.

Marquetta remarked, "You're smiling, but Phillip sounded serious to me. What was that all about? Is there something going on that I should know about?"

"We'll find out soon enough. Bill is coming here with a date to tell us. You better be on your best behavior, because I'll be watching you and Mr. Clemmons."

Marquetta smiled and commented, "You will, will ya! Todd, you're ridiculous. Anyway, I have invited you plenty of times to join the singles group or to go on some of the activities with us, but you always had something to do. It's funny how you joined every business committee I was involved in, but not the church activities."

"I figured you were safe there. I never thought about men being involved in the group or that you would go swimming."

"That I would go swimming?"

"Yeah, swimming! Did Bill go with the group when you went swimming? You never invited me to go swimming with the group."

Marquetta laughed, then asked, "What were you and Phillip discussing on the phone?"

Todd said firmly. "No, Markie, don't change the subject. Why didn't you ask me to go when the group went swimming?"

"Because at the time I didn't think it was a good idea."

"Why not?"

"Todd, you know why not. Just think, not only have you seen

me in a bathing suit, but we've been swimming together, too. So what difference does it make now? That was in the past. Phillip had just finished adding the pool to the house and we got to try it out. Occasionally, a few of us would go over to Phillip's after the singles' meeting and swim."

"Bill happened to be one of them?"

"Todd, what's bothering you?"

"I'm sorry, Baby. I love you so much and, right now, it is so hard for me to look at our pictures without thinking we need to get married really quickly."

Marquetta laughed, then acknowledged the problem, "Bursting at the seams."

Both laughed. Then Todd said, "You're ridiculous." He reached for her and kissed her ardently. Then he said, "Thanks, that should hold me for a while."

The doorbell rang and Marquetta said, "Todd, please get the door and I'll put out the appetizers."

Todd replied, "Okay." He got up and walked to the door. When he opened the door, he decided to play with Barbara and Phillip. He said, "Man, get your arm from around that woman and stop smiling so hard, you may crack your face."

Phillip responded, "You're not the only one in love. Now calm down, ask us in, and show us to our seats."

"Todd laughed and said with a British accent, "I'm sorry. Do come in and you may have a seat anywhere as long as it's not by Markie."

All three laughed and walked into the living room. As Marquetta entered the living room from the kitchen, Barbara asked, "Marquetta, what are we going to do with the two of them?"

"I don't know, Barbara," commented Marquetta as she welcomed her with a hug.

"You look good. I can tell you really enjoyed yourself in the Caribbean," remarked Barbara.

"Yes, we did," responded Todd.

"She was talking to me, and yes, we did," replied Marquetta. Everyone laughed.

"Man, I don't know if I can stand being around you this happy," commented Phillip. Phillip noticed Marquetta's engagement ring and said, "Come here, Little Sister, and give me a hug." Marquetta laughed and walked over to Phillip. Phillip hugged her and said, "Congratulations." He then walked over to Todd, Todd stood up to meet him and they shook hands and hugged. Phillip said, "That's all right, Man. You did good by my little sister."

Marquetta commented, "Barbara, they're worst than us." Then she said, "Thank you, Phillip, your approval means a lot to me." Marquetta, took her seat by Todd on the sofa and Phillip sat in his seat near Barbara on the love seat.

"Yeah, he's all right. Look at him. Stop grinning, Man." Phillip said jokingly.

"We should have known they would be worst than us," remarked Barbara. Then she looked toward Todd and Phillip and asked, "Will the two of you stop grinning for a minute?"

Both responded, "No," in unison. Marquetta and Barbara laughed.

Todd said, "Man, now I understand what you are going through, but I must say it's a nice change for this day and age."

"It is, isn't it? Although, I'll try to remember what you said when I take a cold shower tonight. Here lately, it's becoming more and more regular."

Todd remarked, "I understand. It's the trust, man, that gets ya. They can lie on you, kiss you passionately and even if it seems like they may be weakening, we are expected to be strong. You know when you think about it, that's part of what being a man is all about–making decisions that are best for everyone concerned, even if it appears to be at odds with your personal pleasures and desires. Of course, this can only be done with God's guidance and direction. Boy, is this a learning experience for me."

"For both of us," responded Phillip.

Barbara and Marquetta chimed in, "For all of us."

Marquetta added, "Todd's father said, 'you feel like you're bursting at the seams, but that's good.'"

Phillip said, "Todd, your dad knows what he's talking about—big time, Man!"

They laughed. Barbara said, "It won't be long now for us.

Pastor Green okayed us to be married. We're going to be married in two weeks."

"That's great," stated Todd. "I want us to be married in two weeks, too, but Markie said we have to talk to Pastor Green first. Barbara, you know I've been meeting with him for a while now about me and Markie, but he never gave me any marriage guidelines. Did he give you and Phillip any?"

"No, I think he just wants to make sure you thought it through as thoroughly as possible. In your case, you've been meeting with him individually as long as I have, and that's been for six months. I can't see it being a problem."

Marquetta and Phillip looked at each other. Then Phillip queried, "How did you know I was going to ask you to marry me six months ago? I wasn't sure myself, then."

Barbara replied, "I just wanted to make sure that I understood what marriage entailed. You know, make sure I had a clear picture. Any concerns or questions I had, I discussed with him. Although you were the person I considered marrying, I continued to pray for guidance and acceptance of who God wanted me to marry."

"Barbara, that's similar to the way I thought. As I told Barbara, later Markie, and now you, Phillip, I had been thinking about marrying Markie for a while, but only six months ago was I determined to do what I had to do to be the right kind of husband. So I called Pastor Green and met with him. Sometimes Barbara and I would run into each other between meetings. We would talk briefly about the two of you, so I really wasn't surprised when you proposed, Phillip. I just didn't know when I would, but I knew it would be soon. That night at your place it all came together. Boy, have I thought it through. I feel like Markie has been a part of me for such a long time, I have to make it official," said Todd.

"Todd, Pastor Green had us make a list of all possible concerns and then told us to pray about them," said Barbara.

"That's a good idea. It's just another way of making certain God is the head of your family," said Marquetta.

"Yep. Give all your problems and concerns to God and trust that he will handle them," said Phillip.

Todd said, "There's that word 'trust' again. Boy am I learning, thank you, Holy Spirit."

The doorbell rang and Phillip stated, "That must be Bill."

Marquetta said, "I'll get it." She opened the door and saw Myrna. She hugged her, then invited her in, "I'm glad to see you, Myrna, come in."

"Thank you, Marquetta. Bill let me out; he's parking the car."

"That's fine." Marquetta escorted Myrna into the living room, then inquired, "Myrna, I'm sorry, what's your last name?"

"Thompson," said Myrna.

Phillip James and Barbara Biggins, I would like to introduce to you Myrna Thompson," announced Marquetta.

"Hi, Myrna, just call me Phillip."

"Hi, Myrna, I have spoken with you often over the phone. It's nice to finally get to meet you in person. Just call me Barbara."

"I'm glad to meet you, too. Ms. Logan speaks so highly of you. May I continue to call on you for advice?"

"Sure," replied Barbara.

Todd stood up and said, "Myrna, have a seat." He then moved to his favorite chair where the hassock was and propped his feet on the hassock. Myrna sat in the middle of the sofa, leaving room for Marquetta and Bill on either side. Once comfortable, Todd continued, "I'm sorry if I neglected to tell you, you're a good secretary, too."

"Thank you, Mr. Parker," said Myrna.

"Myrna, please, call me Todd. It's after hours."

"Okay, as long as you understand I must call you Mr. Parker at the office. I feel it's appropriate."

Todd, amused at Myrna's determination to give him the respect she feels he should have, regardless of his own views on the subject replied, "Fine."

The doorbell rang and Marquetta opened it. It was Bill. She hugged him and said, "Have a seat in the living room."

After every one was seated, Bill began with an apology: "Marquetta, I hope you don't mind my discussing work on the weekend but when I spoke with Phillip he thought it best that I meet with Todd tonight."

"That's fine," responded Marquetta. She then turned to address everyone in the room. "Do you want to eat first or talk business?"

Phillip said, "Let's eat. We can talk business later."

Marquetta replied, "Okay. Barbara, would you help me serve?"

"Sure," agreed Barbara.

Once in the kitchen, Barbara commented, "I think Juanita's involved. Phillip wouldn't tell me when I asked, but I think she's involved."

Marquetta said, "Sounds interesting. I want to talk to you about the ownership of Greely's Towing Service, too. But we'll discuss it later. Now, let's eat." Marquetta and Barbara served dinner.

---

Earl was in his den reviewing the last piece of paperwork for the evening. He spent the day reviewing files from both his insurance company and the consortium. Everything seemed to be in order, but he couldn't shake the feeling something was happening that he needed to be on top of. After he put the files back in the file cabinet, he realized if the problem wasn't work-related, it must be personal. He wondered if it was Juanita or Loretta. Then his phone rang. He picked up the receiver. Before he could say anything, Horace commenced talking, "Earl, this is Horace, I need to meet with you on Monday. It's about Juanita and her extortion attempt. I know I told you I wouldn't file charges, but she tried to embarrass me in a public place, and I won't have it."

"Horace, we have been working together for years. I have done nothing but been fair to you. I'm asking you to calm down and let me deal with my daughter my way."

"Meet with me on Monday with the outcome of your meeting with Juanita. If it's satisfactory, I'll forget it, but if not, I'm going to do what I have to." said Horace.

Earl replied, "I understand. I assure you, you will be satisfied. Good bye."

Earl hung up from talking with Horace and immediately called Juanita's condo.

"Hello," answered Juanita. She knew Suzette was packing to go to the mansion when the phone rang, so she answered it.

"Young lady, when Suzette comes over here tonight, I want you with her." Earl said sternly.

197

"Yes sir, Daddy, but what's wrong?"

"We'll discuss it when you arrive. Bring clothes for church, you will be going tomorrow! Good bye." Earl hung up.

Juanita, puzzled, looked at the receiver for a few seconds and thought, "What's wrong with him? This time Daddy has gone a little, too far. He can't tell me what to do. I'm an adult. I shouldn't go over there." Juanita sat in the living room and brooded until Suzette came out of her room and noticed her. Suzette walked over to her and sat down beside her and inquired, "Baby girl, what's wrong? You know I can always tell when something is wrong with you. Are you going to tell me what it is?" Juanita cried in Suzette's arms as she blurted, "I feel so alone."

"You're not alone. You have your Daddy, Violet, and me. We love you, Child, and God loves you, too. Whenever you feel you can't talk to anyone, you can always talk to God. In fact, those are the times I think you really should talk to God.." Juanita didn't say a word but continued to cry in Suzette's arms.

---

Phillip declared, "I'm stuffed. Everything was delicious. I guess I'm ready to talk business, now."

Todd replied, "We better or we may all doze off." Marquetta had prepared roast beef, mashed potatoes with gravy, spinach and homemade rolls for dinner. She topped off the meal with peach cobbler. It was one of her favorite desserts. Bill started, "Myrna was with me, so she'll probably add to what I say."

"That's fine, continue," said Todd.

"Before you get started, why don't we all move back into the living room? That way I can clean off the table while you guys get comfortable," suggested Marquetta.

Todd agreed, "Okay, everybody, let's move to the living room." As they moved to the living room, Barbara assisted Marquetta in the clean up. By the time everyone was settled, Barbara and Marquetta were coming into the living room to take a seat.

As they sat down, Bill said, "It may be nothing, but here goes. Myrna and I went out for dinner and dancing last night. While we were dancing, we heard a commotion, which turned out to be an argument between an older gentleman and a young lady. Myrna knew the young lady, so we thought we would try to assist if we could. The young lady was a friend of yours, Mr. Parker."

Todd asked, "Who?" By the way, please call me Todd."

Myrna looked at Todd and said softly, "Ms. Smith, Juanita Smith."

"I knew it," exclaimed Barbara.

Phillip remarked, "Let her continue, please."

"I'm sorry for interrupting you, Myrna, please continue," said Barbara, as she tried to hide her excitement.

Bill stated, "Mr. Parker...I mean...Todd, the other person was a client of yours, too. Mr. Greely."

Marquetta queried, "William or Horace?"

Myrna responded, "Horace."

Marquetta, now excited, inquired, "Could you hear what they were saying?"

Bill said, "Something like, 'you made my father think I was a prostitute.'"

"First, she said, 'You tell him everything,'" added Myrna.

"Did either of you find out what started the outburst?" Todd asked.

"Not really, just that Mr. Greely told her father something she apparently didn't want him to know," responded Myrna.

"It's probably nothing, but we thought you should know, since both of them are your clients. We didn't want any blowups in the office." Believing he had done his part and now was ready to leave, he put a hand on each leg as he sighed then rose from the sofa. Myrna followed his lead by rising to her feet, too. Bill stated, "Well, it's getting late and I told Myrna I would take her to the movies. Thanks for dinner; it was absolutely delicious. See you in church tomorrow. Myrna's going to visit our church tomorrow."

"Thank you for dinner; it was very good. I may need some pointers from you on cooking, too. Well, I'd better be going. See you later," commented Myrna.

Barbara said, "We'll look for you tomorrow at church. Have a good evening."

Todd and Phillip responded, "Good bye," in unison.

Marquetta escorted them to the door and said, "Both of you are welcome to visit any time. Good night."

Marchette walked back into the living room, took her seat and queried, "Todd, when did Horace Greely become a client of yours?"

Todd replied, "Recently. I picked him up when I went to the dinner engagement with Juanita."

"Did you know he has ownership in Greely's Towing Service, along with Earl Smith?"

"Yes, Markie, but some changes are being made concerning ownership. That's all I can say right now."

Barbara asked, "Marquetta, is Todd's representation of Greely's Towing Service a conflict of interest?"

Phillip inquired, "Todd, why is Barbara asking that question? Don't you work with a lot of companies that receive clients from Second Chance, Inc? Is it because of Tony Davis that she asked that question?"

"Yes," Barbara and Marquetta replied together.

Although Todd was being bombarded with questions, he expected it specifically from Marquetta when he heard Horace Greely's name in the report from Myrna and Bill. "Phillip, it is Markie's and Barbara's belief that Greely's Towing Service is trying to sabotage Second Chance, Inc." He then looked at Marquetta and stated, "I told you, Markie, we have no real evidence to that effect."

Marquetta replied, "We might. What kind of involvement did Juanita have with Horace and why?"

"We know it must be personal and involved sex because of what she said to Horace. 'You made my father think I was a prostitute,'" added Barbara.

Phillip commented, "Oh, Man, you got them going now."

Marquetta reasoned, "'Prostitute' could also mean some type of exchange was given. Maybe money or maybe a favor? Mr. Parker, can you tell me this? Did you know Horace Greely was an owner of Greely's Towing Service when I met with you in your office about the tape?"

"Oh, so it's Mr. Parker now. Well, Ms. Logan, I think you have made an appropriate request in light of the information we just heard. So I'll answer your question. Yes, I did."

"I knew it was something you didn't tell me that day we met at your office. I know you too well, Todd Parker!"

"Markie, at the time it wasn't important. Now I understand it may be, so that's why I mentioned it to you but that's all I will say on the subject for now."

"See, Todd, I knew you were holding out. That's why I did my homework. Now I know exactly what happened," said Marquetta.

Todd smiled and queried, "Oh, you do, do you?"

"So do I," responded Barbara.

"Man, you know how they love to play detective, we better hear them out," said Phillip.

Marquetta said, "Consider this. Why would Horace want to sabotage SCI? He doesn't. I don't even know him personally. But who would want SCI to sink?"

Barbara replied, "Juanita Smith."

Marquetta responded, "Exactly. But why now? She knows something I don't know. But what is it that would be important enough for her to want to sabotage my company?"

Todd chuckled, then remarked, "Detectives Biggins and Logan, I'll give you credit, the two of you are good."

Phillip asked, "You mean you agree with them?"

"Yeah, that's why I jokingly called them detectives. They're good even to the questions they posed. You raised a good point, Markie. I know Juanita knew nothing tangibly about our pending engagement, so it must involve Earl Smith and his consortium. At the last dinner party I went to, I overheard some of the people talking about Earl looking to invite some new businesses into the consortium. I thought I was being considered when I picked up three businesses that were already members of the consortium. But what about you, Markie? I mean SCI. They look for businesses that they think are good for the community, too. Earl Smith likes you and respects your company. With the backing you could get from the consortium, you could expand big time. I'm talking about a serious salary increase."

"To Juanita, a move like that would have made you serious competition for her with Todd," responded Barbara.

"Markie, you told me once, if she thought anything was going on between us, she would probably try to destroy your company. You were right! Wow, she did all this on speculation! Just think, at one time I seriously considered marrying her. Thank you, God, you know what's best for me."

"You know, Todd, I think you're right, because Marquetta received an invitation from Earl Smith's office on Friday. I didn't open it because I thought it was an invitation to another banquet he was sponsoring. I thought I would give Marquetta the pleasure of opening it on Monday as a joke."

"Thanks, Barbara." Marquetta laughed and said.

"Let's assume everything that has been discussed is true. Has a crime been committed? I mean nothing has happened. No more complaints from Mr. William Greely, and Tony's doing fine. It seems to me the problem is solved," said Phillip.

Todd replied, "This is just speculation. However, we do know who the players are in the scheme. So, if anything tangible happens, we know who to look for. But I'm in agreement with you, Phillip, the problem is solved."

"Yeah, I have to agree, too, the problem is solved. What confirms that theory is the argument that took place at the restaurant," responded Marquetta.

Barbara said, "Thank you, God, for hearing and answering prayers."

Marquetta agreed, "That's right. Thank you, God. You are good to us. God really protects his children."

Phillip stated, "Let's praise him in song. Phillip put in a praise CD and they sang.

---

Horace got off the phone, walked into the kitchen where his wife was, and shared the conversation he had with Earl Smith, with his wife. Mattie Greely was dumbfounded. She remarked, "I don't believe you, Horace Greely! You prayed and asked God for help. God heard and answered your prayers. He saved your business and Williams, too. He brought us back together as husband and wife, and now you tell me this. How could you threaten Earl Smith like that? He loves his daughter just like you love our children. How would you feel if the situation were reversed? Give him time to work with her. She was raised without a mother. You need to pray for her. After all, you slept with that young girl and I forgave you. You need to forgive her. God is good to you Horace. You have to share that goodness!" She stormed out of the kitchen, deliberately wanting Horace to know she was not pleased with his decision.

Horace went to the wall phone in the kitchen and dialed his brother's home phone. William answered the phone. As soon as Horace heard Williams's voice, he began talking, "I called Earl Smith and told him what happened with Juanita and me at the restaurant. I told him if he didn't control her I would—basically, let's just say I threatened him. Mattie got on me when I told her what I did. Do you think I should call Earl Smith back this evening and apologize, or tell him when I see him again."

William said, "God blessed us, big time, Man. I've decided I'm changing my ways. We could have lost everything. Mattie stayed with you, Man. Forget about what Juanita did. I don't know about you but I'm going to church on Sunday. I know God is real. I don't think I'll ever forget this experience."

Horace replied, while leaning against the wall near the phone, "Man, I know exactly how you feel. I'll meet you at church on Sunday. Good bye."

Horace dialed Earl's private line. Earl answered. "Hello."

"Earl, this is Horace. Please don't say anything, just listen. I'm sorry for the earlier phone call. I know you tried to do good by everyone concerned. I'm going to forget about what happened with Juanita and me at the restaurant. No real harm was done. But on a personal note, Juanita needs help. I'm telling you this as one father to another."

"Thanks for your concern. Good bye," replied Earl. Earl hung up the phone and thanked God, silently.

# CHAPTER 7

# FORGIVE AND FORGET

Todd queried, "Hey Big Brother, how was your vacation?" Todd was sitting at his desk in his den when he called Sam.

Sam replied, "It could've been better. What's up?" Sam was sitting at his table reading the paper, with the phone on the table. It never failed, the phone always seemed to ring while he read the paper, so he was prepared.

"You're investigating Earl Smith's consortium, aren't you?"

"What are you talking about?"

"You know what I'm talking about. Why? Are you doing this on your own or for the company?"

"Man, you know I can't talk about this with you. You're no longer in law enforcement and you're not an investigator."

"It's for your job. Well good bye, Big Brother." Todd smiled as he hung up the phone. He thought, *What's going on with Earl Smith? I work with three of his business partners and have reviewed their legal documents thoroughly. I double check anything I may find questionable just because they belong to Earl Smith's consortium, and I can't find anything wrong with them or their companies. Now that I'm their attorney, I plan to keep it that way.*

The phone rang. Todd answered it. "Hello."

Sam inquired, "What do you know? You didn't call for nothing."

Todd decided, *I can play games, too. I won't answer his questions.* Todd asked, "How did you enjoy my ex-friend?"

Sam laughed, and then remarked, "Like you care. Marquetta is the only woman on your mind these days. I can give you credit for a nice cover-up. I would've never guessed she looked that good with a name like 'Markie.' You'd better be glad you met her first."

Todd laughed, then stated, "I'm glad on two counts. I met her first, and that I'm smarter than you think."

"I see, you're serious. I'm getting a sister-in-law."

"Yes, you are, and very soon I hope."

"I called home. Mom and Pop are very happy you're getting married. You're not going to believe what Pop asked."

"What?"

"He asked if she liked me. I told him 'no,' then he laughed and said, 'I told Todd his wife wouldn't want anything to do with you and I was right.'"

Todd laughed, then said, "He would always tell me that after you, took one of my girlfriends. Why did you tell him Markie didn't like you?"

"I told Pop the truth. If she does, she doesn't show it. I told him she let me hug her when I congratulated the two of you, however, she faced you the entire time. Todd, does she like me? I think she's all right."

"Let's face it, you're going to be her brother-in-law, so she doesn't hate you. You just approached her the wrong way. But I can tell you this, you will be in her prayers."

"Man, she's tough, brief, and to the point. What are you going to do when the two of you argue?"

"She's not as bad as all that. She just knows how to protect herself and she's not going to be pushed around."

"You know I had to hit on her, right? It wouldn't be me if I didn't."

"She knows how to handle you, and I'm glad. I'm telling you now, if an argument breaks out between you two, I'm on her side—until you can prove otherwise—and then I still am going to go along with her decision. So don't try to separate us, okay?"

"Okay."

"Have you talked to Juanita since you've been home?"

"No, why should I?"

"What kind of investigator are you?"

"You're right, I can't close the door on her, yet. I may be able to get some information from her."

Todd laughed and queried, "The case is closed, isn't it?"

"Yeah," admitted Sam.

"Good, I have a meeting with Earl Smith. I think he's inviting me into his consortium, and I'm considering accepting."

"Just because the case is dead doesn't give you the okay. We may have missed something."

"Not my thorough brother."

"You call me after the meeting, if I haven't contacted you before. Do me a favor, stick with corporate law and leave investigating to me. Bye-bye."

Todd smiled, then responded, "Good bye."

---

Juanita arrived with Suzette at her father's house. She went directly to her old room and unpacked her suitcase. Any other time, she would have waited for Suzette to unpack her suitcase, but strangely enough, she felt she needed to do something constructive, and for the time at hand it was unpacking her suitcase. As she put her clothes in her closet and dresser drawers, she ruminated over her past. She thought of the many problems she had encountered in the past and how she was able to survive them. Everything came back to her father's intervention. The only thing he couldn't do was help her get over the heartache she received because of the separation between him and her mother. But through his constant show of love toward her that heartache feeling left, too. In fact, she had to admit the absence of her mother in this house made her relationship with her father much closer. Juanita smiled because she heard her father's footsteps coming toward her room. She knew her father's walk. She remembered listening for it as a child after Violet had readied her for bed. He walked with such steadiness of pace, she believed he exuded strength and control in each step. The instant Earl entered her bedroom, Juanita stopped what she was doing and began to cry. She ran into her father's arms just as she did when she was a child. Earl patted her head and rubbed her back to calm her.

Finally, she calmed down enough for him to instruct her to sit on the bed. He sat beside her as he held her hand and asked, "Honey, tell me what's wrong. How did I fail you, Baby? I tried to give you everything you wanted."

"Daddy, I love you and you didn't fail me. Every time I asked for something you, Violet, or Suzette tried to give it to me. But, Daddy, I'm a big girl now. I can't continue running home to you every time I have a problem. That's why I tried to solve this one on my own."

"Baby, what's the problem?"

"Who's the problem. Marquetta Logan of Second Chance, Inc.!"

"That's right. She goes out with Todd, too."

"Goes out with? No, Daddy, they're getting married! He went on vacation with her to the Caribbean, remember. I thought he was just fascinated with her because she wouldn't have sex with him. I thought once he got it, he would come back to me. After all, I'm attractive and wealthy. I mean, you're wealthy and have ownership in a lot of businesses in this area and abroad. That gives you quite a bit of clout. Since I'm your daughter, I have clout, too."

"So you tried to use my money and clout to destroy Marquetta Logan to get Todd Parker? Baby, I know all about this. Did you forget our earlier conversation?"

"No, Daddy, you're not listening! It's different now. It's worse. I lost Todd to her. Are you still going to offer them positions in the consortium knowing that I would have to be around them?"

"Juanita, I'm very impressed with Marquetta and her company. Your personal life does not dictate my selection of business partners. You should know that by now. In fact, I want you to get to know Marquetta better."

"Daddy, I love you and respect your opinion, but I don't want to know anything about her. Please don't make me by putting us on committees together, hoping I'll talk to her. I'm warning you, I'll act very ugly!"

"Baby, let's change the subject for now. I want to talk on the subject about your willingness to sleep around. It concerns me, deeply. Maybe I didn't explain it in a way that you could understand or appreciate. I want to try again. I want you to think about the business world. If you want to have a level of control, you have to understand when to restrain. Now, it appears that Marquetta understood that. She obviously has control over herself and she proved it by knowing when to restrain. I want to make another point. If you want a real man, one you can love and respect, you have to let him be a man. Let him do some things on his own. I called Todd and talked to him about marrying you. I even alluded to my business connections to try to force his hand, but he let me know I was not going to intimidate him. The decision he made is the decision he wanted to make. He's in love with her. So don't try to destroy their happiness. I am going to offer both of them a position in the consortium. Oh yeah, before I forget, do not approach Horace Greely like you did in the restaurant, again! He was steamed and almost changed his mind about bringing charges against you. But thanks be to God, he calmed down. I realize I'm putting a lot on you today, Baby, but it can't be helped. I want you to be happy and I want to be happy, too. Living in this big house by myself with no one to share it with, is not happiness to me. I want to remarry."

Juanita looked at her father in utter amazement, then queried, "You do, Daddy? Do you know to whom?"

"Yes, I do, Baby. I want to marry Violet. She has always been so good and loyal to me."

"Daddy, she's your housekeeper. What would people think?"

"Juanita honey, you need to grow up. I am my own man. Violet and I have prayed about this and we are determined this is the right thing to do. Violet and I are in love and have been in love for years, but neither of us wanted to admit it to the other. Each of us was afraid of how the other would take it. Well, a few months ago, we finally admitted how much we enjoyed being with each other. Think about it, we've helped each other weather many storms in our lives. We already felt we were a part of each other. Honey, we talked for hours. After we talked, we knew we were for each other. I don't want to make the mistake I made with your mother. I'm going to serve Violet in the way the Lord would have me serve her, not the way I think I should. God will be the head of our household. Honey, one thing you will learn, money will not buy you love."

Juanita was, too exasperated after hearing her father's selection to hear anything else he said. She remarked, "But, Daddy, the housekeeper!"

"Juanita, did you hear anything I just said to you? Think about everything I said to you and then talk to God about it. Take all the time you need. I'll hold dinner until you come down."

Earl went downstairs, walked into his den where Violet was dusting, kissed her gently on her cheek, then inquired, "Violet, where is Suzette?"

"She's in the living room reading, Earl."

Violet followed Earl as he walked into the living room. The moment Earl and Violet entered, Suzette closed the book she was reading and put it on the coffee table. As if a private in the military, ready to carry out her next set of orders, she poised herself in a sitting position that would enable her to jump into action, upon hearing her new assignment from her boss. Tickled by her decision to position herself for action as a way to elicit a comedic response from Earl, she giggled. She knew Earl had a comedic streak and her responding to him in this manner would make him start telling jokes. She really loved and respected her boss and enjoyed their friendship. Earl was a humble man. He appreciated everything anyone did for him, even if he was paying them. One of the reasons she and her sister had worked for Earl so long was his fairness and love for people. They often wondered about his upbringing. They knew the people that raised him were Christians because he seemed to know how to apply the word of God in his daily activities. To Suzette's surprise, Violet and Earl sat near her on the sofa before Earl spoke. Earl knew how much Suzette hated his serious tone, so he stated as gravely as he could muster, "Suzette, your sister and I want to talk to you." Earl didn't notice Suzette's position because the minute Violet and Earl sat on opposite sides of the sofa, with her in the middle, her position changed.

Curious, Suzette asked, "Yes sir, what is it?"

Earl's tone became happy and joyous when he stated, "Violet and I are getting married."

"That's wonderful," exclaimed Suzette. "Oh you!" Suzette hit him lovingly on his upper right shoulder then replied, "You know I hate that serious tone of yours." All three laughed. Then Suzette's thoughts drifted to Juanita. The smile left her face as she contemplated, *Is this the news that was upsetting her?* She queried, "Miss Juanita has been upset today. Did you tell her? How did she take it?"

---

Juanita reasoned, *This can't be happening! Todd is marrying Marquetta instead of me and now my father is marrying his housekeeper. These men have lost their minds! Todd could never acquire the wealth or the status in the community he could've obtained being married to me. He would have domestics to take care of anything he didn't want to be bothered with at home. Now what is he going to do?* She laughed as she thought, *That's right, he'll have Marquetta—she'll be his wife and housekeeper. She deserves it. But I still don't get it. What assets does she bring to the marriage? That ridiculous company? Please, give me a break! Enough about them, it's Todd's loss. But Daddy has such an eye for business. Obviously, in the female department, he needs help. First, my mother, a loose woman and now a housekeeper. I'm sure I can find a decent woman for him. All he had to do was tell me he wanted to get married. I don't think Daddy understands his money opens a lot of doors for him. He could go anywhere he wants and women would throw themselves at him the minute they knew he was a wealthy man. But no, he wants to stay in this small community and marry his housekeeper. She could damage our image in this community. I'll call Mother. Maybe she'll know what to do.*

Loretta was standing by the side of the bed, folding and placing clothes in her suitcase, when the phone rang. She walked to the night stand near the phone and picked up the receiver to answer it. "Hello."

"Hi, Mother. I thought you should know, Daddy is marrying Violet.

Loretta laughed and asked, "Who told you that?"

"He did, tonight! Mother, I don't think he realizes the impact it will have on his credibility as a businessman. Besides that, she's coming into this marriage with absolutely nothing. The only thing he could save on is her salary."

Loretta screamed, then both laughed very hard. Finally, after they collected themselves, Loretta replied, "No, he'll want the write-off, so he'll let her keep her job."

"Good one, Mom." They laughed again. Still laughing, Juanita inquired, "Can you imagine me introducing her, this is my stepmom the housekeeper?"

Loretta roared with laughter, then commented, "Poor Earl, he's losing it. Well, no one can make wise decisions all the time." The thought of Earl marrying Violet made her roar with laughter again.

That statement made Juanita stop laughing. She queried, "Mother, you give Daddy credit for making wise decisions?"

Loretta could tell by the tone in Juanita's voice that this was a serious question she was raising but she couldn't stop laughing. She was actually holding the phone with one hand and her stomach with the other. Tears of laughter were streaming from her eyes. She finally began to gather herself as she sat on the bed near the

nightstand by the phone. She uttered short words trying to regain her voice. "Wait, wait, I hear ya. Whew, whew." She raised both her feet in the air brought them back down and rested them on the floor; put her hand in her lap, then sighed, shook her head and uttered, 'um, um, um.' Afterwards, she was able to talk. She replied, "Until now! That woman is more than pleasingly plump. She's downright fat!"

Juanita pondered, *That down right fat woman was a mother to me when you left, Mother!* She stated, "Seriously Mother, even though this is far from what I originally thought, after talking to you, I realize Daddy has made a wise decision. She won't leave him. She'll be with him through thick and thin. I know, because she has always been there for me when I needed her. Thanks for the conversation. Bye-bye."

Loretta hung up the phone and decided, *I got my money and I'm outta here. Huh, maybe Earl's right, I should pray. Maybe later.* She finished packing and left.

———

Juanita ruminated, *Violet and Suzette have always been there for me. I could always count on them being in my corner. Just like now,*

*Suzette is mad with Todd because he hurt me. I'm her baby. Violet and Suzette love me, too. That's funny, because I've only thought of them as Daddy's employees. Now I realize they are really part of our family. Whenever they go shopping, they still pick up something for me, although Daddy told them not to. That settles it. I'm going to teach Violet how to live as a woman of means. No more thrift stores!* She chuckled then reasoned, *That's going to be a hard job. Violet only likes to shop at thrift stores, except when she shops for me. I'm sorry, Violet, things are going to change. Change will be good for her. I'll tell Daddy the marriage, is fine but he has to make Violet promise not to shop at any more thrift stores. Earl Smith's wife cannot be seen shopping at thrift stores!* She didn't pray as her father instructed her, but left her room to find Violet and her father. She looked in the normal places for her father and couldn't find him. She thought, *I've checked the living room, the den, the library, and the dining room. Where is he? Violet is probably in the kitchen, I'll ask her.* As she neared the kitchen, she heard laughter coming from the area where the servants prepared the food. The kitchen area had its own wing. The wing was separated into two sections, each with its own entrance and a swing door to link the sections together. The entrance for family and guests was from a hallway that extended to the center foyer of the house. Before entering the kitchen, you walked through an archway which had hand-painted red roses on the wall surrounding the arch. This motif was throughout the kitchen. The floor tile was of red roses. The lovely porcelain dishes were specifically designed with hand painted roses and gold trim. The kitchen windows faced the east. The early morning sun radiated through the kitchen illuminating the gold trim in the dishes detailing the exquisite hand painted-rose design. The east wing where the kitchen was housed was surrounded with palladian windows. Windows were throughout the kitchen area because Earl loved the natural light from the sun. Although track lighting was in the vaulted, cathedral ceiling throughout the kitchen, it was seldom used. The kitchen table seated twelve and always remained set. A wood burning brick fireplace topped off the setting. The workers used two entrances. One entrance was from the back door of the house. This was the way the kitchen staff arrived and left the residence. The door was also used to receive food supplies and groceries. The other door, which could be entered from the family's kitchen area, was a wooden door on spring like hinges that allowed the door to be pushed from either side, using one hand to open it—made similar to those used in restaurants. The door had a window in the shape of a circle for peering in or out. This area of the kitchen was designed on the order of a commercial kitchen. The stove, refrigerator, freezer, and proofer were all of a commercial nature. All foods prepared in the kitchen for the family and guests were made from scratch. A table, to seat up to twelve workers at one time, was also in this area, along with a desk to do household budgeting and hold necessary paper work for ordering supplies. Any time food was prepared the workers were allowed to fix a plate for themselves and take the leftovers home. The table became a place where the workers sat during down time; watched television, talked and played games. In the shelves used to stock food, a place was made to fit a small 9-inch television, and another slot was made to hold games. The favorite of the staff's and Earl's was monopoly. As Juanita neared the workers' area of the kitchen, the laughter got louder. She peeped threw the swing door, saw her father, and used her body to push the door as she walked in. With hands on her hip, she looked at her father, sighed, and asked, "Daddy, why are you in the kitchen?"

"Baby, I'm playing a game. Do you want to play? We can start all over. I'm sure Violet and Suzette won't mind."

'No, that's all right, I don't want to play."

"Why are you looking so concerned? Did you think I was cooking and going to make you eat it?" Violet and Suzette chuckled.

"Daddy, I want to talk to you and Violet. Suzette, you may listen but I don't want to talk in here. Let's go to the den."

"Honey, may we meet you in the den after we finish the game? I'm winning."

"Daddy, really! I want to talk now!"

Earl reluctantly agreed, "Okay, Baby, we'll follow you to the den."

Once all arrived and were seated, Juanita said, "I have decided that the two of you may be married. However, Violet must promise never to shop at thrift stores again."

Violet gasped. She was stunned at the request. Violet collected herself and inquired, "Miss Juanita, why is my shopping at thrift stores a problem? I enjoy shopping at thrift stores and I don't feel I should stop just because I'm marrying your father." Violet looked at Earl for confirmation.

Earl smiled and replied, "I can't make Violet promise to stop shopping at thrift stores to please you. She is a woman with a mind of her own. That's why this house runs so smoothly and household accounts are paid without a problem, whether I'm here or not."

"Some of the dresses you wore as a child and were complimented on came from thrift stores," stated Violet.

Juanita, outraged at Violet's statement, yelled, "No! I won't believe you. Daddy, you wouldn't let her put used clothes on me, would you?"

Earl restrained from laughing because he knew Juanita was upset, but he thought, *That's how that clothing account dropped from $1500 a month per person to less than $500 a month almost immediately after Loretta left. We all looked good. So she knows what she's doing.* He asked, "Juanita, could you tell the difference? I know I couldn't. Did any of your friends notice that you were wearing second-hand clothing?"

"Daddy, that's not the point. You should be asking her what she did with the rest of your money!"

Violet queried, "Miss Juanita, how could you accuse me of spending your father's money improperly? I just decided to save where I could for a rainy day."

"My father doesn't have rainy days!" Juanita stated, looking at Violet with contempt in her eyes.

"Not if I continue to let Violet take care of the household accounts." Earl smiled and continued. "Violet, I must ask, how did you make those clothes look so good? I mean—they looked like new."

"That's because I made adjustments. I customized them to our individual taste. It has become a hobby of mine. Sometimes I think they look better than the original," responded Violet.

Earl grinned. and said, "Lady, you never cease to amaze me."

He grabbed her hand and held it. Earl was sitting by Violet on the brown leather sofa in his den. Juanita and Violet sat in matching leather chairs at opposite sides of the sofa, curved to face the sofa and coffee table.

Juanita declared, "Daddy, this is making me sick! I cannot believe a man of your caliber would want to marry a housekeeper, but I accepted that because Violet and Suzette are unusual people. But to approve of her buying second-hand clothes for your household is ridiculous. Wake up, Daddy, this woman is a pauper, a peasant, a laborer! She'll never know how to represent you as a wife. Sure, she can cook, clean, and manage the household. Yes, she gives good suggestions about some of your business dealings and has even acted as a mother for me. I appreciate Violet, I really do. But I'm talking about your wife. She will be a prominent woman in this community. Violet is not cut out for that position." Juanita looked at Violet and queried, "How are you going to look on his shoulder as he attends important gatherings with other people in his league? Violet, I appeal to you. Daddy won't use his mind you must use yours. You know nothing about wheeling and dealing in the big league, or hobnobbing with the elite. What do you know about etiquette, except for the proper placing at a table? Now, back to you, Daddy. They all know she's your housekeeper. Remember, you entertain quite a bit. Now, do you want to introduce her as your wife before or after she serves the meal?" Juanita thought that was funny, she paused to laugh, then continued. "I'm sorry, Daddy and Violet, I had to say this to you because the two of you needed to hear the truth and it seems I'm the only one who will tell you. I too, thought it could possibly work, but when the two of you didn't understand the importance of Violet not shopping at thrift stores, I realized, Daddy, this woman was going to bring you down to her level of class. Daddy, you have worked too hard to accomplish your goals to let one moment of passion destroy you. I understand you may be lonely, but there are a lot of women in your station in life that would be willing to fill your lonely nights. Besides, whatever she can do, I'm sure somebody can do better."

Earl was livid. He couldn't believe Juanita would disrespect Violet like that. He said, "Juanita, Violet has made many sacrifices to keep you happy. She was a better mother to you than your own and this is the thanks she gets, your disrespect. That's it! I have heard enough from you! As of Monday, you will completely be on your own. I have obviously given you, too much. Now I'm putting my foot down. All of your charge accounts are in my name and they will be cancelled! Get your own! It's time you learn how to live on a budgeted income. You will pay rent for the office space you're using in my building. Buy your own condo. The condo you live in I own and I will now use it for people who come to visit me or my business associates. The car you drive belongs to me, too. I will give you one week to get a car in your name and then I'm taking mine. The furniture in the condo will stay for guests, but the office furniture will be given to thrift stores or auctioned. I paid for the furniture in your office, too. Remember? From now on, Young Lady, you will live off the money you make from your agency only."

"Daddy, you can't be serious! I only have a salary of $50, 000 from my agency and if you take the office furniture, equipment, and make me pay for office space, I'll make less than what I earn now. How can I live off of that?"

"I don't know, Dear. I guess you're going to have to figure it out, but remember, you have class. Perhaps your class will tell you what to do. Oh yeah, anything else I remember belongs to me will be reclaimed. Since the car is mine, you will only be able to use it to get you to and from work this coming week. You should have your own by next week or you will be catching the bus. By the way, Violet and I are still getting married, with or without your approval." Juanita stormed out of the room and thought, *He can't be serious. Where am I going to live? That settles it, I'll stay here until he comes to his senses and, after work, I'll have the chauffeur take me any place I want to go.* She smiled because she thought she had everything figured out. Then she heard Earl's voice as he called her. Surprised that her father yelled for her, she jumped when she heard the tone.

He commanded, "Juanita, come back here, now! I wasn't finished talking to you."

Juanita walked back into the den and, took her seat. Earl continued, "I will permit you to live here until you find a place to stay. However, you will not be able to eat here unless you pay for your food. You cannot use the limo or ask the chauffeur to take you anywhere, either. You can stay here for a month and you will be renting from me weekly during that time. Anything you use in this house has to be cleared by either Violet or me—not Suzette, because she is too lenient with you. Violet or I will tell you what you can and can't use and if there will be a charge. By the end of the week, we will have a list of items and the cost per use. I'll have my attorney draw up an agreement spelling out the conditions of your stay. If you don't sign the agreement, you will not be permitted to stay here. You are an adult and I am no longer obligated to provide for you. I suggest you make arrangements to find your own place, immediately. Our joint account will be off limits to you. If you need a check to pay for your car or the place, give me the cash and I'll write the check."

"Daddy, why are you doing this to me? If I apologize to Violet will you change your mind?"

"You should apologize to Violet, because you want to, not on a condition. But I'm doing this to try to stop my daughter, whom I love very much, from being destroyed. Somehow, you acquired a distorted view of life, Baby, especially when it comes to money and love. Monetary wealth does not give you the right to think you are better than those who don't have it, because you are not. You are not better or more special. Yes, I was blessed to acquire monetary wealth, but with that blessing, as in all blessings, comes responsibilities." Juanita crossed her legs and stilted her body in the seat to look at the wall and not her father. Her lips thrust out as if in a childish pout. "Look at me and listen to me, Juanita! I want you to hear what I'm telling you." Juanita turned to face her father. Earl continued, "There are not a lot of people who acquire monetary wealth and being one of those who has, I have come to understand that what I do with this wealth is very important. First, I wasn't born into this position. So, I've seen and lived another lifestyle. You see, I understand what it is like to have unemployed parents. It is no picnic for them or their children. I'm sure you noticed I very rarely fire employees. That's because I make it a point to find out what they do best, and what their interests are, and place them accordingly. My employees are loyal to me because I'm loyal to them. They know that I recognize their need to provide for their families, as well as my own need to provide for mine. My employees know that in order for them to continue to earn pay increases and bonuses, my company must continue to grow and expand. They do their best to enable my company to achieve its goals. In turn, I recognize I must do my best for them. I see my company and every business I'm involved with, primarily as a means to provide people with a way to provide for themselves and their families. Another thing you need to grasp, money is not a bargaining, tool for love. Real love comes from God, and you can only appreciate love once you know God. I mean, know Him for yourself. I'm afraid, Juanita, I gave you, too many things and didn't talk enough to you about the One who allowed me to achieve, so that I could give you things. God has always been a part of me, so I guess I thought He automatically would be a part of you, too. But now I understand, you must want Him to reign in your life. I realize now, God was a part of me because of my parents' teachings and belief. I could see God operate in my family often. I guess that's why I was so ashamed of my behavior when it came to marrying your mother. I should have prayed, but I decided I knew what was best for me. I wouldn't listen to anyone and I knew better. I was raised better than that. Because of my shame, I never talked to you about my family. It's time I did. As a young child there were times when my father couldn't get work. My mother worked as a housekeeper during the day. I remember she would come home very tired. When I would look at my father, I would see hurt in his eyes as he watched my mother struggle to kick off her shoes at night. But my mother never complained, at least not so I could hear. But she would always pray every night. She taught my brother and me to pray, too. But I never saw my father pray until one night we all went to bed without eating. There was, literally, no food in the house." As Earl continued, tears streamed from his eyes. "You see, my mother lost her job. The family she was working for broke up. The husband and wife got a divorce and both of them moved out of state. My mother couldn't get another job because she was pregnant with my sister, Margaret. Huh, that's strange, I remember that day as if it were yesterday. I can even picture myself playing outside and watching my father as he stared at the corner store in the neighborhood, while mumbling to himself. It seemed like he watched that store all day.

Finally, he called me and my brother, Bob and told us to follow him. When we arrived at the store, the owner told my father that he was closing. My father looked at him and said, 'My wife is having a baby and needs to eat. My boys and I are willing to pay for the food by helping you unload your truck and stock your shelves. I will clean the store, too if you would give me food to feed my wife. We will work as long as you say to pay it off.' The owner looked my father in the face and told him he was sorry, but he didn't need any help. My father left the store a broken man. That same day was the first time I saw him cry. My father used to drive coal trucks for years until the company went out of business. After that, he would do day-work or work as a handyman around the neighborhood just to put food on the table. But this particular day, nothing had come through. Anyway, we went home and my father went to their bedroom to check on my mother. My mother hadn't eaten all day and started getting sick. My father couldn't stand seeing my mother sick; he didn't know what to do. He came out of the bedroom and told Bob and me to come to him. We took seats by my father and listened to him as he talked to us. He told us he was going to do something he hadn't done before, at least not as an adult. He then told us to make a circle. We did and as we held hands, he started to pray. I thought my father would never stop. He prayed for what seemed like hours. Tears streamed down his eyes and he continued to pray. My mother finally came out of the bedroom, saw us, and joined in. By the time my father finished praying we weren't hungry anymore. Everybody felt good. We sang songs and my father told us stories about his family and how they survived through tough times. The time passed by so fast, the next thing I remember was waking up to the smell of food cooking in the kitchen. Mr. Robinson, the store owner, had a brother who delivered furniture for a living and his company needed a truck driver. Mr. Robinson let my father put the food he brought him on a bill of credit. My father got the job with Mr. Robinson's brother, and since that time until he retired, he always had a job. Needless to say, we never went without food again. Juanita, now that I mentioned your grandmother, I want you to know: she was a housekeeper and is a wonderful woman."

Juanita, unmoved, replied, "Daddy, that sounds good, but this is the first time you mentioned your family to me. I thought you were an orphan or something."

Violet and Suzette were moved by the story Earl shared but thought it was, too personal for them to hear, so they decided to leave. As they walked out of the room, Earl said, "Please, come back, Violet and Suzette. I want you to know what happened. I want you to stay and hear this. After all, we are going to be one family. They came back into the den and sat down. "Juanita, your mother wasn't originally from the neighborhood where I grew up. She was from North Carolina. She moved to Maryland when she was 16. She didn't know her way around, so Miss Peabody introduced her to my sister, Margaret. Miss Peabody's family was from North Carolina, too, and suggested Loretta's parents move here. I met Loretta through Margaret. Margaret didn't care for Loretta much because Loretta would do things to get Margaret in trouble. Margaret always tried to carry herself properly but Loretta didn't. Finally, Margaret cut all ties with her when she noticed Loretta deliberately positioned herself so the teenage boys could look under her dress. Margaret never made herself available to go out with her again. Loretta was determined to make Margaret her friend, so she continued to come to our house. By this time, Daddy was doing really well, and we had a house with a yard that connected to the park. We would play baseball often. Both my brother and I were good. Now that I think about it, Loretta probably wasn't trying to befriend Margaret. She knew a lot of the boys hung around our house. She had to have a reason to come over." He smiled. Caught up in thought, he stopped talking.

Juanita replied, "Daddy, I still don't get it. Why am I just finding out you have family members that live in this state?"

"I'm sorry, Baby, let me continue. Loretta always looked so sad on the porch with no one to talk to, so sometimes I would get out of a game just to talk to her. She told me she was lonesome being here all by herself in a new state with no friends. She felt nobody liked her. She told me she tried to be friends with Margaret, but she ignored her. I tried to talk to Margaret, but one thing about my sister, when she made up her mind about something, there was no changing it. One day, Loretta and I were talking and I told her if nobody would be her friend, I would. Loretta was closer to my age than Margaret's, anyway. That's why I thought my mother didn't force Margaret to be nice and play with her. Loretta and I started sharing goals and dreams. We discovered we had similar goals and interests. At least, that's what Loretta told me.

Then we decided to date. We went to the movies and, took long walks in the park. You know—the usual. But one day in my parent's home, Loretta pulled me in the bathroom and showed me her underwear. She literally lifted up her dress. I was dumbfounded. My parents were very strict with us and expected a certain type of behavior. Being in the bathroom with a girl was not appropriate behavior. I kept telling her I had to get out of the bathroom but she told me she was going to say I pulled her in if I didn't kiss her. So, I kissed her and ran. That didn't stop Loretta. She was determined that I see all her new under clothes. She told me she didn't understand why a person would buy something so pretty when no one else would get to see it. Now remember, I'm a young man at this time, with hormones going wild. It, took everything I had sometimes to refrain from having sex with her. She literally tried to push every button she could to break me. I wanted to do right by her. So I decided to marry her. I told my parents my decision to marry Loretta. They told me to talk to Bob because he had some information I needed to hear in making my decision. They also told me after I talked to Bob, to pray, and then come talk to them. I did talk to Bob. I told him I had decided to marry Loretta and the folks said he had some information for me. Bob told me all of the boys that played baseball with us had sex with Loretta. He told me he almost had sex with her but at the last minute he remembered that I really liked her, so he jumped up. I literally flipped. I couldn't believe he was saying such a horrible thing about Loretta. I started punching on him like a mad man. My brother never hit me back. He just protected himself as best he could. Eventually, the noise brought my parents into the room. By that time, Bob was lying on the floor, with blood everywhere. I ran to Loretta's house and asked her to marry me. Then she and I hid in my parents' shed until they came back from the hospital with Bob. He was all right, thank God. But once I knew

Bob was fine, Loretta and I left the neighborhood, and I married her shortly thereafter. On my wedding night, Loretta told me everything my brother told me was true. She told me she wanted me, and since I wouldn't have sex with her; she thought that to be close to me, she had to get close to my friends. She told me she really wanted Bob because he was my brother. She thought being with him would be like being with me. Needless to say, I spent my honeymoon in a daze. I was embarrassed and ashamed. Embarrassed about marrying Loretta and ashamed because I didn't listen to my parents and my brother who I knew loved me and I should've trusted. I didn't even pray about it. I thought: 'how could I ever go back and face them after what I'd done.' They didn't deserve this behavior from me. I knew better. I thought I had brought shame to the family. Everybody in the neighborhood knew what kind of woman I married. I thought to be around my family with her daily would do nothing but bring more shame on them. So, I decided it would be best for everybody if they never saw me again. That's why you don't know your grandparents and your Aunt Margaret and your Uncle Bob. But they are nice, decent people. You would like them. The first day I became a millionaire, I thought maybe my accomplishment would rid my shame and gain Loretta some respectability, but it didn't. I know now it couldn't. Instead, that day, I found my wife having sex with my best friend on my garage floor. That prompted a serious blow-up, which ended in my getting a divorce. I thought I would never get to see my family again! Now, more shame has been placed upon me because my wife committed adultery and I'm now a divorced man. Juanita, you didn't get to meet my family all this time because I have felt for years that I was an embarrassment to them. Now, I see how damaging that thinking was for me and to you. Juanita, if you had had an opportunity to be around my mother and Margaret, you would have been better able to decide the type of woman you wanted to become. Your mother could have changed, but she was trying to fill a void in her life with lust that only God could fill with love. I used to think if I had loved her more, perhaps she would have changed. Instead, she drained me. What she really needed was to know and understand the love of God. That's why I'm telling you to pray. You need to talk to God because only he can help you make it through this time in your life." Earl looked at Violet and grinned, then stated, "Violet, I know what I'm going to do—I'm going to contact my family! I want to invite them to our wedding."

"That's a wonderful idea, Earl," responded Violet.

Juanita commented, "At least I get to meet my family. Daddy, can I go upstairs now?"

"Sure, baby."

Juanita went upstairs into her room and looked around. The loneliness tried to creep back in, but she decided to pray. She got on her knees and said, "Dear God, I need your help. I feel lonely. I need to know your love. I need to understand your love. Because your love is real. Forgive me for my sins, please. In Jesus' name. Amen." Juanita picked up the Bible that was in her room and read it. She read and prayed for hours. She finally fell asleep.

———————

Although it was late, Earl knew he had to speak to his family before he went to bed. He sat on the side of his bed near the night-stand where the phone was sitting and picked up the receiver. He checked his watch before dialing. He discovered it was 10:00 p.m. He started to put the receiver back on the base of the phone, but he couldn't. He knew he had to make the call.

The phone rang at the Logan residence. Mark Logan answered it, "Hello." Mark and Margaret were in their family room watching television. They rarely went to bed before 11:00 p.m. Margaret was resting her head on Mark's chest when the phone rang. She moved her head to allow Mark to answer the phone.

"Is this the Logan residence?"

"Yes, this is Mark Logan, may I help you?"

"Mark, I don't know if you have heard about me. My name is Earl Thomas Smith. I'm Margaret's brother. May I speak with her?"

"Earl, I have heard of you. Hold on."

Mark grinned and said calmly, "Margaret, the telephone is for you. It's your brother Earl Thomas."

Margaret was so excited she grabbed the phone and inquired, "Earl Thomas, is that you? After all this time! How are you, Brother Dear?"

Earl was so happy to hear his baby sister's voice that tears streamed down his eyes, and through a crackling voice, he responded, "I'm fine, now. It's been a long time. I won't do that again!"

Margaret replied, "Please don't stay away from us any longer. I have so much to tell you."

Now composed, Earl said, "First, let me tell you why I called. I'm getting married again. I want all of you to come to the wedding. It will be at my house. It's quite big. Some people call it a mansion."

"Earl Thomas, you live in a mansion! What kind of job do you have?"

"I'm in business for myself. I own an insurance company and other businesses. Are you going to come? I want you to bring your whole family."

"That's wonderful. Yes, we'll come. I want you to meet Mark and my daughter, Marquetta. Earl Thomas, she's getting married, too. May her fiancé come?"

"Sure, I know your daughter and her fiancé. She is quite a businesswoman, and just as pretty as she can be. I started keeping an eye on her, and Todd when I noticed he was on every committee she was on. When I first saw her I knew who she was, even though, I checked to make sure. She looks just like you."

"You know her all right and Todd is her fiancé. Everybody says when they see her she reminds them of me. I can't wait to see you. I missed you so much!"

"I missed you, too, more than you'll ever know. I want to call Mom and Pop before I lose my nerve. I'll talk to you again, okay?"

"Okay, I love you, Brother Dear."

"I love you, too, Margaret. Good night."

Margaret hung up the phone and said, "Thank you, God."

———————

Todd went home after church to change and, as he turned the key to enter into his townhouse, he heard the phone ringing. He made a dash for the phone. He wondered, "Who could that be?" He answered the phone, "Who is this?"

Sam asked, "Where have you been? I've been calling you for hours. Ever since I found out the news."

"What news?"

"First, tell me you won't get angry."

Todd queried, "I won't get angry, why? You checked on Markie, didn't you?"

"Do you want to hear what I found out or do you want me to hang up?"

"I don't care what you say or do, I'm marrying her."

"That's fine with me if you want Earl Smith as an uncle."

"Who? Earl Smith, Juanita's father. Come on, Sam. Give me a break. I think you need to do a little better than that."

"Oh, so you're doubting my investigative ability."

Todd laughed and inquired, "You mean, you're serious?"

"Little Brother, I'm trying to tell you Juanita—the girl you have been sleeping with off and on for two years— her father is Marquetta Marie Logan's uncle."

"No way!"

"Let me ask you this question. Is Marquetta's middle name Marie?"

"Yes, so what does that mean?"

"I didn't know that until I started digging in some files in the office."

"What kind of files?"

"Let's just say Tom is very thorough, even in getting clients."

"So you're telling me that Marquetta listed Earl Smith as her uncle."

"No, it wasn't that easy, but I know that Earl Smith is her uncle. Ask her!"

"If that were true, she would have told me. She knew I was sleeping with Juanita. I think you're wrong."

"Look, her mother has two brothers, Bob and Earl."

"Maybe you're right about Earl being her uncle; but maybe she doesn't know it. She told me they don't talk about her mother's siblings around her grandmother and mother. So, maybe she doesn't know their names."

Sam laughed and replied, "That family is strange! You think they disowned him because he's wealthy?"

"Don't be silly; and I don't like talking about Markie and her family with you."

"Well, talk to her about them. Anyway, she looks good, other than having Earl as an uncle and Juanita as a cousin. Boy, Little Brother, you really know how to do it." Sam laughed again.

Todd responded, "Good bye, Sam," and hung up the phone.

---

Marquetta was on the phone with Barbara when she asked, "Did you see who was at church today?"

"Yes, I did. William, Horace, and Juanita. Prayers are being answered. We don't know how, but God is working or has worked it out. God is good," replied Barbara.

"Yes, He is."

Barbara inquired, "Did you see how Todd lit up when the Pastor gave the scripture reference?"

Marquetta replied, "'Psalm 139:14.'" That passage of scripture stands out to me, too. It lets me know who I am in the Lord and tells me why I should praise God. Marquetta recited the verse: "'I will praise thee; for I am fearfully and wonderfully made: marvellous are thy works; and that my soul knoweth right well.'" ""Psalm 139:14 (KJV)'" After she recited the scripture, she said, "When I think about what this verse of Scripture is saying, I can't help but take a second look at myself. I understand that I am important to God and that he, took time to make me."

"Wow," replied Barbara, now deep in thought about the scripture and it's meaning to her.

Marquetta asked, "It's powerful, isn't it?"

"Yes, it is! If we stay on this conversation, we'll have church all over again. I need to get off this phone and prepare dinner."

"Oh, before I forget, we got the okay to be married in two weeks by Pastor Green."

"Do you think we can do it together?" Barbara said.

"If not, we'll wait and marry the following week."

"That would be nice, but I don't know how Todd would feel about that."

Both laughed. Then Marquetta replied, "I'll talk to him about it."

"Sounds good. I'll talk to you later. Good bye."

---------

Marquetta looked out the window and saw Todd entering her building. The minute she opened the door for Todd, the phone rang and her food timer went off. She said, "Todd, do me a favor and answer the phone, while I check the food, please."

Todd reluctantly answered the phone, because he wanted to talk to Marquetta about Earl Smith being her uncle. Todd said, "Hello."

Margaret asked, "Does Marquetta Logan live here? I'm so excited. I may have dialed the wrong number."

Todd replied, "Yes, you have the right number. May I ask who's calling?"

"This is her mother. Is this Todd?"

"Yes ma'am. Markie had to check the food so she asked me to answer the phone."

"That's fine. May I speak with her?" Margaret was sitting on her sofa beside the phone, with her legs crossed at her ankles and a broad smile on her face, waiting excitedly for her daughter to pick up the receiver. She was so elated she had finally talked with her brother she was still dressed in the clothes she wore to church, including her pumps. She usually changed into jeans as soon as she returned home from church. When Mark came in the living room and saw Margaret holding the receiver in her hand, with a smile like a Cheshire cat, he knew she had called Marquetta. Knowing how she hated wearing heels in the house he left the room and came back with her house slippers. She mouthed the words 'thank you' as she bent over to take her shoes off and to slip her feet into her fluffy lavender closed toe slippers with the back out.

"Hold on. Todd pushed the hold button on the phone and said, "It's your Mother. I'm innocent. I answered your phone because you asked me and I still felt like I should have explained to her why I answered your phone. I don't want her thinking I'm presumptuous."

Marquetta laughed, then stated, "Don't be silly, you can answer my phone." She, took the receiver from Todd, pushed down the hold button and inquired, "Hi, Mom, what's up?" Marquetta hadn't heard her mother this excited in a long time. She commented, "Mom, slow down. What did you say? We are invited to your brother Earl Thomas' wedding? Really, Mom, I thought you said he eloped and refused to have anything to do with the family. What happened to change his mind?"

"I don't care how it happened. We know God hears and answers prayers. I have always prayed for both my brothers, Earl Thomas and Bob, even though I haven't seen or heard from either of them in years. Until now, that is. Marquetta, I'm so glad I spoke with your Uncle Earl Thomas last night, I don't know what to do. If it weren't so late, I would have called you afterwards. Marquetta, he's going to have his wedding at his mansion."

"Your brother lives in a mansion. Is he loaded?"

"From our conversation, I would say so. He told me he could afford the mansion."

"If he can afford a mansion, he must be rich."

"Where does he live?"

"Near you, dear."

"He's rich and lives near me. You said his name is Earl Thomas. I don't know him. Hold on, I'll ask Todd if he knows him.

Todd had walked toward Marquetta and was standing by the phone by the time she put her mother on hold and stated, "Your mother's brother is Earl Smith, the insurance magnate."

Marquetta looked at Todd in disbelief and replied, "She said his name is Earl Thomas. Earl Smith doesn't use a middle initial, so he probably doesn't have a middle name. Besides, I'm not sure if Smith is her maiden name. Wait, I'll ask her his complete name."

"Marquetta pushed down the hold button on the phone so she could talk to her mother and inquired, "Mom, what is his full name?"

"Earl Thomas Smith. Did you forget my maiden name again? Why do you have problems remembering my maiden name? I wasn't always a Logan. We should have made you call my parents by their last name like we did Mark's. I think that's why you always have a problem remembering."

"I'm sorry Mom. I won't forget again. So, you are saying that your brother's name is Earl Thomas Smith."

"Yes, he said he owns an insurance company and other businesses."

Marquetta, shocked, said, "Mom hold on." She put her mother

on hold and stated, "Todd, my mother's brother is Earl Smith, Juanita's father." Marquetta picked up the phone, now collected, and asked, "Mom, why didn't you tell me your brother's name was Earl Smith?"

"Honey, I knew you knew him because he said he knew you and Todd. By the way, you and Todd are invited to his wedding. He told me he kept an eye on you and Todd. He said he spoke with Todd about being on every committee with you."

"Mom, I need to call you back for the details." The reality of Earl Smith being her uncle finally set in and she wondered how this would impact her and Todd's relationship. She needed to talk to Todd..

"What's wrong, Dear?"

"Mom, it's just that Todd had been dating his daughter Juanita for some time. I don't know if we should attend the wedding."

"Nonsense, he invited you last night and he knew you were marrying Todd."

"He did?"

"Yes, he did! You, Juanita and Todd are family and you're going to have to learn to get along. On that note, I want his entire family invited to your wedding. Talk to Todd about it and get back to me. Good bye, Baby."

"Good bye, Mom."

Thoughts began running through Marquetta's mind. She remembered, both her mother and Todd were explaining to her that Earl Smith was her uncle.

Marquetta, now upset with Todd because he knew about Earl Smith being her uncle, said, "You knew and didn't tell me. How could you, Todd? You knew Juanita was my cousin and you still slept with her? I guess you did feel guilty the first time you slept with her!"

Todd responded, "Markie, calm down and listen to me, please.

"No, I don't want to listen to you. In fact, I want you to leave. I need to think." Marquetta walked to her entry door and opened it.

"Markie, I'm not going anywhere until you hear me out." Todd sat in the chair near the hassock and refused to move. In fact, he put his feet on the hassock and folded his arms.

Marquetta closed the door; walked over to where he was sitting; gave him a harsh look, then began pacing the floor. She stopped pacing and walked to where Todd was sitting and inquired angrily, "What do you have to say for yourself this time, Todd Parker?"

"Markie, please sit down and listen to me."

Marquetta refused to sit down, but responded, "Go on, and make it snappy."

"Markie, I found out today just before I came over here. Sam called and told me."

"Sam, how did he know? Did Juanita tell him?"

"No, Sam was investigating you and found out."

"Sam was investigating me! I don't believe your brother! Who does Sam think he is, investigating me? Todd, you didn't ask him to, did you?"

"No, I wouldn't do that. I've been knowing you, too long and know you, too well. That's what Sam does, he likes to investigate people."

Marquetta's tone softened as she inquired, "Sam is an investigator?"

"Yeah, but he doesn't want anybody to know because he works for Investigations Unlimited and their policy is to reveal it only when necessary."

Marquetta, now composed, apologized to Todd, then sat down on her sofa with hands in her lap and said, "Todd, Earl Smith is my uncle. How do you feel about that? We're invited to his wedding and my mother wants him and his family invited to ours. This means—Juanita is family."

Todd, took a seat beside her, then reached for her hands. He covered her hands with his as he spoke, "I know. I thought about that on the way over here. I'm sorry, Markie. Of all the women I could've slept with, why did I sleep with Juanita? This is one time I understand why it's best to wait until you're married. You did say ours, meaning our wedding. You mean you'll still marry me?"

"Yes, I'll still marry you. Unfortunately, this is one of many things that could develop when you fornicate. After this experience we are obligated to tell our children the importance of celibacy before marriage. This could have been a lot worse."

"You're telling me," agreed Todd. He brushed his forehead as if wiping sweat.

"Since Sam is so curious, maybe he knows where my mother's other brother lives. The next time you talk to him, ask him?"

"Okay, what's his name?"

'I think Bob Smith. It may be Robert Smith."

"How about Robert Thomas Smith, like your Uncle Earl Thomas?" Todd smiled.

"Give it a try, my Grandpa's name is Thomas."

"Okay, I'll ask him. Boy, you're taking Sam's behavior better than I thought. I'm glad. I thought if you decided to go ahead with the wedding you probably wouldn't allow Sam to come over our house, and I would have to meet him at the neighborhood bar or something."

"No way! I want Sam to visit you at our home. That way I'll know what he's doing. Anyway, I'm happy my Mom is so happy, I can't get angry with him. Todd, I want to tell Barbara. Do you mind if I call her before we eat?"

"No, go ahead. It should give her and Phillip a laugh at dinner."

Marquetta smiled and called Barbara. "Hello," answered Barbara.

"Barbara, are you sitting down?"

"No, I answered the cordless phone in the kitchen. Wait, I'll walk into the dining room to sit down." Marquetta laughed, then said, "Don't get the popcorn. I don't want you choking." They both laughed. Barbara replied, "I'm sitting down now with one elbow resting on the table and the other arm holding the phone. I hope you're satisfied. I really think I may need my popcorn, but go on."

Marquetta stated, "You're not going to believe this. Earl Smith is my Uncle Earl Thomas Smith."

"What? Are you serious? Earl Smith, Juanita's father, is one of your mother's brothers? I don't believe it."

"Yes, he is. He called my mother last night and told her he was getting married and he invited us to the wedding."

"Unbelievable! Juanita's father invited you to his wedding."

"Yes, Todd and me. He told my mother he knew we were getting married. He also told her he questioned Todd when he noticed he was on every committee I was on."

"So he knew all the time."

Marquetta pondered that statement as she responded, "Yes, he did."

"He never gave you any indication?"

"No, not really, I just thought he was a nice man."

Marquetta, do you think Juanita knows?"

"I don't know. How did Todd feel about this new development?"

"He's okay now. We talked. We still haven't decided to go to the wedding. But I think we should, after all, he is my uncle and my mother would be very happy. I explained to her that Todd used to date Juanita, but she basically said 'get over it and work through it.'"

Barbara replied, "She's serious. She wants to be a family again with her brother, huh?"

"You got that right."

Marquetta, you didn't think about cancelling the wedding at all, after you heard the news?

"The thought crossed my mind but I know Todd and I are for each other. So I say forgive and forget. Barbara, remember, it could have been me."

"That's true. The wedding should be interesting, though. Who is he marrying?"

"I don't know. I never heard anyone talk about his dating. But we'll find out soon enough. I'll keep you posted. I better feed Todd now. Good bye"

———

Tom searched through the obituary and wedding announcements for information. He found something interesting and called Sam. As soon as Sam answered the phone, Bob inquired, "Have you finalized your report on the consortium established by Earl Smith?

"Man, what's up with you? You had me investigate your own brother's consortium. Why?"

"We were paid to investigate his company, remember? How long have you known Earl Smith was my brother?"

"A few days now."

"Did you know he's getting married soon?

"Yeah, Todd told me. He and Marquetta are going to the wedding. Man, what's wrong with your family? You people don't talk to each other for decades. I mean, my future sister-in-law didn't even know who Earl Smith was and she has been involved with him for years. Well, for that matter, she's been associated with you, too, for a long time. Do you know she asked Todd if I could find you?"

"She did?"

"Yeah, that's how I found out it was you. She wasn't sure of your complete name so one of the names Todd gave me was Robert Thomas Smith. As I played with and shuffled the name around I thought, wouldn't it be funny if Tom was the other brother. She and Earl do business with him all the time on the phone. That would be a laugh. But it wasn't a laugh, Man. I didn't know what to do when I found out it was you. So I didn't do anything. I haven't even told Todd. I wanted to talk to you first."

"Thanks, Man."

Sam queried, "I don't understand. What caused the separation? I love my brother. Sometimes I may be overly protective—that's why I investigated Marquetta. I mean, she's nice enough, but Todd's my brother. I don't want him getting a bad deal."

"Now you know why I started this company, Investigations Unlimited. This was one way I knew I could protect my brother. You see—when we were young we could protect each other by communicating with each other about everything. But one day Earl decided he wanted to marry Juanita's mother, Loretta. I told him that she was sleeping around with other guys we knew and she even asked me to sleep with her. I wouldn't because of him. Well, that was it. No longer did my brother trust me to tell him the truth. He started punching on me like crazy. I couldn't believe it. I wouldn't fight him because I loved him, too much to hurt him. I just tried to protect myself."

"Are you kidding? I never thought a girl could come between two brothers."

"Well, this one did, at least as far as Earl was concerned. My parents, took me to the hospital and I had a broken nose and a busted rib. At first my father was mad at Earl Thomas, and then he became angry with me for not defending myself. That same day, Earl Thomas left and I never heard from him again, at least not as brother to brother. I never trusted Loretta, so I decided, although my brother doesn't want my help, I was going to help him the best I could. I pondered how I could keep tabs on him without him knowing it. A man on my job told me to hire a private investigator. I did, but after a while it became very expensive. Not wanting to give up the surveillance, I inquired about the qualifications needed to do the work myself. The guy I was paying introduced me to his boss and that's how I became involved in the business. I ended up taking other assignments and became good at it. Other investigators would ask me to assist them on cases. Once I completed the case, the employer would refer me to some of his/her associates. After a while I made a very hefty sum on referrals alone. I lived off of the money I made from working new cases and assisting other investigators on their cases. I was single and working most of the time, so I decided I could bank the money I earned through referrals. So, when the owner decided to retire to Florida, I bought the firm. The rest is history. My original plan was to tell Earl who I was after he and Loretta divorced, but I sent out one of my investigators to get a feel for where he was in his thinking and he wasn't ready to receive family, yet. He was, too embarrassed and ashamed. At this time a lot was happening with me, too. I was now an owner. I had gained the responsibility of making certain that my employees could eat and feed their families. I had to structure Investigations Unlimited in a way that investigators weren't solely dependent on a case to earn a salary. I kept investigators on my family while I developed my own niche. My family couldn't know where I was or what I was doing, because of Mrs. Peabody. Mrs. Peabody runs the neighborhood paper and has connections all over the country. She's one of those types that believe all news must be reported. One slip up on my part and Earl would know that I was the owner of Investigations Unlimited—which could have made matters much worst. You see, even though Earl caught Loretta in the garage with his junior partner, my company had been investigating her. Surprisingly enough, it wasn't for free, either. Earl had hired Investigations Unlimited because he was told by his housekeeper that Loretta was acting suspicious. Before that week was out, we had given Earl everything he needed to take Loretta to court and win custody over Juanita. Girlfriend had become reckless with her adulterous behavior. I couldn't take a chance on Earl knowing I knew the intimate details of his life. He was embarrassed enough. That information I believed could have destroyed him as a man. So, in order to keep my secret from Earl, I needed to keep it from the rest of the family. The less my family knew about me and my whereabouts, the less Mrs. Peabody would know. She tried to find out about Earl's and my whereabouts, but she contacted my firm. I was able to throw her off the track.

"Wow, Tom. I didn't know, Man." Your parents must have really taught you the value of love and respect. I don't know if I could still respect Todd if he married someone like Loretta."

"Remember, you tried to convince him, too."

Sam responded, "Oh yeah, that's right. Wait a minute! Juanita and Marquetta are your nieces. You knew Todd was trying for both of them. How did you feel about that?"

"I have done work for Marquetta for a while now. I figured she could hold her own, and unfortunately, Juanita acts like her mother, Loretta, but in her own way she could take care of herself, too."

"You're right on both counts. I guess you're really pleased with Marquetta."

"She acts like my sister. By the way, if you had checked further you would have found out, Earl had Todd investigated just before you started working for me."

"Why? He didn't start dating Juanita until two years ago."

"It wasn't because of Juanita. It was because of Marquetta. Just because Marquetta didn't know he was her uncle didn't mean that Earl didn't know she was his niece. She looks just like my sister."

"Really, your sister must have been a hot number."

Tom replied, "She was an eyeful but she was never a hot number. I'm telling you this because now you're going to be a part of my family. Just don't get the wrong idea. We will help each other even if the other one doesn't know they need help."

"That's all right. I think Todd and I can fit right in with one exception."

"What's that?"

"Not what, who? Juanita—Man, she's a trip."

"She can handle herself. You better make sure you can." Tom chuckled.

"Did your father try to find the two of you?

"Yeah, but he used Investigations Unlimited. I couldn't reveal myself until Earl did or I would lose my edge. Now, let's get back to a girl coming in between two brothers. In our business we have come to understand it's not necessarily the people, but the behavior, that causes the problem. If the behavior changes, there would be no problem. One of the things I have learned about love is that we must respect people's decisions even if we know in our hearts, it's not right. We must pray that God will reveal his truth to them and teach them how to work through their problems. I know that's what has happened to my brother because he has changed his thinking. He was ashamed he made a mistake, but we all do. Once you give the situation to God, he will work it out. My family are praying people. I knew eventually we would all get back together. Even when one of our investigators told me that Earl Thomas told him to tell my father to stop looking for him because he didn't deserve to be his son. I knew he would come back to the family. You know he dropped the name Thomas. Thomas is my father's name. Both of us had it as a middle name."

"Boy, I never realized relationships could be so complicated, yet so important. Choosing the right mate is critical. Your decision will somehow impact the entire family. Um, maybe I need to pray about selecting my wife when I'm ready to marry," said Sam.

"That's what I said, too. I just never got around to it. Your brother is blessed to become a member of my family. We're a God-fearing people who love and protect each other, even at sacrifice to ourselves. I haven't been back home in a long time. I couldn't take the chance of Miss Peabody's finding out I'm the owner of Investigations Unlimited. If she had found out, Earl could have found out, and it wasn't the right time. But now I think it's time. I'm going to a wedding."

———————

Margaret remarked to Mark, "Do you know, in all the excitement,

I never told Momma and Daddy about Marquetta getting married?" What's wrong with me? I've been holding on to some of this happiness. No wonder I feel like I'm going to explode. I need to share."

Mark laughed, then commented, "You've been sharing, believe me! Since we've approved Marquetta's marriage and you've talked to Earl Thomas, you haven't done much around the house but share. You went into the attic; found your parents' family album, which your dad and I thought we hid from you and your mom, then proceeded to make me look at every page and hear the stories that went along with all 50 pictures."

Margaret waved her hand in front of her face, then stated, "That's not true. I couldn't remember all the stories. Oh, leave me alone, Mark Logan. I'll be back. I'm going to my folks' house. I love you. See ya later." She kissed Mark on the cheek and left. Mark smiled as he watched her walk to her parents' home. After 32 years of marriage, he still liked to watch his wife enter and exit a room. Margaret arrived at her parents' house to find Miss Peabody with them. Margaret thought. "Oh no, she couldn't have found out about Marquetta. I wanted to tell them."

Miss Peabody said, "It's about time you come and tell your parents the good news."

Tom Smith stated, "Speak loudly, Margaret, so your mother and I can hear you."

Miss Peabody remarked, "I told your parents that Marquetta was at your house with a handsome young man this weekend."

"Miss Peabody, may I tell them what happened?"

"Sure, Honey, help yourself." Miss Peabody put her hand in front of her mouth with one finger pointed at her lips and moved the finger from one side of her mouth to the other, giving the sign she had zipped her lips.

Margaret thanked her with a nod and a smile, then proceeded, "Well, Daddy and Momma, Marquetta brought a respectable young man to the house. He is nice and handsome, just like Miss Peabody mentioned. He asked Mark and me for Marquetta's hand in marriage."

Tom Smith asked, "What did Mark say this time, Margaret?

"Daddy, he...I mean..., we both approved. Our baby's getting married in two weeks."

Kate Smith inquired, "Why so soon?"

"She's okay. Apparently, they've been knowing each other for 10 years and her fiancé, said it's time they marry and she's in agreement. They are very happy. I think he's going to be good for her. I don't think it's going to be a big wedding, though. Momma, did you and Daddy talk to Earl Thomas?"

Kate Smith, beaming, replied, "Yes child, we sure did. He's getting married, too. We finally get to see our other grandchild."

"We may have more than two if we ever hear from Bob," commented Tom.

Margaret dreamed aloud, "Wouldn't it be nice, if we could hear from Bob and get the whole family together again?"

"We might. Things are happening. Prayers are being answered," said Kate Smith. After Kate Smith's statement, they all thanked God and cried tears of happiness, including Miss Peabody.

---

Juanita remembered she wanted to investigate W&Z realty to find out how they worked with minority firms, so she walked into the den where her father was home working, and asked, "Daddy what is the number for Investigations Unlimited?"

Earl stopped reading the file he was working on, looked up from the folder, and reached for his Rolodex. Once he found the number, he called it out to her. Then he stated, "Ask for Tom, he's the owner and tell him I referred you. That way you'll get a discount. Tell him exactly what you want. He's good."

"Thanks, Daddy." She went to the study and called the agency.

Tom's secretary answered and Juanita asked to speak with Tom. His secretary buzzed him and told him what line to pick up.

Tom picked up the phone and answered the line. "Hello, Tom Smith speaking."

"Hi, Tom. My name is Juanita Smith, Earl Smith's daughter. He told me you would give me a discount on my bill if I made you aware he referred me to you."

Tom chortled, then queried, "How can I help you? What or who do you want investigated?"

Juanita told him and Tom replied, "I'll have some information for you in the next couple of days."

Juanita demanded, "I need it today."

Tom stated, "You'll get a discount, but it's going to be on our emergency rate for services. Where do I send the bill and how do I contact you?"

"Send everything to Earl's home address. He'll give me the bill."

"Very well. Do you have a fax number?"

"Sure." Juanita gave him the fax number, then said, "Thanks a lot. Good bye."

Tom got off the phone and walked to Sam's office, and stated, "I need a rush on this."

Sam looked at the assignment, who ordered the work, smiled, then remarked, "Now, this niece of yours, is something else."

"She's like her mother and the only way she will change is if she gives her life to the Lord. But until she does, I want you to be careful. Personally, I was glad when Todd got away from her. I knew he was your brother. Marquetta is good for him, though. I've been monitoring them for a long time, even before Earl hired me."

"What?"

"Don't play me, Sam. You couldn't wait to get to the East Coast when you knew your little brother was getting serious. While you were in Maryland, Nancy and Walter were in the Caribbean. I gave them the trip for their honeymoon. They did a little work for me while they were there."

"Man, I can really learn from you. My brother didn't stand a chance." He ruminated, *Well, what do you know, he hasn't slept with her yet. I know what he'll be doing on his honeymoon. That's all right.* He remarked, "Hey, you pay for some of these investigations out of your own pocket. You are good to your family."

"My family is good to me. My Dad taught me about love, respect and forgiveness. He told me, although my brother and I had the fight, my brother loved me and he wanted me to never stop loving my brother. He told me to learn from his mistake. Be prayerful, especially when you are selecting the woman you want to marry. Members of my family pray, and so do I. I have to admit, I pray only about the business, never about women. But that's because I'm not ready to marry. Although, I have to admit I'm starting to feel uncomfortable about my present relationship, or should I say, relationships. He chuckled, then took on a grave look when he said, "Sam, I want you to remember real love comes from God. You need to get to know God personally, too."

"I'll take that under advisement."

---

Juanita was in the study reading when she heard the fax machine cut on. She waited until it stopped and went over to the cherry wood table where the fax machine was sitting and, took the pages out of the page holder on the machine. The fax was from Investigations Unlimited, with a history on the company she wanted investigated. A notation was placed on the first page of the fax suggesting that Juanita's company decline representation. The first page of the fax also had a recommendation of a similar company with equal monetary value. As Juanita scanned through the pages of the fax she saw a dossier on the recommended company.

Juanita was impressed as she thought, *They are good and worth all the money I had to pay.* Juanita buzzed her father, who was still working in his home office, and told him what happened. She then said, "Thanks for the referral." She hung up and called her office. She instructed them to stop work on the project for W&Z Realty. She told them to use the package that was put together for W&Z Realty for another company. She stated, "I'll fax over the name of the company and its dossier. Make the necessary adjustments and make them aware they were referred to us by Tom Smith of Investigations Unlimited. Thanks, goodbye." Juanita hung up the phone then dialed W&Z Realty. She gave her name and company to their secretary before leaving a message telling Mr. Zooks that her company was not interested in representing them. She then rose from her seat and walked to her father's office. Once in his office, she took a seat by his desk in a mahogany wood straight back chair. The back of the chair had wood carvings in the design of leaves. The padded lime colored seat was made of velvet. She tucked one leg under the other as she normally did when she was relaxed and talking to her father. She inquired, "Daddy, could we talk?"

"Sure, Baby, what's wrong." Earl smiled, eager to comply to his daughter's request.

"Nothing really. I wanted to tell you I prayed last night, read scripture, and I enjoyed church on Sunday, too. I think I'm going to go more often. I want to know more about God. I'm going to try to do better."

"Well, Honey, I'm glad you feel that way. I have something I want to tell you, too."

"Dad, is this another one of these things I may not want to hear?"

Earl laughed, then said, "Yes, Baby, but I know now, you can handle it. Remember my conversation on Saturday night, about my family?"

"Yes sir."

"I called them. I want to be involved with my family and I want them involved with us. So I invited them to the wedding. I don't want to wait for the wedding, though. So, I'm going to invite them to dinner on Saturday."

"Daddy, that's fine. I want to meet them, too. I've had you all to myself for a long time. I can share you now—

especially with your family. After all, they're my family, too."

"Honey, I'm so glad you said that but I don't want you to be overwhelmed when they arrive. I have prepared a copy of the guest list for you. You will see a couple of names that are familiar but I'm sure you can handle it." Earl handed Juanita the guest list and escorted her out of his office, smoothly. He thought, *If she wants to scream this is a good place for her to do it.* Earl listened for about five minutes at his door and to his surprise Juanita didn't scream, and come back into his office to complain. He said, "She did better than I thought."

Juanita, bewildered, wondered, *What's wrong with Daddy?* She went into her father's study to draft a letter to send to Land and Sales Investment Realty, which was the name of the company Investigations Unlimited gave her. She called her secretary, dictated the letter over the phone with instructions to use her signature stamp because she wanted the letter and package in the mail that day. She then requested a copy of the entire package be faxed to her after the original was mailed. After she finished talking with her secretary, she sat on the couch in her father's study and contemplated, *I wonder if Daddy would mind if I invite Tom Smith over on Saturday. He has such a pleasant voice. I know he's older, but I would like to meet him. Sometimes older men can be enjoyable. Besides, I could use him as an excuse to get away from my family, if necessary. I'll wire him an invitation.* She picked up the phone near the couch and called her secretary. She said, "Hello, Lucille, this is Ms. Smith. I want you to send a wire to Tom Smith of Investigations Unlimited inviting him to my father's home for a family gathering and celebration on Saturday. Oh yeah, tell him he won't need a date. I'll be it. Let him know there is no need for him to RSVP—just be here at 7:00 p.m. Thanks, goodbye." She hung up, then considered her actions, "I better tell Daddy what I've done." She buzzed her father in his office.

"Hello," responded Earl. He knew it was Juanita so he put the phone a little away from his ear so her yelling would not hurt his ears. When he heard her tone, he moved the phone closer to his ear.

"Daddy, don't get angry, but I invited Tom Smith to the family gathering. I may want to sneak out after I meet everyone. I thought I could use him as my excuse. Is that all right with you?"

"Sure, Juanita, that's fine. My baby's growing up." Earl was very pleased.

---

Barbara, with calendar and steno pad in hand, was sitting in her favorite cushioned chair in Marquetta's office. Marquetta was sitting behind her desk reviewing the last of the updated files Barbara had placed on her desk. She was so pleased with the way Barbara ran the office, she said, "Barbara, we had no emergencies and everything was handled perfectly. That's great. I knew you could do it."

"Praise God. I tried to check and double check everything since you left. Now, since the work is fine, tell me have you heard from Juanita?"

"No and Todd hasn't either. We decided we will contact each other if she calls. Oh yeah, where's the envelope from Mr. Earl

Smith's office?"

"You mean Uncle Earl don't you?" Barbara queried then snickered.

"It's so hard to get used to. I mean, he's always been nice to me, but my uncle. Boy, that's something. Remember, it was hard for me to believe he was Juanita's father when I first met and talked to him. Now I have to get used to Juanita being my cousin."

Barbara opened the envelop and announced gleefully, "It's an invitation for you to come to a consortium meeting next month!"

"Wow, let me see that." Barbara handed Marquetta the invitation. Marquetta read it, then stated, "That's nice, SCI has been considered for membership in the consortium." When she made that statement, she grasped the impact of what that would mean for her business. She exclaimed, "Do you know the weight his consortium carries? We could expand!"

Barbara, not wanting to put a different spin on their happy occasion, but felt she had to mention, it stated, "Marquetta, I hate to bring this up, but this also confirms our theory."

"You're right. But there's no reason to worry about it because God protected us."

Barbara and Marquetta said, "Thank you, Jesus."

The phone rang and Barbara answered it. "Second Chance, Inc., may I help you?"

"This is Earl Smith. May I speak to my niece, Marquetta Logan, please."

Barbara held in her laughter as she said, "Hold on." She got off the phone, laughed, then stated, "It's Earl Smith and he asked to speak to his niece, Marquetta Logan."

"No, he didn't!"

"Yes, he did! You better pick up, you don't want to keep your uncle waiting."

Marquetta, took a deep breath, then, took her phone from Barbara, "Hi, this is Marquetta Logan."

"Hi, Marquetta. This is Earl Smith, your uncle. I hope you've talked to your mother and plan to attend my wedding."

"Yes sir. I was really surprised to find out you were my uncle."

"I hope pleased, too. I always wanted to tell you. You make me very pleased to be your uncle, especially at our business meetings. You are a smart businesswoman. That's why I make certain your company is on the list to attend meetings that would affect the business community. I told your secretary that you're my niece today. I'm looking forward to announcing it at the next business gathering I sponsor. I want you to sit across from Juanita, near me at the head of the table. After all, we're family. Of course, Todd will sit beside you. I heard you're engaged to be married. He's a nice boy and he loves you. I know, because I deliberately forced his hand. I'm happy for you. By the way, I'm having a family gathering on Saturday because I want us to get together before the wedding. We've been separated long enough. I'm hoping you'll attend. I'm sending a car for your parents and grandparents. Should I send one for you and Todd?"

"No sir. We can drive ourselves."

"I've talked to Juanita about the family gathering. However, I must admit, I didn't verbally tell her about you and Todd being part of the family, but I gave her a copy of the guest list with both your names on it. She invited Tom Smith as her guest, so it appears she has handled it well. She didn't say anything about the list. So she knows you're invited. Please come. Don't disappoint us. You, Juanita, and Todd can work it out, I'm sure. Tom can keep Juanita occupied on Saturday. It will be rough at first, but if we stay honest and above board as a family, we'll get through it. I do love you, you know. You look just like your mother and act like her, too. I've been watching you. Let's decide to be patient with each other, okay? Give Juanita time, she'll be all right. Now, I want to hear it."

"Hear what, sir?"

"Uncle Earl. I've been waiting for you to say that for years. Whenever I see you, I think of your mother and Bob."

"Uncle Earl, why don't you ask Tom Smith to see if he can locate Uncle Bob?"

"That's an excellent idea. We'll make him work for his dinner. Thanks for calling me Uncle Earl, please continue. Tell Todd I want him to call me Uncle Earl, too. I'll put Tom on that assignment and I'll keep you posted. Your grandparents and mother will really be surprised if we can locate Bob."

"Sounds like a winner to me. Uncle Earl, if you need me to talk to Juanita, I will."

"Thanks, Baby. I knew I could count on you. See you later, Marquetta."

"Good bye, Uncle Earl."

Marquetta got off the phone, smiled then commented aloud but to no specific person, "That sadness in his voice has left. His voice has such a calm, peaceful note to it, now. Wow, thank God for his reconciliation and restoration power. I had no idea how quickly your life could change for the better. This man is at peace with himself again." Marquetta then looked across her desk at Barbara and responded, "Barbara, close your mouth. I'll tell you what happened, but let me call Todd. You can pick up on the extension. That way I won't have to repeat myself." Marquetta dialed Todd's office number and Myrna answered. "Todd Parker and Associates, may I help you?"

"Hi, Myrna. This is Marquetta. Is Todd in his office?"

'Yes ma'am. Congratulations! Mr. Parker held a staff meeting and told us you two were being married. Of all the women he's dated, I knew he would eventually marry you. He's so excited. I've never seen him like this. I think he'll be faithful to you. I guess Ms. Smith knows, because she hasn't called."

"She knows, but we are expecting her to call. This has been an informative weekend for us. I found out Ms. Smith was my cousin, and even though it was a hard pill for me to swallow, it may be harder for her, considering the circumstances. Please keep her in your prayers along with the rest of my family. One other thing, please be patient with her."

"I have prayed for her and I'll continue to do so. I'll add your family, especially you and Mr. Parker, to my prayers."

"Thank you. May I speak with him?"

"Sure, hold on." Myrna buzzed Todd and told him what line Marquetta was on. Todd pushed down the button then queried, "Hey, Babe, what's up?"

"Todd, are you sitting down?"

"No, I was on my way out the door. I was coming to see you. Can it wait until I get there?"

"It'll wait. But you may not like what I agreed to. So I prefer telling you now. You can ponder it while driving over here."

"What is it?"

"It's concerning my family. Barbara giggled on the extension and Todd heard her. Todd knew her giggle and asked, "Barbara, what are you and Markie up to? I'm on my way." Todd hung up the phone and left for Marquetta's office.

Barbara got off the extension, walked into Marquetta's office and remarked, "Todd will be all right."

"You think so. Let me tell you about my conversation with Uncle Earl. He's inviting the family over on Saturday for a family dinner. I don't think Todd is going to be pleased that I accepted for both of us. How could I refuse? Uncle Earl, took my advice and is going to ask Tom Smith of Investigations Unlimited to find my Uncle Bob. Hopefully, he'll be at the dinner, too. If he's able to locate my Uncle Bob, my mother and grandparents would be elated. Oh yeah, another thing Todd may not like, Uncle Earl would like both of us to call him Uncle Earl. At his next business meeting, I am to sit across from Juanita, which is on the other side of him, and Todd is to sit beside me."

Barbara queried, "So Juanita knows you're a part of her family?"

"We think so. Uncle Earl gave her a copy of the guest list with our names on it. He told me Juanita didn't say anything, so he thinks she knows and is handling it well. She did invite Tom Smith as her guest."

Barbara stated, "I'm surprised she's this calm. Maybe she didn't read the list."

"Barbara stop it. How do you think Todd will react to calling Earl Smith 'Uncle Earl?'"

"At least it's not 'Dad,'" Barbara responded, as she began to cackle.

"Very funny, but somehow I don't think I could use that statement to appease him. Barbara, this is no laughing matter. My family is trying to reunite after all these years. I want them to, even if that includes accepting Juanita as my cousin. My grandparents and mother will be very happy."

"I know, but it is kinda funny. I know Todd regrets sleeping with

Juanita now."

The new clerk-typist buzzed Marquetta to announce Todd's arrival. "Mr. Parker is here to see you."

"Thank you, Carol. Send him in," replied Marquetta. She looked at Barbara and stated, "Keep the staff away from my office, please. Thank you." Barbara laughed as she left.

Marquetta stood up and walked over to Todd as he entered the office. She kissed him and said, "Remember, you love me and you want me to be happy."

"I don't need to be reminded of that. What's up and don't stall?"

"Todd, Uncle Earl called me today."

Todd interrupted, "Uncle Earl. You didn't know this man was a relative before this weekend—now it's Uncle Earl. Come on, Markie!"

Marquetta laughed, then responded, "Todd, he asked me to call him Uncle Earl. I don't see anything wrong with it and besides he wants you to call him Uncle Earl, too."

Todd had just sat down as he heard that statement, he rose from his seat and stated, "He's not my uncle! He likes to throw his weight around, too much for me."

Marquetta replied calmly, "Todd, he will be your uncle by marriage. When he talked to you that day, he did that deliberately to force your hand. You can't hold that against him. Anyway, he wants us to sit near him at the next business meeting he sponsors as a family unit."

"Oh man, what a sham. Markie, I thought when I chose you to be my wife, I wouldn't have to put up with Earl Smith and his family. I can't believe it. I'm still in it."

"Well, if you feel that way, I'm not going to tell you the rest of our conversation." Marquetta sat in her cushioned mahogany leather chair near her sofa, across from Todd. She crossed her legs at the ankle and folded her arms as if in a stand off.

Todd said gravely, "Honey, I thought about my sleeping with Juanita and her being your cousin! Earl Smith knew all the time you two were family. He could have prevented it from happening. I would've never slept with her if I had known she was your cousin."

"Baby, let's forget about it. You can't continue to beat yourself up about sleeping with Juanita. That's another thing, we may need to be more tolerate of her behavior because she probably is uncomfortable with this, too."

Todd remarked, "Honey, there are going to be so many people at his wedding, she can overlook our presence if she wants to. Anyway, we can leave early. Most of the time, we travel in different circles."

Marquetta replied, "Baby, I'm not talking about the wedding. Uncle Earl has invited us with the rest of my family to a family gathering on Saturday. He asked if we wanted a car sent for us, but I told him we would drive ourselves. He's going to ask Tom Smith to try and locate my Uncle Bob. Isn't that nice? We haven't heard anything from Sam to that effect. He said Tom will be Juanita's date. He also said Juanita didn't say anything about the guest list and our names were on it. He really wants us to come. Todd, I think we should. My parents and grandparents will be thrilled if the family were together again."

"Markie, do you understand what you're asking me? Boy, this is one time I should've kept my pants zipped. This could only happen to me. I'm going to be sitting with my future in-laws and family who consist of Earl and Juanita Smith. Not to mention your grandparents, whom I haven't met. Markie, we both know Earl knows me personally and knows I slept with his daughter. He also knows that I have been chasing you for years. Remember, he questioned me about you before I started seeing Juanita, and when I started seeing her, he questioned me again. Markie," Todd paused. He hit himself on his forehead with the palm of his hand and queried, "Was that his way of telling me to choose one or the other? That you two were related? I should have asked him why he was interested, but I thought he wanted you for himself. I knew he was protective of Juanita because she was his daughter. That settles it—I love you, but I can't go. Suppose Juanita plans to use the gathering to make a scene in front of your parents and grandparents. What would they think of me?"

"Todd, things happen. They were young once, too; plus, people make mistakes. Uncle Earl understands. He just asks that we be patient with Juanita. Besides, you've changed, you're no longer a womanizer. I don't care what they think, we know we're for each other and we're getting married. I love you and my family loves

Uncle Earl and Uncle Bob. My mother and grandmother couldn't stand hearing their names without getting sad and teary-eyed. I'm happy and I want them happy, too. Please Todd, let's go to the gathering to support my family."

Todd acceded, "Since you put it that way, I'll go." The intercom buzzer went off and Marquetta answered it, using the phone on the coffee table near her. "Yes, Barbara."

Barbara responded, "It's Todd's brother Sam. He said it's important that he speaks with him."

"Okay, thanks Barbara." Marquetta got off of the intercom and stated, "Todd, it's Sam, for you."

Todd, reached for the phone from, picked up the receiver and said, "Hello."

Sam replied, "Hi, Little Brother, I'll be at the dinner on Saturday. Prepare to be surprised. Tell Marquetta I said hello. Bye-bye." Sam hung up.

Todd looked at the phone receiver strangely, then stated, "Markie, I don't know what's happening on Saturday but that was Sam and he's coming, too. He told me to prepare to be surprised."

"Sam! Why is he coming? Juanita invited Tom Smith as her date."

"Tom Smith, the private investigator who owns and operates Investigations Unlimited? Are you serious? How does she know him?"

"I don't know. I told you earlier she invited him. That shows you weren't listening to me. He's going to try and locate my Uncle Bob."

"Oh yeah, that's right. That's probably why Sam is coming."

"You mean you think Sam is handling this case? But we asked him to try to locate Uncle Bob already and he never got back in touch with us; or did he tell you something that you haven't told me?"

"No, he didn't tell me anything, but that may be why he's coming. Maybe he found out something."

"That would be great. This will be one time I'll be happy to see your brother."

Todd said, "I think we need to pray about this family gathering." Marquetta replied, "That's a good idea."

Todd led the prayer. "Father God, please forgive us for our sins, especially for the sin of fornication. Please unite our families in love. Please let us forgive ourselves and each other and be the family you would have us be, respecting one another and putting you first. We want to please you. We understand that in pleasing You, we will be pleased with our lives. In Jesus' name. Amen."

---

Juanita couldn't get any of her work done. She kept thinking about her father's dinner party on Saturday. Juanita decided she would help Violet with the family dinner, so she called her.

"Hello, the Smith residence. May I help you?"

"Hi, Violet. I'm calling because I want to help you prepare for the family dinner."

"Your father approved the menu. He made certain I fixed his parents' favorite dishes and ordered his sister's favorite flowers. He's going all out."

"There must be something I can do," said Juanita.

"Oh, I know, you can adjust the seating chart. We received confirmation from Tom Smith and he's bringing a guest."

"I hope not female."

Violet chuckled, then replied, "No, it's a male. I'll tell you what, I'll fax the revised copy of the guest list to your office. That way you can work on the seating chart there. I've already grouped the couples together, but you can take a look and tell me what you think."

"That's fine. Fax it now. I can work on it while I'm eating lunch."

"Okay, good bye."

Juanita buzzed her secretary and stated, "I'm expecting a fax. Bring it to me as soon as it comes in."

Lucille surmised, "She has been pleasant today. She must have convinced Todd Parker to marry her." She heard the fax, picked up the paper from the fax, and took it to Juanita.

When Lucille handed the fax to Juanita she acknowledged receipt by saying, "Thank you, Lucille."

Lucille, stunned Juanita thanked her twice in one day, said, "Excuse me, Ms. Smith. May I ask you a question?"

Juanita answered, "Sure, why not?"

"Are you engaged or something? You seem to be in such a good mood today. I mean you seem rather peaceful."

"No, quite the contrary. Mr. Parker is getting married to someone else. I guess I realize he isn't the person for me. Mine will come around some day."

Bewildered, Lucille replied, "You've changed."

"I went to church on Sunday. I've been talking to God and reading the Bible. I know I feel better. Thanks for noticing the change and telling me."

Lucille walked out of the office and said, "Thank you, God."

Juanita looked at the list in wonderment and thought, "I finally get to meet my grandparents and other relatives. I know I have an aunt and an uncle. I don't know if they're married or have children, but if they are and have children, I will have some cousins, too. Let me look at the names of my relatives. She tried to picture her grandparents and her aunt and uncle as she came to their names, and then she saw Marquetta's name. She couldn't believe it. She reread the name aloud. "Marquetta Logan with the word niece written beside it. It must be a different Marquetta Logan. Let me check the next name on the list. No way are they coming to my father's house! Future nephew, my foot! I don't care if it is written by his name. He is not going to be my father's future nephew! I can't believe Daddy would do this to me. How could he have Marquetta Logan as my cousin? He probably knew all this time she was his niece. I thought he was a little, too friendly with her. He always, took up for her. 'I want you to get to know her better,' he said. "No way!" She couldn't look at the list any more. She rose from her desk and started pacing up and down her office. She finally calmed down enough to pray. "Father God, help me. I'm trying, but I don't know if I can be at this dinner. Keep me calm, please. I don't know what to do." Tears streamed from her eyes as she continued to pray. "I know Todd isn't the one for me, but it still hurts. I want to stop hurting. I need your strength. I can't do it alone. I was feeling at peace. I thought everything was under control. But when I saw their names together, the reality of their impending marriage hit me and I began feeling hurt all over again. Then to discover Marquetta and I are family, which means, when she and Todd marries, he'll be family, too. I don't know if I can be around them. Father God, I tried to destroy her business. Please forgive me. Thank you for not letting me succeed. Teach me to love. Forgive me for my sins, including the sin of fornication. I don't want to have sex before marriage again. I see the problems it has caused in my life. Please let me wait until I get married to make love again. Select my husband, please. In Jesus' name. Amen." Juanita felt better after she prayed and decided to take a walk. She unlocked her lower desk drawer with the key she had mixed in her paper clip holder, then opened the drawer. She, took her pocketbook out, then locked the drawer back. She placed the key back in the paper clip holder, shook the container to mix the key in and left her office. As she walked outside, she noticed people walking and fanning themselves. It was a hot summer day but the heat didn't matter to Juanita. She was glad to be outside in the fresh air. She noticed the color of the sky; it was an aqua blue. The clouds looked as soft as cotton and as white as snow. She heard the birds chirping as she walked toward the park near her office and smiled. She continued to smile as she watched two squirrels chasing each other around a tree. The tree leaves and the grass were a beautiful shade of green. She looked to see if they were the same shade and decided they were. She realized she was enjoying God's creation. She thought, *I'm blessed just to be alive.* She remembered the scripture verse the Pastor spoke on the past Sunday; it was Psalm 139:14. She lingered on that scripture, after which, she knew she had to make a decision. She said, "I will praise thee." She knew it was no longer about her and what she wanted but it was about fulfilling her purpose in this world. God made her for a reason, just like he made everything else. She wanted Him to get the glory out of her life. She left the park feeling stronger than ever.

She got into her car and drove to Todd's office, but he wasn't there. She decided it was time to face Marquetta. She drove to SCI. She was wearing a red pant suit with a white silk shell top. As she got out of her car, she buttoned the middle button on her suit coat and began the walk toward SCI. At the door she pushed the buzzer to be let in and saw Barbara sitting at her desk, facing the door. Barbara buzzed her in the main office. Juanita walked to Barbara's desk, and introduced herself, "Hi, I'm Juanita Smith, Marquetta's cousin. Is she here?"

"Yes, she is, but Mr. Parker is with her now."

"I know you and my cousin are best friends. Todd told me. Please buzz her. I would like to speak with them both."

Barbara responded, "Just a moment. Would you like something to drink?"

"No, thank you," replied Juanita. Juanita, took a seat on the sofa near Barbara's desk, waiting to be seen.

Barbara buzzed Marquetta and stated, "Ms. Juanita Smith is hear to see you and Todd. May I send her in?"

"Sure," answered Marquetta.

As Juanita walked toward the office door, she prayed, "I need your strength." Marquetta and Todd held hands and Marquetta prayed, "Father God, please let us reflect your love." Juanita reached the door just as Marquetta opened it. Marquetta, wanting to break the ice, spoke first, "Hi, Juanita. I'm glad you came by. I know your being here takes a lot of strength. Have a seat."

"I prefer to stand." Without hesitation, Juanita began her congratulatory apology. She hadn't planned what she was going to say but she knew she needed to make a fresh start. "I want to congratulate the two of you on your engagement. Tears streamed down her face as she talked but she stood firm and strong. She continued, "Todd, I realize you are not the man for me because if you were, you would be marrying me and not Marquetta. The person for me will love me and there won't be any doubt. Marquetta, I probably never really loved Todd, but I saw a decent man in him. There are not, too many decent men around, in my opinion, so I tried to convince him that marrying me would be to his advantage. I think he has loved you for a very long time. I know at least for two years. I don't know what happened between the two of you that night two years ago when I called your house looking for Todd, but when he picked me up from my father's, I knew I had lost him. That is, if I ever had him. Now, I know I didn't. I tried to insist on sex that night, but he wouldn't bend. He slept in the guest room. Todd, I set my alarm so I could give you a couple of hours to complete the work you brought with you and then I hoped we could get together before you went to sleep. But when I went into the guest room with plans to arouse you sexually, you were praying. I tiptoed out and peeped through the door, waiting for you to finish, but when you got up, I noticed tears coming down your eyes. I couldn't understand what had made you so upset you felt the need to pray. The only thing I could think was that you thought being with me made you lose out on being with Marquetta, and that disturbed you. Marquetta, after that night, we continued to go out, but sex was very seldom. Marquetta, I want you to know that Todd and I haven't had sex in six months. I knew he was trying to make a decision about his life, and I knew I wouldn't be in it. Todd, that's why I began pushing even harder for marriage. I couldn't accept it. Marquetta, I knew I had something that you didn't—access to my father's wealth and his business partners. But all of a sudden, my father was going to blow that by recommending you and your business become a part of his consortium. I knew he was going to recommend Todd's law firm, too, so I panicked. I convinced Horace Greely to use his brother's company to sabotage your company. I persuaded him by sex. But, my mother, Loretta, came into town to get me to invest in a business venture. I waited, too long to respond to her, so she started watching my condo. Early one Sunday morning, she noticed Horace leaving my condo, and guessed I was sleeping with him. She decided to blackmail him, not knowing that was what I was doing. We both had him frightened because he believed we would tell my father that he was sleeping with me. Finally, the pressure became, too much for him and he told my father. That's how the plan was aborted. Now, Marquetta, knowing all this, do you still want to receive me as your cousin?"

Marquetta, took Juanita's hand, then responded, "Yes, we're cousins through the good and the bad times. After all, none of us is perfect. We just thank God because he is!" They hugged each other hard and long. When they finally let go of each other, Marquetta, took Juanita's hand and said, "Juanita Smith, I would like you to meet Todd Parker, my fiancé. Todd Parker, I would like you to meet Juanita Smith, my cousin. They each said, "Hi,." Then Todd stated, "Markie and I have decided that we want all of us to be a family that love and respect each other. We are doing this by establishing a policy of 'forgive and forget' as our motto. Are you with us?"

Juanita smiled, then agreed, "Yes, you can count me in."

All three hugged and Marquetta said, "Father God, we thank you for your mercy and your grace."

Todd and Juanita said, "Amen."

———————

Walking through the Los Angeles Airport, Sam queried, "Man, you mean you are not going to tell them until you get there that you're Bob Smith. Tom, do you think that's fair?"

"Earl and I look just like my father. I won't have to tell them I'm Bob. I just have to tell them I'm Tom Smith, too."

"I still can't believe you had me investigate your family."

"We were paid by Mattie Greely to investigate my family, remember. It was a job! Anyway it's good to be certain that the consortium, after all these years, is still a legitimate business organization—which is just what I thought all along."

"Yeah, but you also found out Horace was sleeping with Juanita."

"I thought it was either Loretta or Juanita that was involved with Horace because he has always liked Loretta, and Juanita looks just like her mother. When Earl was establishing himself in the business community, Horace was trying to get close to Loretta. However, Warren was always around her, so Horace eventually had to stop trying. Remember, I've been keeping an eye on my family for a long time."

"You're telling me that you knew Loretta was in town, too? So not only did you have Nancy and Walter watch Marquetta and Todd, and have me check up on Earl and Juanita, but you had someone on Loretta, too. Talking about 'covering all bases.' Man, you are good! You're this thorough with all our clients, too, aren't you?"

"I owe that to my family. While keeping an eye on them, I have learned to watch for certain situations in other investigations. That's why I involve more than one investigator on all our cases. Think about it, how else am I able to feed each of you more information than you give me?"

Sam replied, "I thought it was because you always did your own investigating, too."

"I do, but I have discovered that it never hurts to have people approach the problem at different angles. In the end, we all look good and no one person has all the answers. That way we work better as a team. Do you agree?"

Sam answered, "I never thought about it that way before, but it makes sense. I may not think a bit of information is important and someone else may. You never know what will help a client."

Tom, took a seat in the section stipulated on his ticket and Sam followed suit. Once seated, Tom stated, "I don't know why I'm talking so much. I guess it's because I'm nervous. I haven't seen my family as a family member in a long time."

"That shouldn't mean anything. You have been helping them in more ways than they know. You even give them good referrals. You help to keep money in all of their pockets, too. Besides, I'll be with you. If it gets tough, we can leave."

Tom replied, "Thanks, Sam. But I'll be all right. How do you think I should tell them?"

"Once we get there, you'll know when, but I can't tell you how. So I'll tell you like you tell me—pray about it," Sam smiled.

# CHAPTER 8

# FAMILY REUNION

Phillip was sitting by Barbara on the love seat in Marquetta's condo. He put his arms around her before he declared, "You girls can plan the wedding by yourself, if you like. All I know is one more week and I'm a married man." He spoke loudly enough to be heard in the kitchen where Todd was assisting Marquetta with the dinner dishes.

"Me, too, but I get to meet Marquetta's family tomorrow," announced Todd as he walked into the living room..

Marquetta was still in the kitchen finishing up the last bit of dishes when she heard Todd's announcement. She yelled from the kitchen. "You met everybody but Uncle Bob, Grandpa Tom and Grandma Kate. You'll be fine. Remember, I haven't met Uncle Bob either."

"No offense, Baby. But I'm more interested in meeting who's bringing Uncle Bob, and that's Tom Smith. Phillip, did you know he has one of the top agencies in the nation? Most of his people work from their homes, too. You call his headquarters in California and he can assign an investigator to you from all over the country."

Phillip inquired, "Is that right? But why would you call California for an investigator when you can get one from this area?"

"That probably does happen. People look for location but I think most of his business comes from referrals. He's really thorough. He also recommends companies to you with a copy of their dossier, especially if he thinks the original company you had investigated and wanted to do business with, wasn't good for your company's image," responded Todd..

Marquetta walked into the living room, took a seat by Todd, then commented, "With him you usually make money, learn how a company does business, and become more educated in your field of expertise."

"He's smart. A real business man," replied Phillip.

"Although his specialty is corporations and businesses, he will do other types of investigations for his clients," stated Todd.

"I can see why a person would continue to use his services," commented Phillip.

Marquetta jokingly said, "Hey, Barbara, maybe we could work for him on the side. Todd thinks we're good investigators."

"Sorry, Barbara has her hands full working with you at Second Chance, Inc. Not to mention the volunteer work you talked me into doing. You work my family enough. However, you and Todd have made Tom Smith sound interesting. I would like to meet him," responded Phillip.

"Maybe I can set it up," stated Todd.

Barbara wasn't involved with the conversation because her mind was on the planning of the wedding. She was going over in her mind the processional. She envisioned both her and Marquetta in white silk, traditional wedding gowns with matching veils. The men would be in white tuxedos with white shoes. Both fathers would wear red carnations in their lapels. Phillip and Todd would have red roses in their lapels. The groomsmen would also be wearing red carnations in their lapels. Both bouquets would have white orchards. She and her father would lead, then Marquetta and her father would follow.

Marquetta chuckled, then said, "Come on, Barbara, you'll going to let Phillip speak for you. How about it?"

Barbara, hearing her name this time, broke her concentration. She still didn't hear what was being said. She responded, "Hey, look, you guys, we have a double wedding to plan in only one week. We need to get busy," urged Barbara.

"I forgot. Juanita wanted me to ask you if you would be willing to wait until the end of the month and get married with her father and Violet. She also wants to be in on the planning process. She gave me a list of suggestions. Wait, I'll get the list." Marquetta walked to her bedroom, picked up the list off her dresser, and brought it back to the group.

"No way," determined Todd. "I've been checking the days off on the calendar. Baby, it's got to be next Saturday."

"I'm in agreement with Todd," declared Phillip.

Barbara responded, "Let's think about it. No. Better yet we need to pray about it." They agreed.

Phillip led the prayer. "Father God, let us marry when and where you want us to. Let us not be selfish, but be in one accord with you and your plans for our marriages and our lives. In Jesus' name. Amen."

---

Juanita was in her bedroom in her father's house, looking through her closet for something to wear on Saturday. Normally she would have bought a new outfit for the occasion, but since her last conversation with her father, she wouldn't dare ask him to let her use his charge card. Although he was still the same loving father to her, she knew he had not reversed his decision which meant she was still in the dog house. Her eye landed on a navy blue pantsuit. When she pulled it out of the closet for a better look she noticed the price tag was hanging from one of the sleeves. She had never worn the suit. She tried it on and loved the way it looked on her. It was settled. She would wear the pantsuit. She determined she would wear pearl earrings with matching necklace and bracelet as accessories. The navy blue pumps would accentuate the pantsuit beautifully," she thought.

After being successful in selecting a lovely outfit for the occasion, Juanita stated, "Now that I'm calm, let me review all the names on the list and the seating arrangements. She picked up the list from the dresser, walked over to her chaise lounge and lay down. She had her head resting on the pillow and both legs on the lounge. She bent her right leg at the knee, with foot still on the sofa, and crossed the left leg, placing the foot with ankle resting on top of her right knee, then commenced reading. As she went down the list, she noticed Sam's name and decided, "If I don't hit it off with Tom—after all he's probably an old man—I could go to a club with Sam. Her mind drifted to the last time Sam was in town and how alone she felt when he left. She commented, "I'm not lonely now, but I would like to see Sam again. Though not the way I saw him the last time he was in town. Boy, won't he be in for a surprise. He'll get to meet the new me." She grinned.

———————

As Sam, took a seat at Gate B, waiting for the flight for Maryland to arrive he inquired, "Why are we taking this flight?"

Tom, took the seat next to Sam, then responded, "I want to make sure no one will see me when I arrive in Maryland. This late, most people I know are asleep."

Sam downplaying Tom's concern, remarked, "Tom, I can assure, you Miss Peabody will be nowhere around Todd's place."

"Look, I just want to make sure my family will be the first to know I'm here," responded Tom.

"You're the boss," acknowledged Sam.

"Does Todd know we're using his place?"

"Yes, I mean, he knows I'm using it. I didn't want him to know you were with me. Remember, Marquetta thinks I'm bringing Uncle Bob with me."

Tom chuckled and said, "She's right."

"But you don't want her to know that yet. Todd, on the other hand, admires you as Tom Smith and has been wanting to meet you for some time. If he knew Tom Smith was going to be staying at his townhouse, he probably would have prepared some kind of gathering for your arrival. I knew you didn't want that, so I didn't tell him."

"Good thinking. But how are you going to get me in the townhouse without disturbing him? Anyway, he would see me in the morning."

"That should be okay, shouldn't it?"

"No, it isn't okay. Todd would know before the rest of the family. I told you I don't want that to happen. I want them all to see me at the same time."

"When we get close, I'll call Todd and see if he could let me use his townhouse for business.

Tom stated, "I don't know why you didn't think of that earlier.

---

As soon as they arrived in Maryland, Sam called Marquetta's house. Marquetta left her living room to answer the wall phone in the kitchen. "Hello," responded Marquetta after she picked up the receiver.

"Hi, Marquetta. Is Todd there? This is Sam."

"Hi, Sam. Did you find my Uncle Bob?" Marquetta asked excitedly.

Sam, not wanting to answer her question, stated coldly, "Marquetta, you'll have to wait. May I speak with Todd, please?" Marquetta put the phone on her kitchen counter and called Todd to the phone. Although she had a phone in her living room, she felt it would be rude to be talking on the phone in front of her guests. As she walked back to the living room, she met Todd walking toward the kitchen. With disappointment in her voice, she said, "Todd, it's Sam. He won't tell me if he found Uncle Bob!"

Todd, trying to console Marquetta, commented, "Honey, you know Sam takes his job seriously. You'll find out tomorrow, okay?" Todd kissed Marquetta on her forehead and then answered the phone. "Hello, Sam, what's up?"

"I need to use your place for business. Can you sleep over Marquetta's tonight?"

"You can use it for business. I'll be fine. Good bye," replied Todd. Todd walked back into the living room, took a seat by Marquetta, then asked, "Phillip, may I sleep at your place tonight? Sam needs to use my place for business."

Todd, you and Marquetta behaved yourself in the Caribbean. I think you can sleep in her guest room. But I don't mind if you stay with me."

"You can sleep in my guest room," responded Marquetta.

Barbara, wanting to get back to the wedding plans, queried, "Guys, what is it going to be?"

Phillip looked at Marquetta and said, "Marquetta."

Todd followed suit, "Markie."

Marquetta, feeling the pressure, responded, "Next week. I'll tell Juanita tomorrow."

Todd and Phillip, with the same thought in mind, leaped to their feet and gave each other high fives. Both said, "Thank you, God." Then they jumped up and down. Barbara then commented, "You two are ridiculous. You guys must have serious plans for us."

Phillip and Todd nodded their heads in agreement. Then Phillip smiled and replied, "It's all good."

"I know that's right," remarked Marquetta as she laughed. Then she stated, "Now, you guys have to remember although we are not virgins, we have been out of commission for some time. Remember, Todd, I've known you for ten years. Do you get my drift?"

Barbara commented, "Five or ten years, it doesn't matter. Patience will be the order of business on our wedding day."

"Man, we're scaring them," remarked Todd.

"Trust us—we know what we're doing," said Phillip.

Barbara, wanting to finish the plans, stated, "Let's get back to the planning process. Although the wedding is informal and small, who is going to be your best man, Todd?"

"My brother Sam."

"Mine will be Bill Clemmons," responded Phillip.

Marquetta, who will be your maid or matron of honor?"

"I don't know. I always hoped for you."

"I know, I wanted you, too. Let's skip that part and go on. We can get back to it later," replied Barbara.

"Okay," agreed Marquetta. They planned for hours, then agreed to meet at Phillip's house after church to finish.

After Barbara and Phillip left, Marquetta said, "Todd, I'm tired. I'm going to bed. The guest room is ready for use. I don't have anything for you to sleep in so I guess you're going to have to sleep in your shorts.

Todd, walking toward the guest room, remarked before entering the room, "Or nude." He closed the door behind him as he smiled to himself.

Marquetta, not wanting him to have the last say, yelled so Todd could hear through the closed door. "Whatever! Good night."

Marquetta, riding in Todd's car, pulled up just as her parents arrived. Marquetta and Todd waited for her parents and grandparents to get out of the limousine, then walked with them toward the house. In the center of the circular driveway was a display of azaleas—red, white, and pink azaleas in full bloom. Marquetta's grandparents stopped as they neared the flowers, which halted the remaining family members and Todd. Marquetta knew the flowers were her grandmother's favorite; in fact, they were not only in her grand-mother's yard, but also in her mother's yard. Now in her Uncle Earl's yard. As she looked back on the hoopla that was made every year about Earl Smith's azaleas she wondered why she never made the connection. "Well, that's water under the bridge now," she reasoned. She said, "Grandpa Tom and Grandma Kate they're wait-ing for us at the door. She nodded her head in the direction of the doorway. Earl, Juanita, and Violet were standing in front of the door-way waiting to greet them. Marquetta's grandparents then began to walk toward the house and the others followed. When they reached the first steps leading to the house, Earl met them there with arms extended. Juanita and Violet followed. Hugs and kisses began on the outside and then they went inside. Juanita and Violet lead the way with Earl taking up the rear. Suzette, peered out the door, saw Juanita put her hand on the doorknob and opened it. She held the door open with a smile on her face as the family members passed by but when Todd and Marquetta entered, just before Earl, she grunted loudly. When Todd looked in her direction, she presented him with a harsh look. Todd, determined not to be intimidated, decided to intro-duce Suzette to his fiancée. "Hello, Miss Suzette, this is my fiancée, Marquetta Logan." Earl noticed the look Suzette gave Todd and decided if harmony was to prevail he needed to address her. "Suzette, I would like to introduce you to my niece, Marquetta Logan and her fiancé, Todd Parker. We're family." Suzette, getting the message, responded by giving a half-smile, then speaking politely, said, "Hi." Earl then led them into the great room with the rest of the family. He had dinner catered and hired additional help. Marquetta surveyed the place with her eyes as best she could and thought, *He must have hired additional help because maids are all over this place.* Marquetta's thoughts were interrupted by her grandfather. "Come here, Baby Girl, and give your grandpa a hug."

Marquetta loved her grandfather and wanted to please him. She knew she hadn't been home in months and only called on him and her parents one day a week. Even though they were in the same state, they had different exchanges, which made the calls more costly. Marquetta looked at Todd and said, "Excuse me." She went to her grandparents and hugged both of them. After she hugged her grandfather, he held her, and remarked, "You know, Earl, Marquetta is my baby. I love this child. I have to admit your Momma and I smothered her by not giving her enough freedom to grow. You know why? Because of you and Bob. We taught you right from wrong; the importance of making the best choice for your life; and gave you the freedom to apply your learning. We love you boys deeply. Never in our wildest dreams did we think we wouldn't see you for decades. Now I find I have another grandchild; one you didn't permit your Momma and me to know as a child. We're hurt, Boy. You and your brother hurt us badly. Tom Smith's eyes searched the room for Juanita. When they landed on her, he said, "Come here, Child. Give your Grandpa Tom a hug."

Marquetta left her grandfather's side and, took a seat near Todd. Juanita walked over to her grandfather, gave him a hug, then her name. "My name is Juanita, Grandpa." Hearing the word 'grandpa' coming from her mouth caused a broad smile to break out on Juanita's face. She was experiencing the excitement of having an extended family. Her heart was overwhelmed with joy. Tears filled her eyes. As they began to stream down her face, Tom Smith patted the space between him and his wife, instructing Juanita to take a seat between them. She responded without saying a word. Once seated, Tom Smith stated, "Juanita, don't be afraid of me and your Grandma Kate. We want you to get to know us. We have looked forward to the time we could hug and hold our sons' children. We feel very blessed to finally have the opportunity to meet you." Brimming with emotion, Juanita hugged Tom Smith, then Kate Smith. Kate Smith kissed her on her cheek, then held her hand. Tom Smith, took the other hand as Kate introduced Juanita to Marquetta's parents. She pointed her index finger toward Margaret and Mark Logan, then announced. That's your Aunt Margaret and Uncle Mark. They're Marquetta's parents. Marquetta's father is a good man. He helps Grandpa Tom with things around the house and anything else we need. Now, go hug them, Juanita. We're a hugging family." Both Kate and Tom released their grip so she could leave their side. Juanita hugged both Margaret and Mark, then took a seat in the chair near her father.

Margaret then introduced to her parents Marquetta's fiancé. "Momma, Daddy, this is Todd Parker." Margaret was pointing her index finger in Todd's direction. He's Marquetta's fiancé."

Tom Smith commanded, "Come here, Boy. Give me and your new Grandma a hug."

Todd grinned, glanced at Marquetta, then rose from his seat and walked over to her grandparents. He hugged each one, then took a seat by Marquetta and held her hand. Marquetta smiled.

Juanita thought, *Grandpa Tom and Grandma Kate are the type of people that like to take charge. Daddy hasn't been able to say much of anything. They're in charge now. I like that. My grandparents don't play. They're tough. Now I see why Daddy acts the way he does, blunt and to the point.*

Marquetta looked around the room, contemplating, *This is my family.* Before she could grasp its meaning, she noticed the happiness in her Grandpa Tom's eyes. She, too became overwhelmed with joy. A sense of security and value swept over her. She was a part of this wonderful God fearing family. She thanked God for letting her be birthed through this group of his children and for letting her come to understand and appreciate the love she has and is receiving from him through this family. She knew she must continue sharing His love. Before getting back to the others, she took another glimpse at her grandfather. She noticed his facial expression had changed. His chin seemed to have stiffened. His cheeks were no longer filled with a smile. His face, took on a serious reflection. That look was also one she was familiar with, and the thought of it made her grimace. She reasoned, *Uncle Earl is going to get a scolding. Well, after all these years, I guess he's due.*

Tom Smith declared, "Boy, your mother and I want to talk to

you privately. Where can we go?"

Earl had also read the facial expression of his father and knew what was about to happen. Surprised at the emotion swelling up in him, he smiled to himself. He missed being advised by his father. Unlike the past, he welcomed it. He now realized his father was a man with great insight and he wanted to hear what he had to say. Earl, trying to keep a solemn face, looked at his parents and replied, "Yes sir, we can go into the library. Please follow me." Earl turned to look at the other guests, then said, "Excuse us. Please make yourselves at home. If you want to look around, you may. Help yourself to the hors d'oeuvres." As soon as Earl and his parents left, Juanita walked over to Marquetta, took a seat by her on the sofa, then asked, "What do you think they're going to say to my father? They seem nice but firm. They remind me of how my father handles me when he feels its necessary."

"Where do you think he got it from? Marquetta grinned then looked in her mother's direction as if for confirmation, then responded, "Uncle Earl is going to get a good talking-to; at least that's what they call it. I know my...I mean...our grandparents." Once again she looked to her mom, but this time she waited for an answer after she queried, "Right, Ma?"

Margaret, enjoying the conversation between her niece and daughter, sat quietly by listening to what she believed was the start of a lasting relationship and family bond. She thanked God for being a witness to this new-found friendship. She was so happy she knew she was glowing. Then she thought about Bob and hoped he would rejoin the family soon. She realized she was, too happy to become sad. She was very thankful for the happiness she was experiencing right now. She spoke softly but aloud, "Thank you, Father God, you are truly good to me and my family." Marquetta's interruption came immediately after she finished praying. She smiled, then replied, "Right, Marquetta! Juanita, your father hurt us very much and my father is the kind of man that tells his children and grandchildren what's on his mind. Whether we want to hear it or not. Your father expected this, believe me. He's okay. You will get used to your grandparents and their behavior because they are not going to give you any slack. You'll learn what they expect from us, but we are a loving and God-fearing family. I'm sure you'll like being a part of this family."

Juanita said, "Now, I see where Daddy gets his directness."

Todd chimed in, "And Markie."

Marquetta laughed, then remarked, "I thought you said you liked that about me."

"I do, but a whole family like that, wow!"

Mark joined in, "It's not as bad as all that. We respect each other but sometimes we need to discuss, in love, actions and/or behaviors that are affecting those we love."

Todd agreed, "Yeah, that's Markie, all right."

Margaret stated, "Todd, my husband assured me you knew our daughter very well. I see that's true. Now that you know that about her, I'm confident the two of you will be fine."

"Mom, I'm not that bad," responded Marquetta. Looking first at Todd then at her mother.

Margaret replied, "No, you're not, dear. Now, did the three of you solve the problem you had with each other?

"Yes ma'am," replied Juanita. Juanita, not understanding why but wanting to be honest, answered in a soft tone. There was a certain pitch in Margaret's tone that relaxed Juanita. She liked her directness and believed she was a fair person like her father. Juanita knew she wanted to get to know her family better, but more specifically, she wanted to get to know her Aunt Margaret. She decided to continue dialoguing with her, "Aunt Margaret, I saw my mother recently and I discovered I look just like her and you look, I mean…Marquetta…looks just like you, too. Daddy told me you were an eye stopper. Now I know he was right. I used to act like my mom, too. But I'm changing."

"That's good. If you ask God for help, you can change your behavior."

"Yes, Aunt Margaret, I know," answered Juanita.

---

After they were seated in the library, Grandpa Tom commenced, "Son, you knew the type of girl Loretta was when you wanted to hook up with her and you made your choice. As your family, our job is to tell you the truth as best we know it and advise you. But we have to respect your decisions, even if we don't agree with them. I thought you knew how we operated as a family."

Earl replied, "I did as far as other people were concerned. But I knew you wanted what was best for me and I didn't respect that. I wondered how then, could I expect you to respect me. I was so ashamed. She confessed on our wedding night everything, Papa. She named all the boys she had slept with in the neighborhood. Don't you see? I couldn't come back there to live. Besides, I hurt Bob. I beat him up and told him he was a liar when he told me the truth. I felt so dumb, so stupid. But I knew you would want me to make my marriage work. I tried very hard to make it work. I missed you and Momma so much. Sometimes I would call just to hear the sound of your voice and then hang up. The day Loretta and I were divorced I called, Momma you knew it was me because you said, "Earl that's you, isn't it, Honey? I love you, Son. I cried when I hung up."

"Tom, I told you that was Earl! We heard word of your divorce. I thought we were going to see you soon then,

Son," commented Kate.

"Earl Thomas how could you hurt your mother and me like that? Money doesn't take the place of us, being able to spend time with our children. I know you call yourself helping us by keeping money in our savings account.

Our savings account stays high. Every time we think we're broke, we go to the bank and find we have more than we thought. We figured it was true what we heard, that you had money."

"I instructed the bank to let me know when your account was under a certain limit or if you needed a loan, but I found out some-one else was depositing money into your account, too. I had it investigated and discovered it was Bob. So Bob is doing well, too."

"Well, we're mad at him, too. We want our family back. Money doesn't cut it, Son. You know what I mean, don't you? Boy, a family needs to communicate with each other, regardless of the problems. Just give the problems to God. He'll know how to fix them. I thought we taught you that."

"You did. I guess I wasn't ready to receive it then. But I am now. I love you both very much. Please forgive me," asked Earl.

"Your mother and I have already forgiven you. That's why we came. We just wanted to remind you of what we taught you while we could."

Earl laughed, then rose to his feet. He walked over to his father, held out his hand, and when he stood up, he hugged him. He then turned to where his mother was sitting and held out his hand, and when she rose from her seat, he picked her up as he held her. When he put her down, all three hugged and kissed each other while tears of joy streamed down their faces. Once collected, Earl queried, "Daddy, may I bring Margaret in, now?"

"Sure, I know she's ready. You know she hates to feel left out."

Earl went to the great room and beckoned Margaret and Mark to follow him to the library. They did. Once in the library, Earl asked, "Baby Girl, will you forgive me for not contacting the family until now?"

"Yes, but it really hurt me. I missed you very much," declared Margaret.

"I missed you, too," replied Earl.

The two of them hugged, then Margaret, took a seat on the sofa near Mark. Earl sat beside Margaret. Margaret said, "I'm so glad we're together again as a family. If only Bob were here." The excitement of being with his family again made him forget his surprise to his parents and sister—Bob. The moment Margaret mentioned Bob, he remembered. He decided it was time to tell them of his surprise. He announced, "Before we go back in the great room, I want you to know that, I, at Marquetta's request, hired an investigator to locate Bob, and they found him. He's going to be here today, along with Todd's brother Sam. Sam works for the agency I hired to find him. The owner of the company is Tom Smith and he'll be here as Juanita's date. This may be an interesting night. Juanita has dated Sam, too."

"Juanita has dated Todd, too," remarked Margaret.

"Todd, Marquetta's fiancé?" queried Kate Smith.

"Yes, but I talked with the three of them and that part has been taken care of, Momma. She told me she was like Loretta, but she's changing," replied Margaret.

"That's okay, she's my granddaughter. If I could handle you

during puberty, and Marquetta, I sure can handle her. No matter how old she is. I have a lot of love in my heart for that child. She'll be all right," responded Kate.

"Yes, Momma, I know," said Earl.

How old is this Tom fellow anyway? I'll look him over," stated Grandpa Tom.

Earl looked at his watch, now expecting the other guests to arrive, and said, "Let's go to the great room before the youngsters get bored."

"All right, I want to talk to Juanita before this Tom fellow arrives," declared Grandpa Tom.

Immediately upon entering into the great room and taking his seat, Grandpa Tom said, "Juanita, I hear you have two dates tonight. Tom Smith and Sam, Todd's brother. I do like the first characters name. However, how old is he?"

"He is an older man, I guess, Grandpa Tom. I never met him in person, just over the phone."

"That's okay because I'm going to check them out anyway. You may be staying here with me and your Grandma Kate, if I don't like them. I want you to spend time with us anyway."

Juanita smiled and replied, "Yes, Grandpa." She then looked at her father for assistance.

Earl responded, "I'm sure you have noticed how your Grandpa takes control of a room. That conversation is between you and him."

Juanita then glanced at Marquetta and asked,"Are you going to help me with this?"

Marquetta laughed and responded, "No, I've learned not to argue with Grandpa Tom. When he says something he means it."

Anticipating Bob's arrival, Earl peered at his watch. Then he looked at Todd and inquired, "Have you heard from your brother? Tom Smith of Investigations Unlimited assured me they located Bob and he would be with Sam.

"I know he's here," responded Todd. "But I didn't know your brother would be with him."

Marquetta, trying not to be rude, but spoke very softly so only Todd could hear, asked, "Do you think my Uncle Bob was at your townhouse last night?"

Todd responded in a low voice, "I don't know, but now that I think about it, probably. That's why Sam so easily brought my clothes to your place today without my having to call." The others didn't notice Marquetta's and Todd's private conversation because Grandpa Tom had begun updating Juanita on family history. Whenever Grandpa Tom told family history, the other members of the family never knew where or when he would embellish. He did this to get a rise from the others. It ended up with all the members present listening very carefully and taking part. When Suzette walked into the room, she noticed everyone was focused on Grandpa Tom while he was talking and gesturing at the same time. Suzette cleared her throat loudly, then excused herself to get the attention of those in the room. She then made her announcement. "I was asked to announce the arrival of Tom Smith and Sam Parker of Investigations Unlimited. Should I send them in?"

Earl replied, "Sure." Then he queried, "Did they mention the name Bob Smith or is there another person with them?"

"No sir," responded Suzette. She left the room and sent the new arrivals into the great room. She had them waiting near the entryway of the great room when she announced their arrival. The moment Sam and Tom entered the room, Earl and Margaret jumped out of their seats and ran to Tom and hugged him. Grandpa Tom and Grandma Kate walked over to Bob (Tom) and hugged him. Earl said, "I'm sorry. I love you, Man." He repeated those lines over and over again as he hugged his brother. At this time Bob was surrounded by his siblings and parents. He was inundated with hugs and kisses. The minute Bob walked into the great room, Margaret jumped up very quickly and with great excitement. The force pushed Mark on the floor. Margaret at the time was seated in the center of the chaise lounge leaning on Mark, who was sitting at the open end. Todd ran to help Mark Logan get back on his feet. The room emanated with joy as parents and children reunited. Marquetta and Juanita sat on the sidelines watching this wonderful spectacle unfold. Needing clarity, Juanita asked, "Marquetta, is that Uncle Bob?"

Marquetta responded, "I thought Suzette said it was Tom Smith of Investigations Unlimited."

Juanita replied, "I did, too, but look at how they're behaving. That must be Uncle Bob, but where is Tom?"

Todd, listening to Marquetta's and Juanita's conversation, commented, "Markie, you're better than that. Think!" He then walked over to where Sam was standing and continued to watch this joyous reunion. Marquetta finally made the connection. She shouted, "Unbelievable! I got it. Uncle Bob is Tom Smith of Investigations Unlimited. He used Grandpa Tom's name."

Marquetta's outburst interrupted the reunion. Realizing they were standing in the middle of the floor near the doorway, Earl led the group back to their seats. Bob and Sam, took seats near Grandpa Tom and Grandma Kate. Once seated, Grandpa Tom leaned toward Marquetta and stated boldly, wearing a smile that stretched from one ear to the other, "That's his name, too. That's both of my boys' name—their middle names anyway."

Todd, took his seat by Marquetta, held her hand, then remarked in a low tone, "See, I told you, you could've been a detective."

Marquetta grinned, then commented, "Right, it's in my blood."

Bob addressed Juanita. "Hi, Juanita, thanks for the invitation. I brought Sam along to escort you if you want to leave after dinner."

"Thank you, but Sam is going to have to be cleared by Grandpa Tom first," stated Juanita.

Grandpa Tom responded, "Sam, you can go out with her provided Marquetta and Todd go, too. If not, you're going to have to court her here tonight."

Sam looked at Todd and then Grandpa Tom, then replied, Yes sir."

Todd, Marquetta, and Juanita laughed.

Sam asked, "Todd, would you and Marquetta go on a double date with Juanita and me?"

Todd peered at Marquetta and queried, "What do you think?"

Marquetta smiled and replied, "Okay, provided we get home early. We have church tomorrow."

Sam said, "That's fine."

Bob, sensing it was time to seek forgiveness from his family moved closer to his parents and sat on the hassock. He, took his mother's hand, kissed it, then rubbed his father's hand and said,

"Daddy, Momma, I'm sorry. Please forgive me."

Grandma Kate looked at her husband, then stated, "Tom, we agreed I would talk to Bob first. Earl, take us to that room again. Margaret, you and Mark come, too. Now you young'uns stay put until we come back."

Marquetta, Todd, Juanita, and Sam laughed. Sam said, "Todd, Man, they act worse than our family. Are they for real?"

Todd replied, "Well, Brother Dear, they are going to be a part of my family and they are for real."

"That's right, they are, and you still want to go through with it? Just kidding. Now, Little Brother, you don't really have to double-date with us. In fact, we can just go to your place, right Juanita?" Sam rose from his seat and walked to the sofa where Juanita was sitting.

To his surprise, Juanita's response was negative. "Not really. My father hasn't officially given me the condo back. We can stay here if you want."

Sam looked at her in disbelief, then stated boldly, "No way! I think that old man is serious. He'll be watching me like a hawk."

Marquetta, displeased with the way Sam referred to her grandfather, declared, "That old man is my grandfather and he is serious. He's smart, too. He figured you out within minutes. Besides, I don't lie to my grandfather, so if he told me to go on a date with you and Juanita, I'm going, or I'm telling him and Juanita's not going."

Sam asked, "How old are you?"

"I'm old enough to appreciate and respect the wisdom of my elders," replied Marquetta firmly.

Juanita chimed in, "Me, too. I'm trying to get my condo and car back. I'm not going to get my father upset over disobeying his father. No way! I know Grandpa Tom may be old, but he's no dummy. He knows exactly what your plans are for me. Right, Sam?"

Sam couldn't believe what he was hearing coming from Juanita. This had to be a front for Marquetta and her new-found family, but he had plans for them tonight and he wasn't going to let her ruin them trying to impress her family. He decided he needed to bring her back to reality. Sam said, "Come on, Juanita! We've had sex before, so I don't need this garbage from you tonight."

Juanita replied, "Just because we've had sex doesn't mean every time you want sex, I have to comply to your wishes. Does it?"

Marquetta responded, "No, it doesn't, Juanita. Sam, how dare you insinuate that she is obligated to satisfy your needs. You're not her husband. Really! Marquetta folded her arms and rolled her eyes in disgust.

Sam was getting angry and he didn't want to hear anything from Marquetta, so he looked at Todd with a stern look on his face, then demanded, "Todd, talk to Marquetta, please. This conversation is between Juanita and me." He turned to look Juanita in her eyes, then said in a commanding tone, "Juanita, don't start acting like Marquetta because I'm not Todd. Do you understand me?"

Juanita was taken aback by Sam's tone. It through her off to the extent she replied in a docile manner. "Yes, Sam, I understand." Hearing her response frustrated her. She knew Sam had done it to her again. Puzzled about the effect Sam seemed to have on her, she questioned herself? *Why does Sam seem to know how to make me do and say things I wouldn't normally do or say?* Determined to gain control, she continued, "Nevertheless, Marquetta is right. I'm not your wife and I don't owe you sex, and I'm not having sex with you tonight!" At a time when her strength seemed to be wavering, she needed a strong support network. Marquetta's assistance was desperately needed and Juanita was grateful to have her in her corner. She smiled at Marquetta, acknowledging her new-found confidence that they were cousins and would protect each other. Marquetta, understanding the glance and the smile, sent the smile back, assuring her she read her loud and clear. Then Juanita said, "Marquetta, I think I would have been a lot different if I were around Grandpa Tom and Grandma Kate. I really want to get to know them.

"You will; there's no getting away from them now," replied Marquetta.

"They still have a lot of energy and get around well for their ages. They must be in their eighties," responded Juanita.

"They are—Grandpa Tom is 84 and Grandma Kate is 82, approximately. You'll love them. They're good people and you'll find that they really want what's best for you."

"I can tell that already," replied Juanita. She moved her eyes in

Sam's direction then she and Marquetta laughed.

———————

Once in the library, Bob took center stage. Earl sat on the maroon leather sofa with Margaret and Mark. Grandpa Tom and Grandma Kate sat on the loveseat leaving Bob to sit in the maroon leather rocker that faced them. With all eyes on him, Bob proceeded to explain his absence from the family. He stood up, then sat down, then stood up again before he began talking. "Momma, Daddy, Earl, Margaret, and Mark, I sincerely apologize for not being in contact with you physically for many, many years. I just couldn't see how I could help Earl any other way. Once we heard he had married Loretta, I knew he was in hot water. Somehow this woman had blinded you, Earl, and you weren't able to see the truth. I tossed and turned the night before I left, trying to come up with a way to bring you back home, once I found you. However, I didn't know if you would be willing to talk to me. You were so angry with me when you left. Besides, I felt I played a big part in your leaving. After all, I was the one who told the family about Loretta's extracurricular activity. I hired an investigation agency to find you, but decided I wouldn't tell the family until they had located you. But, coming home each day, watching the look on Momma's and Margaret's faces hurt my heart badly. Poppa seemed to be dealing with it better, but every now and then, I would look at him and see a tear gently fall from one of his eyes. I did the only thing I could do without getting Mrs. Peabody involved. It was bad enough she was the one who told us you and Loretta had married. Apparently, Loretta wrote her folks and her folks told Mrs. Peabody. But Loretta, just like you, never gave an address. When my money started running short, I decided to do part-time work as an investigator. That way I could look for you and get paid, too. The closer I came to locating you, the more I had to go into seclusion. Man, you didn't want to be found by the family. Because I had already experienced how easy you were willing to take flight, alerting you to me or the family before you were ready I thought would force you to leave the state. I couldn't take a chance on Mrs. Peabody finding out where you were because, if she knew, she would put it in the paper—which could have made you leave the area. At least I knew where you were and would keep an eye on you. Poppa, you told us we had a responsibility to care for and protect each other when the occasion presented itself. Earl was, too blind to see the truth. He was willing to leave the comfort and protection of his family for a woman that couldn't be trusted. I couldn't let her destroy him, could I? I had to keep an eye on him. I never really planned to lose contact with the family, but the more involved I became in my business and in tracking Earl and Loretta the more I realized I needed to stay clear of the family. I couldn't take a chance on the word getting out that I was the owner of Investigations Unlimited. That was how I was staying in touch with Earl. Perhaps I could have told you but I honestly didn't know how Mrs. Peabody received her information. I couldn't take the chance. Now my reasons seem flimsy, but at the time it seemed very real to me. Please forgive me. Oh yeah, by the way, Little Brother, don't ever hit me again, because the next time I'll hit you back. Right, Pop?" Every one in the room laughed.

Earl replied, "Man, this is a big sacrifice that you made just for me. Thank you, Man. I missed you very much. Man, the day Loretta and I were married, she confirmed everything you said. I was embarrassed and ashamed. I thought bringing her back to the neighborhood would just put more shame on not only me, but the whole family. When I finally thought my financial status could bring us the respectability we needed, so I could come back home, I found Loretta in the garage on the concrete floor having sex with my junior partner, Warren. I couldn't take it any more. I divorced her, but that to me added additional shame on the family. I didn't think I would ever get to see any of you again. Then Marquetta walked into my life. She had just finished school and had decided to start her own company. She saw a space in my building that she wanted to rent and came to see me. Listening to her talk was like hearing you, Margaret. I knew at first glance she was your daughter, Margaret. To make sure, I had her investigated. When it was confirmed, every time I was around her I thought of our family. I couldn't help but smile every time she walked into the room. Mark and Margaret, she's something else. She has a mind of her own and it will not be swayed. I have tried, and so has Todd for that matter.

She's sharp, too. You should hear some of her suggestions. Wait a minute! Bob, your company was the company who checked into her family history for me. You knew we were together! What a fantastic way to keep track of the family. Your idea for your company was ingenious."

Margaret, not wanting Earl to think that Marquetta was a perfect child or that Juanita couldn't be helped, said, "Earl Thomas, the Marquetta you see is what she blossomed into. She has experimented with men as well. I'm telling you this to let you know, Juanita can and will change, so don't worry about that."

Grandpa Tom said, "Bob, I'm not going to fuss with you because I told you to love and protect your family as best you could, and you tried to do that, but don't you ever stay away from us again." He then turned his gaze from Bob to Earl. He continued, "Earl, you were wrong when you hurt your brother, and I told him he should have fought you back. We saw you and Loretta running out of the yard after we returned from the hospital. We knew you were checking to make certain your brother was okay. However, that response didn't free you of your responsibility to leave without saying good-bye. But enough of that now. It seems we all have learned a lesson to remind us that each family member is important. Now, we need to learn how to forgive and forget so we can continue to develop as a family unit."

Grandma Kate decided to comment on Margaret's statement to Earl. "Yes, Marquetta had her growing pains, too, but the Lord put her on the right track, and now we will pray that the Lord will put Juanita on the right track, too."

Margaret replied, "Momma, I can tell God is working with Juanita now. Maybe we can convince Juanita to come and stay with us for a while. That way we can get to know her and she can get to know us. She can stay with Mark and me. Right, Honey? She turned to look at Mark, with a smile on her face, waiting for a response."

Mark, without hesitation, responded, "Sure, it will be good to have her around the house."

Earl chuckled, then agreed, "Then it's settled. She'll stay with you for a while. I'll spring that on her later this evening." He looked at his dad lovingly, then asked, "Daddy, may we go back into the great room? I want you to talk with Violet and Suzette, my future wife and her sister. Violet and Suzette have worked for me for years as my housekeeper and cook, until Juanita moved to the condo. Suzette went with her, as a chaperone of sorts, but she wasn't firm as I had hoped."

Grandma Kate remarked as she rose to her feet to leave the room, "Honey, I'm glad this money hasn't made you forget your background."

Sam, determined to convince Juanita to sleep with him, moved closer to her on the sofa. As he took her hand, he whispered in her ear, "Let's go upstairs. I want to talk to you privately."

Juanita said loudly, "I'm not having sex with you, Sam. I'm not doing that anymore until I get married."

Sam blurted, "What? I don't believe this. You mean I have been looking forward to seeing you for what? To hold your hand—I don't think so."

As Marquetta rested her head on Todd's shoulder, he stroked her hand gently, then said, "Big Brother, don't worry, you'll get used to it—holding her hand, I mean."

Sam, now agitated, looked at Todd with eyes that could cut glass and said, "Right!"

As the older generation entered the room, Bob walked near where Marquetta and Juanita were sitting, then said, "Juanita and Marquetta, give me a hug." They both walked to him, stood on each side of him and wrapped their arms around him. He put his arms around both of them and gently squeezed them, then said, "My two nieces. Keeping an eye on you two have kept me very busy." Both Marquetta and Juanita laughed as they continued to hug Bob. Bob continued to talk, "Marquetta, so you're marrying Sam's brother, huh?"

"Yes sir," answered Marquetta.

"Call me Uncle Bob."

Juanita, took her original seat and Marquetta, took her seat near Todd while Bob continued talking. "Todd, I heard a lot about you. Nancy and Walter said you behaved yourself like a gentleman in the

Caribbean. I like that, you respect her."

Mark asked, "Marquetta, did you tell your mother Todd was with you in the Caribbean?"

"No, Daddy. I knew I was going to behave, so I didn't want her to worry."

"You'd better be glad you're getting married, Young Lady," remarked Margaret.

"Yes ma'am. It was perfectly innocent, just like Uncle Bob mentioned earlier," replied Marquetta.

Todd asked, "Mr. and Mrs. Logan, may I explain? I surprised Markie. She didn't know I was going until the last minute. I proposed to her over there and we both behaved properly."

Everyone laughed except Todd and Marquetta.

Marquetta waited until the family members were looking and listening to Grandpa Tom, then she whispered in Todd's ear. "I feel like a child."

"Remember, you are their child. Just think one day, hopefully, we will be able to have a similar conversation with our child or children," Todd said softly.

Marquetta replied, "Thanks, I feel a lot better."

Grandpa Tom turned to look at Todd and declared, "That boy is all right. I like you, Todd. So, have the four of you decided where you're going to go this evening?"

Juanita responded, "No, not really, Grandpa Tom. I guess we'll stay here and hear you guys reminisce."

"Sounds good to me," replied Marquetta. She looked at Todd and said, "Get relaxed, it's going to be a long night."

Grandpa Tom, after having taken care of much needed family business, decided it was time to introduce himself to Violet. He stated, "Violet, I hear you're marrying Earl Thomas. That's good; and I'm making you responsible for his visits to see his Ma and me regularly. Can you handle that?"

Violet answered, "Yes sir, I think I can."

"Well, either you can or you can't. Which is it?"

Violet, recognizing Grandpa Tom was a man who didn't mince words, stated firmly, "I can!" The room roared with laughter.

Grandpa Tom waited patiently for the laughter to stop because he wanted to make a sincere statement to his son. When the room had silenced again, he said, "Earl Thomas it's about time you got on with your life. Your Mom and I are glad to be here and to be a part of your life again. We want all of our children and loved ones to be happy. Now it's time to thank Father God for this joyous occasion he was allowed us to share with each other." All together everyone said, "Thank you, Father God." Afterward, the room was so quiet you could hear a pin drop. Grandpa Tom hugged and kissed his wife, wiped tears from his and her eyes, then remarked, "Well, Earl Thomas, I see you finally learned to get a woman with some meat on her bones. She'll be soft and warm when you need it."

Juanita, now sitting on the other side of Marquetta, commented softly, "They get real, don't they?"

Marquetta responded with a low voice, "You'd better believe it. They don't want you to have sex until you're married but they sure make it sound interesting."

"So that's why Daddy was never afraid to talk to me about sex. He talked and talked and talked. I guess I just wanted to do it my way," replied Juanita.

"Me, too, until I understood it was better to wait," said Marquetta.

It was after midnight and the reunion was in full swing. Sam inquired, "Todd, why don't the four of us go to your place?"

Juanita heard Sam, touched Marquetta's hand to get her attention and mouthed the words, "Say no."

Todd responded, "Man, I'm enjoying this. Look at the love being shared. They are trying to recapture all they missed. Sam, I don't care who you marry. Right now, let's agree to forgive and forget. You'll always be my brother."

Juanita ruminated what happened to divide the family and began to cry, "Just think, their unhappiness was caused by my mother. I feel so ashamed."

Before the others could respond, Margaret had already come to Juanita's aid. She walked over to the sofa where Juanita was sitting and grabbed her hand, leading her to the chaise lounge where she was sitting with Mark. She put Juanita's head on her chest and stroked her hair as she said, "You are family and have no reason to be ashamed. Just think, if it weren't for Loretta, we would have never received you, and in order to have you as a member of our family, we would welcome Loretta any day. Remember, you are not your mother; plus, we all have made and will make mistakes. We're not perfect, God is. Just remember to put God first and he'll lead the way."

Bob went to where Juanita was sitting and sat on her other side. He patted his hand on his shoulder, letting Juanita know he was there for her, too. She then leaned her head on Bob's shoulder, buried her head in his chest and said, "I'm trying."

Bob replied as humorously as he could muster, trying to stop the tears. He hated to see a woman cry. "Honey, we're all trying. If you need anybody investigated, you can call me." Laughter filled the room again.

Earl, noticing the bond that had developed between Margaret and Juanita, believed it was time to spring the plan on her. He stated, "Juanita, your Aunt Margaret and Uncle Mark want you to stay with them for a while. If you agree to stay with them, you won't have to look for a place and you can get to know them and your grandparents better. In addition to that, you won't have to worry about transportation because you can keep the car." Less formally and with sincerity in his voice, he said, "Besides, Honey, I don't want you alone right now."

Juanita was happy the family had accepted her and since she wanted to get to know them, too, without hesitation she replied, "Sure, I'll be glad to stay with them. That's a great idea. When do you want me to come?"

Margaret was impressed with Earl's and Juanita's relationship. It was very similar to the way she and Mark reared Marquetta. They gave them the freedom to explore, yet never letting them forget to respect authority and their elders. Margaret smiled as she responded, "Whenever you're ready. But make it soon. By the way, you will not be staying in Marquetta's old room. The room you will be staying in will be your room and you can decorate it to suit your taste."

Even more excited now that decoration became part of the arrangement, excitedly she answered. "Okay, that sounds wonderful!" Pleased with Juanita's response, Grandma Kate smiled, clasping her hands together under her chin. Grandpa Tom smiled as he rubbed Grandma Kate's thigh happily. Todd remarked to Marquetta, "Your family is all right."

Marquetta replied, "I told you they have a lot of love to give."

Sam, wanting to get away from the others, said as innocently as he could, "Juanita, would you show me around your father's house?"

Marquetta chimed in, "It would be nice if we could walk the grounds. Although it is very late. What time are you leaving, Grandpa Tom?"

Grandpa Tom responded with a broad smile on his face, "I've decided we're going to stay the night and go to church with Earl Thomas tomorrow. Momma Kate, Mark, and Margaret, is that all right with you?" They nodded their heads in agreement.

Earl said, "Daddy, that's a marvelous idea."

"If that's the case, I'm going home now. I'll see you tomorrow at church," replied Marquetta.

"Todd and I are meeting Barbara and Phillip to finish planning our wedding, so we won't be able to come tomorrow."

Earl asked, "Juanita, have you gotten everything out of the condo?"

"No sir, I haven't."

"Why don't you get the rest of your things and stay here until you're ready to stay with Margaret and Mark."

"Okay, Daddy. I can get them after church tomorrow. Aunt Margaret, may I move in with you and Uncle Mark after the wedding?"

"That's fine, Dear," said Margaret.

Earl replied, "Margaret, you can send her packing whenever you're ready. Did you hear what she said? Move in."

Margaret laughed and then said, "She'll know when she's ready to leave. Right, Juanita?"

"Right, Aunt Margaret. Daddy, you're going to miss me."

"True enough, but your stay with Margaret and Mark will be good for all of us. I'm taking Violet and Suzette on a cruise. Suzette needs a break and I'm sure she knows better than to bother Violet and me on our honeymoon."

Bob said, "I heard that. I'm in need of a vacation, too. Maybe

I'll keep Suzette's company."

Grandma Kate hollered, "Boy, that woman just met you. Stop being so fresh."

Bob respectfully replied, "Ah Ma, I could have had a date, but you blew it. Suzette, would you like to see a movie tomorrow evening?"

"Sure, that will be nice,"answered Suzette.

Todd stated to Marquetta, "Tom...I mean Bob... is too much." As he was making that statement he began to yawn. He apologized, then said, "Honey, are you ready to go? I'm sleepy."

"Yeah, I'm ready." Marquetta rose from her seat and Todd followed. Standing by her seat she said, "Mom, Dad, family members and soon-to-be family members, Todd and I are leaving. I'll keep in touch. Nice meeting you, Suzette and Violet." After Bob and Sam arrived, Suzette joined the family in the great room. She sat quietly by Violet, never saying a word until Bob began hitting on her. She was concerned about Juanita but by the time the evening was over, she was at ease. Sam, making his last attempt for the evening to get Juanita alone, stood to his feet, walked to Juanita, took her hand, then asked, "Todd and Marquetta, before you leave, could Juanita and I see you in the foyer, please?" Marquetta and Todd agreed. Once they entered the foyer, Juanita suggested they walk the grounds to the pool house. As they walked, Sam said, "Juanita, I'll leave with Todd if I could help you gather your things at the condo tomorrow."

Todd replied, "That doesn't have anything to do with Markie and me. Why are you wasting our time?"

"I know, but I needed to make it look like the four of us were planning something together," responded Sam.

Marquetta, annoyed at Sam's apparent one-track mind, said, "Sam, the girl told you 'no sex.' Leave it alone."

Juanita, trying hard to avoid Sam's question, changed the subject, "Marquetta, could I assist with the planning of your wedding?"

Juanita, I'm sorry I forgot to get back to you. Sure, but we're still getting married next week. So the plans will be limited because we're operating on short notice. Okay?"

"Okay. That should make the planning fun, yet challenging."

Sam, wanting to see Marquetta naked and wanting to get Juanita in the sack, noticed the water and the lights around the pool. He believed he had come up with an idea to get his wants satisfied. He said smoothly, "Since we're at the pool house how about the four of us skinny-dipping?"

Todd stated boldly and without hesitation, "I am going to be married in one week, so this game is not for me. Besides, that I'm tired, and you're not skinny-dipping with Markie! And you should have known better than to ask."

"Sorry, Little Brother, but can't we all go swimming? I'm sure they have swimsuits in the pool house. A dip in the water may wake you up."

"No way! Markie and I are leaving. If you want a lift, we're leaving right after we walk Juanita back to the house." Todd, angry at Sam's attempt to see Marquetta nude, decided he would make certain Juanita got back to the others before he left. Sam was livid but knew it was not the time to act. He still had tomorrow. He made mental plans to call Juanita early to make arrangements to meet her at the condo." Sam stated, "Todd, I'll leave with you and Marquetta. The three left together.

---

To Marquetta's surprise, Todd drove directly to his townhouse, dropped Sam off, then, took her home. She sensed he was upset, but she didn't know to what extent, so she waited until Sam had been dropped off and they arrived at her condo before she spoke. She was trying to give him an opportunity to blurt it out but he wouldn't, so she turned to him, then asked, "What's bothering you?"

Todd parked the car in a space near the entrance to her condo; turned off the ignition, propped his left hand on the driver's side door and leaned on it. Then he replied with an exasperated look on his face, "Correction, who's bothering me? It's Sam. I know Juanita wants to try to abstain but he's not going to give her a break." Tonight I could see she really wants to live differently, but she's very insecure in her ability to carry out her new found goal. This is not the time for her to be around my big brother."

Marquetta, seeing the love in Todd's heart for his fellow man, replied, "She'll be all right. We'll just have to monitor Sam while he's here."

"I know but I don't like doing that. After all they're grown and if he can convince her, is that our business?"

"Well, if she wants to, that's not our business, but you told me Sam could be very persuasive. Remember, she already had sex with him and enjoyed it. This is going to be tough for her. But if she does refuse him and he tries to force his affection on her, we should be there to help if we can."

Todd asked, "How will we know the difference?"

Marquetta yawned, then answered, "We'll know. Thanks for the ride. I have to go to bed. I'll see you tomorrow."

Todd leaned toward her and kissed her lightly on the lips, then said boldly. "Markie, I don't want you in the pool with Sam unless I'm present, at least, until we're married. Do you understand what I'm saying?"

Marquetta smiled before she answered Todd. Hearing the boldness in Todd's voice took her by surprise, but once collected, she replied, "Yes, I understand completely."

"I think after we're married he will respect you as my wife."

She kissed him on the cheek, then said, "Don't get out of the car; you can watch me go into the building from here. Good night."

# CHAPTER 9

# A NEW DAY

S am queried, "Come on, Baby, how long are you going to keep this up? Sam had one arm around her shoulder with his hand barely touching her breast and the other he used to unbutton her blouse. Juanita had one arm around Sam's back, which she was trying to retrieve, while she was using her other hand to prevent him from unfastening her blouse. When she sat on the couch with him and agreed to kiss him, she put her arms around him. Not realizing Sam had every intention to get one of her arms out of use. When she placed her arm around him, Sam eased into a position that placed a small portion of his side and back against the back of the sofa. He then began kissing her fervently.

Juanita exclaimed, "Sam, I told you no!" Juanita's outcry surprised him, so he moved his back enough for her to remove her arm. She stood up and buttoned her blouse, then walked to the door.

Sam, grinning inwardly, thought to himself, *The games have begun*. He had no plans to leave until he emerged the victor. With deceit in his mind and trickery on his lips, he said cunningly, "Juanita, you led me on. Now you expect me to leave like this." He walked to where she was standing near the door and grabbed her hand swiftly to try to make her touch him.

"Stop, Sam, I don't want to touch you!" Unsure of how she should carry herself now that she had made the decision to abstain, she wondered if she had led him on. She decided to apologize while backing away from him, "I didn't mean to arouse you but you kept rubbing yourself against me. I told you to stop. I have my clothes packed now; let's go to my father's. We can eat there." She turned toward the condo door, turned the lock, and opened it.

Sam, not ready to move to a new battlefield, said, "I want you to cook for me. Can you cook?" Juanita couldn't understand the strange feeling that came over her when she was with Sam. If any other man had suggested she cook for him she would have told him a few choice words and kicked him out of her place. But Sam seemed to bring out a domestic side in her she didn't think she had. It bothered her that he could do that to her, but it was such a pleasant feeling that she didn't want to fight it. She replied, "Yeah, a little."

"Well then, cook for me. Let's see what's in here to eat." Sam walked toward the kitchen. Juanita followed.

"We have plenty of food. Suzette keeps the refrigerator and cabinets full with different types of food. Do you think I should pack up the food, too?"

"No, Suzette can do that later if your father wants it done. Just prepare something for us to eat now."

"Okay. You want steaks. I'm not the best cook but I can cook steaks and bake potatoes."

"That's fine for me, but I thought you didn't eat meat."

"I do but very rarely. I'll fix the salad now."

"That's fine." Juanita opened the refrigerator door to take the salad fixings out of the refrigerator. Sam held the refrigerator door open as she, took the food from the refrigerator and placed them on the table. Juanita walked to the cabinets under the sink; opened one of the doors, then, took a big salad bowl from the lower shelf and placed it on the table. She then proceeded to tear lettuce leaves from the head of lettuce that was on the table and place them in the bowl.

Seeing the domestic side of Juanita aroused Sam greatly. He knew he had to bed her again. He rose from his seat across the table from where he was watching Juanita and walked around the table to where she was standing. He positioned himself behind her, then put his arms around her waist then whispered in her ear, "May I at least kiss you?"

Juanita felt stupid denying him a kiss so she replied softly, "Sure."

Sam began by kissing her on the side of her neck and when she turned to him he kissed her passionately while using his hands to explore her body. Juanita felt herself succumbing to his touch. She tried to pull away from him but he held her tightly. She heard herself moan with pleasure and she thought, "Oh no, I can't." She squirmed, trying to break free from his hold, but she couldn't. Sam put his hand under her blouse and unhooked her bra. Juanita finally regained her strength and blurted, "Sam, I told you, 'no!' Now, if you want to eat here, you will have to keep your hands to yourself and let me finish preparing the salad." Sam, challenged by Juanita's new attitude, decided in order to stay in the game he had to maneuver a little differently. He, took a seat near her and replied nonchalantly, "Finish the salad, then. But I don't want all that stuff in mine. Tomatoes and lettuce is all I want."

Juanita shrugged, "If that's the case, it's finished."

"Come here, let me fasten your bra." Hesitantly, Juanita walked over to him and permitted him to hook her bra.

She then put two steaks in the oven and two potatoes; after which Juanita followed Sam to the living room and sat on the sofa beside him. Juanita, ruminating the events of the evening, determined it wasn't wise for her to be alone with Sam although she really enjoyed his company. She considered her choices silently. Before she could suggest they go someplace else, Sam proceeded with his next plan of action. He kissed her on her back and neck softly then tickled her earlobe with his tongue as he watched her body react. He then moved her toward him and kissed her on the lips. Juanita became absorbed in the kiss. After they finished kissing, she noticed her blouse was opened and he was trying to unbutton her pants. Vehemently, she said, "Sam, stop. You are not taking me seriously. I told you 'no' and you won't listen. You fastened my bra but you unbuttoned my blouse. Sam, we've had sex before so I thought you would understand when I said no, I meant it."

"Look at me. You will have to satisfy me now. My body's aching for you."

"No, Sam. I'm not going to have sex with you." Attempting to change the subject and place, Juanita said, "I know, let's go over to Phillip's. Barbara invited us, plus Todd and Marquetta will be there. Phillip has a pool, too. I have the address."

"Give me a glass of water and I'll think about it," replied Sam. Juanita walked to the kitchen to get Sam a glass of water while continuing to contemplate her choices. She determined she could spend time with Sam, but in a safer environment. She decided to call Phillip's house to talk with Marquetta. She didn't realize Sam was following behind her until he cornered her against the refrigerator and said sensuously, "Let's do it right here." He pulled at the button on her jeans and pressed himself against her as he kissed her fervently. He fondled her gently as she moaned to his touch. She thought, *I can't do this.* She felt his hand unbutton her pants when she silently prayed, "God, help me." She finally got the strength to withdraw her mouth from his and pleaded, "Please don't do this to me. I don't want to do this. Can't you understand? This isn't me anymore. I don't want to." Sam let go of her so quickly she almost lost her footing. He proceeded to walk away from her and into the living room as he aggressively cut her off, "You want me to kiss you because you enjoy it but you don't want me to have any enjoyment. I have needs, Juanita. I'm not a high school boy. I'm a grown man. Do you think this is fair?" Juanita followed behind him, trying to make amends. "Look, Sam, you're right. Let's not kiss, either." Juanita, questioning her ability to refrain from having sex with Sam, determined it would be best for her not to kiss him.

"You said earlier I could kiss you." Sam, recognizing her confused state, decided this is the time to come in for the kill. This time he decided to sit in a chair. Juanita sat in the love seat near the chair. She sat on the end of the cushion so she could lean towards Sam in the chair as she talked. Juanita, with sincerity in her voice, responded, "I did, but it's more than I want to handle right now."

"Juanita, you're a grown woman. This is not high school. You're telling me, you can't handle a kiss. Come now!"

"Sam, I'm just trying to recover from your brother. I can't handle you right now. I know you like women to respond to you when you want them to, because I used to be the same way about men. But your brother broke me out of that habit and now that I met you…."

Sam cut in, "Give me a break! You slept with Todd and me, not to mention that old man I saw coming out of here one Sunday, so stop playing games. You're not innocent. You know how the game is played. If Todd hurt you, he just got you before you got him. I'm not Todd and I think you know that by now. Do you?"

"Yes, I know you are not Todd. With Todd I felt I had some control but with you I am afraid I won't have any. Being with you frightens me, because I like being around you, but I don't think I should right now. I did sleep with Horace Greely but Todd hadn't slept with me in months. I slept with you to get back at Todd. I was going to let him know that I slept with you. But I don't want to play the game anymore. I'm telling you all this because I want us to be friends and I want you to know me."

"You have the wrong man, Juanita. I want sex, that's it. I don't have female friends."

"So, you're saying we could never be together as a couple or friends?"

"Exactly."

"So why did you have sex with me?"

"I make it a point to have sex with as many of my brother's girls as possible. It lets Todd know the type of woman he's dating. I do it to protect my brother, although I enjoy it, too."

"Thanks for the information," Juanita said disappointedly.

"Oh, don't act hurt. You got something out of the deal, too. Did you enjoy it?" Sam grinned slyly.

Juanita felt like Sam had just put a knife in her heart. This man seemed to have a handle on what made her tick and it frustrated her. She was being as honest with him as she could, pouring out her feelings, and he had no respect for her honesty. All she knew was she wanted to leave his presence and remain in his presence at the same time. She mustered up the strength to leave. Forgetting about the food she had in the oven, she stood up, walked toward the sofa, grabbed her purse which was on the end table near the sofa, and stated, "Sam, just leave me alone. I'm ready to go."

"The food is still cooking. Come here, Baby. You didn't answer me. Did you enjoy it?" He knew she was at a very vulnerable point and it electrified him. Normally, it's at this point he moved in for the kill, but for some odd reason he wanted to hear what she had to say. So he let her talk without making a move toward her.

"Sam I deserve what you did. But it still hurts and yes I enjoyed being with you."

Sam, intrigued by her honesty, walked over to her and held her in his arms. Juanita thought, *His arms feel so good around me. I know he's not good for me now but he knows how to touch me in a way that makes me want to scream! I can stand here all night with his arms around me.*

Sam lifted her chin, kissed her softly on the lips and said, "The food should be ready. Let's check it."

The food was ready so they ate. After the meal, Sam relaxed on the couch and dozed off. Juanita looked at him and remarked silently, *He is one handsome man. He looks just like a big baby lying there.* When she leaned over to kiss him, he woke up and pulled her to him. He responded by saying, "Let's take off our clothes and take a nap."

"No, Sam."

"Do you want me to kiss you?" Sam, now wide awake, put his plan of action back into gear.

"Yeah." Juanita said reluctantly.

"Okay, but don't complain later."

Sam kissed her gently on her lips and queried, "Did that satisfy you or do you want more?"

"I want more," replied Juanita.

He kissed her again gently on her lips and asked, "Do you want more?"

She giggled, then responded, "Yeah."

Sam kissed her on her lips and slowly eased his tongue in her mouth. He teased her with it first and then they kissed passionately. She found herself wanting more of him. She became so heated by Sam and the games he played with her earlobes, neck, and breast that she almost lost control. When she felt her zipper come down and Sam's hands enter her pants she prayed silently, "God, help me, please." She regained her strength and jumped off the couch. As she looked at herself, she realized how much of her was exposed. Before she could say anything, the phone rang. She answered it. "Hello."

Marquetta could hear panting in her voice. She asked, "Juanita, are you all right?"

She gathered her composure and replied, "I am now."

"Good. We decided to come to you. Do you need any help getting your clothes?"

"No. Sam is here, but you can still come over."

"Okay we will. Good bye." After Juanita hung up the phone, she took a seat in the chair near the sofa.

Sam queried, "What kind of game are you playing? You want me as much as I want you. Cut the game, I'm not Todd. You are an adult, so act like it. Come here. Let's make love now. You know I can make you feel good." Sam walked over to the chair where she was sitting, took her hand and escorted her to the sofa. He then put his arms around her and moved his body towards hers as he continued talking. "If you want me to marry you, you're going to have to show me how good you can treat me in the sack. You gave me a taste but I want you to show me what you can really do to keep me happy. Will you do that for me tonight? I want you, too."

"Sam, you're not going to marry me. You don't even like me." Juanita was surprised at her boldness. She smiled after she heard her response. She decided, *I haven't become a wimp. I've become more honest.*

"I do like you, Baby. I like you a lot. I thought about you when I went home."

"You didn't call me."

"I knew I would be back for the wedding."

"You wanted to see me again?"

"Yeah, Baby, you know I did. I spent my last day here with you, didn't I?"

"Yeah."

"Now, show me that you like me. I want to share myself with you. Do you want to share yourself with me?"

"Sam, I don't know you as a person. I like when you hold me. It feels nice. But I don't want to be an easy lay, anymore. My father told me men, decent men, don't like that. I know with you I have been easy but I don't want to be that way anymore. Do you understand?"

"I understand, you're still selfish. It's what you want, not what I want. I'm not Todd. If you want to be with me, you will satisfy my needs." She had her head buried in his chest. He lifted her chin until she was looking him in his eyes and queried, "Do you want to be my girl? If you do, you have to satisfy my needs."

Juanita couldn't understand why she felt so domesticated by Sam. She replied, "I do want to be your girl. You can check on me and everything. I won't sleep around on you but I don't want us to have sex until we're married. Sam, I just can't have sex now. Please understand." Sam distracting her with conversation had unzipped her pants and unbuttoned her blouse. After he heard Juanita's response, he decided to give the appearance of a frustrated man, he said, "Zip up your pants, Juanita, and button your blouse. They should be here. I'm leaving when they arrive." He tried to move away from her but Juanita put her head in his chest and cried. He said harshly, "Stop crying and go clean your face. I'm telling you if we don't make love tonight, I'm not going to visit you again while I'm here. So if you want to see me again, you need to get rid of them as fast as you can. Because, when I say I'm leaving, I want you to know that's the end of us. Do you understand me? I've had you and you haven't given me a reason to want to marry you. I thought maybe you would do that tonight."

"Sam, I'm not trying to force you to marry me. If I didn't satisfy you before, I won't be able to do it now. I just don't want to have sex until I'm married. Sam, I'm sorry I didn't satisfy you before. I wanted to."

"You satisfied me, Baby, or I wouldn't have come back. But I want more from my wife. Can you give me more?"

Juanita, recognizing Sam's bogus attempt to get her into bed, stood up, looked him directly in his eyes, and stated angrily, "Sam, you're making me very angry. You're one of the few people I told how I really feel and this is the way you treat me. You have no respect for me or any woman, for that matter. My feelings mean absolutely nothing to you. I thought you would be different. We could really date—you know—enjoy other things together because the sex was out of the way. I enjoy being in your arms and feeling you close to me. I enjoyed it when you held my hand last night. I thought it was cute how you were trying to persuade me to sleep with you, although I was afraid of being with you alone. But tonight you ruined it. You're selfish and egotistical. You want what you want when you want it and forget everybody else and their feelings. I know, because that's exactly how I was. But Sam, that's not the way to live. I mean really live. I want to really live. I want to enjoy life. Sam, please change."

The doorbell rang. Juanita stood up to open the door. Sam looked at Juanita, noticed her pants were still unzipped, and zipped her pants. He then stood up to button her blouse.

She smiled and said, "Thank you." She walked to the door and opened it to let Barbara and Phillip in.

Barbara said, "Marquetta and Todd are parking the car."

Juanita replied, "You can have a seat. I'll be back." Juanita went into her bedroom to look for Sam. He was in her bathroom nude. She closed her bedroom door and inquired, "Sam, why are you preparing to take a shower?"

"I need to cool off. Look at me." He turned on the water then asked, "You want to get in, too?"

"No Sam, but I will tell you this, you don't make this easy. You buttoned and zipped me like you didn't want any one else to see me exposed—making me think you cared about my decision. Now you ask me to take a shower with you while Barbara and Phillip are here."

"Would you get in the shower with me if they weren't?"

"Sam, please don't do this to me. You don't understand how hard you are making this."

He kissed her on her neck and rubbed her bottom and said, "Go on, I'll be out shortly."

She left the bedroom and thought, *If I can stand up to him, I can stand up to any man!*

Marquetta and Todd came in as Juanita entered the living room. Todd noticed her button was open and determined, "Brother either broke her or is working on her, big time. I'll find out soon enough."

Todd queried, "Juanita, where is Sam?"

"He's taking a shower," responded Juanita.

Todd leaned close to Marquetta and said, "She's all right. They haven't done anything yet. He's trying to break her. This is one of his tricks."

Marquetta replied, "Todd, Sam is ridiculous. You need to talk to him."

"Markie, he's been doing this for years. You need to talk to Juanita."

Marquetta asked, "Juanita, could Barbara and I see you in your den?"

"Sure." Once they entered into Juanita's den and were comfortable, Barbara commenced speaking. "Juanita, has Sam tried to convince you to have sex with him."

"Yes."

"Button your pants. Have you given into him?" Marquetta queried.

"No, but he's so sweet. When you came, my blouse was open and my pants were unzipped because we came close. I prayed and we didn't. I talked to Sam and although he wasn't happy about my behavior, he didn't want you to see me like that so, when the bell rang, he buttoned and zipped me. I guess he forgot the button on my pants. I saw him go in my bedroom and I wanted to check on him. He's taking a cold shower. Isn't that sweet?"

"Don't trust him. Sam is determined to break you," remarked Barbara.

"Do you think I teased him because I let him kiss me?"

Marquetta inquired, "You told him 'no sex,' right, and he persisted?" Not waiting for a response, Marquetta continued, "He has no one to blame but himself. Don't let him put you on a guilt trip. You are not obligated to have sex with him. I told him that last night."

Juanita confessed, "Abstaining is hard. I like Sam. He's good in bed. I enjoy making love to him. He knows just how to touch me. I love the way he kisses and when he holds me I could stay in his arms indefinitely. He was holding me as we talked. This is tough!"

"Yes it is, but if it's something you want to do and you know in your heart it's right, then you have to do it. The choice is yours. For me it's been ten years and for Barbara five years. It's tough but if you ask God for help you can do it."

"I want to do it. I know I shouldn't be fornicating. I saw the damage it caused in our family, Marquetta, and almost between you and me. I like it better this way when we work together as a family.

Thank you, Barbara, for befriending me. I also see how Todd treats you, Marquetta. Yeah, I may have slept with him but I don't know half as much about him as you do. You two really know how the other thinks. I've been watching the two of you together. You're happy; I mean really happy. It amazes me to see how content the two of you are. I'm starting to get an understanding of real love. Phillip behaves similarly to you, Barbara. Phillip trusts you. He never looked to see you and Sam on the dance floor. He was busy trying to help me. But he never disrespects you. That's how I want my husband to feel about me. I want him to be able to trust, love, and respect me."

Sam called Juanita to the bedroom. Todd walked to the den and said, "Juanita, I'll help Sam; you can continue talking to Barbara and Markie." He kissed Marquetta on the forehead and walked into Juanita's bedroom. Sam was standing nude in her room. He was shocked when Todd came in and said, "Big Brother, give the girl a break. You've had her. She wants to change; let her. Leave her alone."

"Oh, this family thing is getting to you, I see. You are a Parker! Act like it, or is Marquetta going to give you orders to carry out for her from now on? Are you going to become her messenger boy? I called Juanita, not you."

"Sam, come on; give her a break, Man. What are you trying to prove?" Sam refused to answer Todd so Todd went back to the living room and, took a seat. Sam got dressed and looked for Juanita in the living room. When he noticed Sam looking around the room, he said, "She's in the den."

Sam called her. "Juanita."

"Yes, Sam, I'm in the den."

Sam, wanting to send a message, refused to walk into the den as he stated, "It was nice seeing you again. Bye-bye."

When Sam left, Juanita burst into tears. Barbara said, "Juanita, if Sam really likes you, he will see you again before he leaves town. If you don't see him until the wedding, then you don't need him. At least, not now. We'll take you back to the mansion, tonight."

"A few helpful hints. Don't invite any man to your place unless you know someone else will be there. Eventually, you'll know whom you can trust to behave and who you can't. Personally, I don't trust Sam. Believing you can handle him and trusting him are two different issues. At this time and in this situation, he is not trustworthy. Remember, he's had you, and his ego is playing a part in this, too. He's wondering how you can resist him. He thinks if you enjoyed him once you wouldn't be able to resist him. Since you did enjoy being with him, it will be harder for you to refuse him. But you can, if you remember to pray when you're around him," commented Marquetta.

---

Juanita arrived at work early Monday morning with the determination to put all her energy into her business. Perusing one of the files that was on her desk, she was interrupted by the buzzer attached to her phone. She pressed down the button and heard Lucille, her secretary's voice, "Ms. Smith, a Mr. Samuel Parker is here to see you."

Juanita, elated, replied, "Send him in."

As soon as Sam entered Juanita's office, he turned on his boyish charm. His grin sent chills to her body as he said, "Hi, Juanita."

Juanita smiled and said, "Hi, Sam, I'm glad to see you. Would you like to eat lunch in the park? I'm not really hungry but I can take lunch now."

"Good, take lunch now. I want to talk to you and I have the perfect place."

"Where?"

"Can you cancel your appointments for the rest of the day? "

"Yeah, but I don't know if I should."

"Are you afraid of me?"

"No," She said as she, took her purse from out of her drawer and walked toward him. She gave him a curious look, then walked to her office door, backed away slightly to allow him to open the door, then walked through—never giving him a second look until she spoke to her secretary. "I won't be back today. You can reach me on my beeper."

She then turned to him displaying a sexy smile. Sam rushed to open the main door, so Juanita could exit her place of business.

They rode in silence, neither wanting to turn the other off before they arrived at their destination. Sam, took her to Todd's townhouse. When they arrived, there was a dozen red roses in an open box, on the small marble table sitting in the foyer. Normally, there is a fake plant that Todd had sitting on it but Sam removed it specifically for this occasion. She accepted the box, smelled the roses, then put them back on the table. Sam directed her to the living room. where she took a seat, and he went into the kitchen, returning with two flutes filled with champagne. He handed her a flute. Juanita thought, *This is so nice.* She asked, "Sam, do you remember the first time I met you here for lunch? It was nice, wasn't it?"

"It sure was. Now, if you want to eat, you have to go to different rooms to get your food.."

"What do you mean?"

"What do you want to eat?"

"Fruit."

On the coffee table, covered up, was a tray of various types of fruits on it. Sam took the covering off the tray and said, "Voilá" Juanita ate some fruit, smiled, and then queried, "Suppose I wanted some cheese?"

Sam walked her into the den. There was a platter with an assortment of cheeses on the cocktail table. Juanita giggled then said, "Sam, this is so sweet. What if I had requested salad? He led her to the kitchen and there was a big garden salad on the table. She replied, "This is, too much. I know you don't have a favorite food of mine."

"What is it?"

"Smoked fish."

"Do you want it if I have it?"

"Yeah, where is it?"

"We have to go upstairs."

"Okay."

Sam had a tray of different kinds of smoked fish in the guest bedroom on the nightstand by the bed. When she saw it she kissed him and when she did, Sam responded fervently. After the kiss they both were lying across the bed. Sam asked, "Can't you see I care about you?"

"Yes, I care about you, too. I'm sorry we started off the way we did. I left a watch here so I could tell Todd we were together, I'm sorry. It didn't matter anyway. He and Marquetta caught us together." As Juanita talked, Sam was undressing her. She knew, but at the time, she didn't want to fight him anymore. She was enjoying the attention he was giving her. Sam, I want to continue to see you even when you go back to California. Do you have someone special there?"

"Juanita, you are nude now. I'm going to undress. Do you understand why?"

"Yes, Sam. Because you want to have sex with me. Sam, you didn't answer me. Do you have a special friend or can I be it?"

"Juanita baby, you are special to me but I don't want one woman in my life. We can have fun together though. That won't change. Whenever I come to see Todd and Marquetta, I'll check on you, too. Both were nude and Sam decided to play with her body with his fingers. He enjoyed watching women squirm to his touch. As Sam positioned himself over Juanita, Juanita remembered her conversation with God. She decided, *I can't do this!* She shouted, "Sam, get off of me! I can't let you. I can't put you before God in my life. I'm sorry."

Sam, startled, got up and queried, "What's wrong with you?"

"I can't, Sam. I'm sorry. Everything you did was great. The food, how you set it up, the attention, but I can't." Juanita was dressed and out of the bedroom before Sam could think of anything else to say. He dressed and went downstairs. Juanita asked timidly, "Would you take me home, please?"

"Come on. He, took her to her father's mansion and said sternly, "I want to come in; we need to talk."

Juanita responded, "Okay." Once in the house, Juanita asked, "Where do you want to sit?"

"Anywhere but the great room. I don't need reminders of your family gathering."

"How about the living room?"

"Fine."

"Juanita, sit over here by me." Sam sat on the two-seated sofa in the living room and patted the seat next to him.

"Okay," replied Juanita, as she sat near him but leaving some room between them. She turned to look at him as she apologized. "Sam, I'm sorry. I really am. Will you forgive me? I know it seemed like I teased you deliberately but I didn't. I thought I would be able to go through with it. You were so thoughtful to do all that for me, but I couldn't."

"Juanita, I'm trying to understand you and I'm trying to be patient, but I'm not going to continue to put up with this behavior from you. Do you understand me? You asked if I had a special girl and I don't. But you're not going to be it acting like this; I mean it."

"Sam, I like you to touch me and I enjoyed you when we made love, so don't ever think that's the problem. But I want to please God now. I lived an ugly life in the past. I don't want to live like that anymore. I never want to do to you what my mother did to my daddy and my uncle. I bedded both you and your brother. To tell you I like you may make you think there was something wrong with Todd. If Todd wanted to marry me, I would have married him. I didn't realize how much I had attached myself to him. But I feel differently about you. Sometimes when I'm with you, I want to stay in your arms, indefinitely. I feel comfortable and secure. I can't explain it. I feel like I have to tell you the truth. That first time we had sex and I called for you, you brought back feelings I had when my mother left. I don't know why. I do know that a lot has happened since we met. Do you think if we married, you and Todd would still be close? If not, let's not try getting to know each other. I like having family around. How would your family accept me, knowing I've already slept with Todd? You know what? I never had female friends before. I like having female friends, too. Marquetta and Barbara are really nice and they care about me."

"Juanita, this is about us. Besides, if I married someone Todd had been with, my dad would probably find it funny. Since, I slept with many of Todd's girlfriends. Wait one minute. I'm not saying we're getting married!"

"Sam, how do you feel when you hold me? Is it the same way you feel when you hold other women?"

Sam, not wanting to reply, said, "You ask too many questions, Juanita."

"Will you hold me now?"

"I'll hold you but, you'd better understand, we are not getting serious. I'm not ready for a wife.

What you want isn't for me. I'm not one for long walks in the park and holding hands. When I travel, I look for someone who can keep my bed warm while I'm there. I thought you would be that person for me here. If you don't want that, I have nothing to offer you." He noticed tears as they streamed from her eyes and he kissed her and said, "I want us to enjoy each other while I'm here and I don't like women who cry."

"I'm sorry. It's just that I want us to really get to know each other. We don't have to walk in the park or hold hands if you don't want to. But can't we share what we like with each other?"

"Juanita, you're acting like there is going to be a future with us and I'm not sure there will be."

"Neither am I. I understand you may have sex with other women because we aren't having sex. Although, I really don't want you to. I don't know if Marquetta told that to Todd, but I'm telling you because I think seeing you with them would hurt me. But Marquetta hasn't had sex with Todd, so I guess that's the difference. If only we hadn't had sex. I guess I wouldn't hurt so much."

"Juanita, when I leave for California, I don't know when I'm going to see you again. I may be married the next time you see me. How would you like that?"

"I wouldn't but, if you are, I know you're not for me."

"Oh, so you would just brush me off like that, like you did Todd, huh?"

"I guess so. Can you forgive me for sleeping with Todd?"

"Can you forgive me for deliberately sleeping with you because I knew you slept with Todd and wanted him to marry you?"

Both smiled and then Sam kissed her passionately. Juanita whispered, "I think it would be best if you don't use your hands. You know I can get loud when you touch me. Anyway, I'm not ready for you to touch me like that again until we're married."

Sam hadn't had honest dialogue with a woman in years. He enjoyed this type of communication. So he said, "I'm not agreeing to marriage, however, I think I will enjoy holding your hand and walking in the park for the time being."

"You mean it, Sam?"

"Just while I'm here, understand?" Juanita didn't speak she just smiled.

---

"Hi, Barbara, is Marquetta in her office?" Juanita was resting her feet on top of her desk as she spoke to Barbara on the phone.

"Hi, Juanita, you sound very happy today." Barbara said while glimpsing through one of the magazines for the company. She was searching for an article that may be useful to their organization.

"I am. Barbara, guess what?" Juanita said excitedly.

"What, Juanita? She queried then laughed.

"Sam picked me up for lunch yesterday and we didn't have sex. Thank God. But we talked and it was a nice evening. You know—I haven't had one like that for a long time. It was like when I was in high school. You know before sex."

"I told you if he liked you, you would see him again. I'm happy for you. Hold on."

"Okay." As Barbara put Juanita on hold, she found an article she believed would be useful, so she grabbed her scissors with one hand and buzzed Marquetta with the other.

"Hi, Cuz. Daddy wants me to ask if you, Todd, Phillip, and Barbara would be willing to have the reception at the mansion this Saturday. We have everybody on stand by. All you have to do is say yes!"

"I can't answer for them but I'll get back to you with an answer. Now, about you—Todd told me that Sam saw you last night. How are things going?"

"Really well. No sex. But I like him as a person. I know he's rough around the edges, but I sure can't talk. I guess I like him because we think so much alike or at least used to. I feel comfortable talking and being with him. I already told him, if our being married someday would affect his and Todd's relationship, then I wouldn't want to marry him. You know at one time I wanted their brotherly bond to be broken, but after what happened between Uncle Bob and Daddy, I wouldn't want that to happen to anyone."

"I know, but that's behind us now and you wouldn't break up their relationship. Remember, Sam had something to do with that, too. Besides, he's slept with enough of Todd's old girlfriends, it's time Todd had one of his, if you ask me."

"That's how Sam said his Dad would feel if we married. Mind you, he has not committed himself to marrying me. But we talked for hours at my father's house. Uncle Bob and Daddy even joined us for a while. I think he likes me."

"Being with you and no sex, I would have to agree. But please, take it slow."

"Okay, Cuz. I hear ya. Do you believe that your parents have a schedule made out for me when I come to stay with them? Every hour is accounted for, even when I visit Grandma and Grandpa Smith. I'm not complaining, because it looks like we're going to have a lot of fun. We may go to Uncle Bob's ranch, too."

"Really, he has a ranch? When are you going?"

"Right after your wedding. Boy, your parents are thorough."

"That's their way of keeping tabs on you. I guess I shouldn't say that but that was the way I felt in high school. I always had family activities, so I couldn't do anything with my friends unless they wanted to join in with my family. Most times my friends joined in and we did have fun, now that I think about it."

"They love you and want to protect you, like they're doing for me now. You know—I get to fix up my room at your folks' house any way I want to."

"I can tell you are enjoying their plans for you. I'm glad. You're making me appreciate my childhood more. I think I needed you around then."

"No, you didn't. I'm a much better cousin now."

Marquetta glanced at the stack of folders on her desk, then said, "Let me get back to work but I'll ask Todd, Barbara, and Phillip and call you as soon as I get an answer. Thanks, and tell Uncle Earl thanks, too."

"Okay, good bye."

"Barbara, could you come in here for a second, please." Marquetta said, when she buzzed Barbara at her desk.

Barbara walked into Marquetta's office and asked, "Marquetta, is everything all right?"

A broad smile came over Marqutta's face when she answered, "Everything is wonderful. How would you like to have the reception at my Uncle Earl's mansion?"

"What?"

"You heard me. Juanita told me they have everybody on standby, just waiting for our answer."

"I would love it, but how much would that cost us? Phillip and me. It's your family's house. They wouldn't charge you."

"Barbara, Juanita wanted me to ask you, Phillip, and Todd about this. Think about it and ask Phillip, please. I'll talk to Todd. Although it's informal, it could be nice. What do you say?"

"I'm fine with it but I have to talk to Phillip."

"I understand. I'll call Juanita and tell her we love the idea and we'll try to persuade the guys, okay?"

"Okay."

Marquetta called Juanita's office and thought, *I never dreamed I would be calling her for pleasure. God can work things out.*

"Hello, may I speak with Juanita Smith, please?"

"Hold on," responded Lucille. Lucille buzzed Juanita and told her she had a call. Juanita answered the line. "Hello."

"Hi, Juanita, it's Marquetta. We love the idea and we'll try to persuade the guys."

"Good, may I be your coordinator? It's not part of the deal. Daddy wants the reception at the house but I would love it if you said, 'yes.'"

"That's fine with me. I'll ask Barbara. I'm sure she won't mind. She's been trying to do everything pretty much by herself. I have to admit, planning weddings isn't my thing."

"That's what Aunt Margaret said."

"Did my mother put you up to volunteering your services? I'm sorry if she did, you don't have to."

"No, she and I found out what we have in common and we both like to plan weddings. I would like to do it, if it's all right with you."

"If it's what you want, it's fine with me. Don't let my mother push you into anything. I love her but she can be very ingenious when she wants to persuade you to do something."

"I know she's smart. Marquetta, remember when Barbara said, if Sam likes you, you'll see him again. I have to admit, I almost blew it. He had different types of food for me in different rooms in Todd's house. He picked me up and, took me there. Roses and champagne were waiting for me. That's what we had the first night we had sex. I thought he was so sweet I decided to have sex with him, but at the very last minute, I remembered my conversation with God. I knew I couldn't. I jumped up and got dressed so fast that Sam couldn't say anything. I just kept telling him I couldn't and apologizing. I told him I wanted to please God now. Sam didn't say anything on the drive to my father's house but when we got there he told me he wanted to talk. I prayed and remembered what your mother told me about how to phrase the questions to see how he felt about me? She was right. He called me today. He's going to meet me at my daddy's this evening. I'll put him to work on the wedding, too." She laughed.

"You mean you told my mother and she told you how to pose questions?"

"Yeah your mother is something else. I told her everything about Sam and me. She said to take it slow. You'll find out soon enough how he feels about you. In the meantime, enjoy the experience of being a free woman. She told me you don't have to feel obligated to any man when you're not married and don't have sex with them. You can date anyone you want without feeling guilty. I'm going to tell Sam tonight that I'll go out with other men but I won't have sex with them either. I told him he could have sex with other women, though I probably would be hurt by it. Your mother also told me. I'll be all right. She said, "'Just think, if he wants you in the bed with him again, it will be as his wife. He knows it's a difference, although he may act like it isn't.'"

"I can't believe my mother told you that."

'Yep, I enjoy talking to her. I've been calling her just about every night since we met."

"Good, I know you're making her happy. Are you calling Grandma Kate and Grandpa Tom, too?"

"Yeah, but not every night. Your mother is good to talk to, especially now that I'm trying to get my life together. She gives me good advice."

"That's true. I'll call you after I talk to Phillip and Todd. Good bye."

Marquetta thought as she hung up the phone. *My mother is something else. I'm really blessed to have lived with both my parents and to have lived so close to my grandparents. I sure didn't appreciate it, then. Oh well, you live and learn.*

# CHAPTER 10

# WORTH THE WAIT

Sitting beside Marquetta on the veranda in a swing built for two, Todd peered through the glass doorway, quietly admiring the design of Phillip's house. His eyes were mentally scanning the areas he could see and he was enjoying the layout. Finally, he commented, "Man, I love the design of your house. Do you think you could get the person who designed this house for you, for Markie and me?"

Phillip replied, "Obviously, you forgot who I told you designed this house." Phillip was sitting at his wicker table with matching chairs. Barbara was sitting near him. The table was near the center of the porch.

"Who?"

Barbara and Marquetta stood up and, took a bow, then took their seats before Marquetta responded, "I think you could use our services. How much do you think we should charge him, Barbara?"

"Oh since he's a friend and your soon-to-be husband, nothing."

Marquetta said gleefully, "You heard that, Todd. Are you going to request our services?"

Phillip asked, "Todd man, did you think I was kidding when I told you Barbara and Marchette were the designers?"

"I forgot. So much was happening then. So when can you two designs a house for us, Marcie?"

"Well, we've already been working on it," answered Barbara.

"I was going to spring it on you after we were married a few months. I didn't know how hard it would be to separate you from your specially designed bachelor's pad," said Marchette.

"Man. Barbara had me laughing about the set-up. She said the plans you had in mind were obvious when you walked in the door," remarked Phillip.

"Barbara, when did you come to my townhouse? I don't remember."

"You weren't there. It was last year when you were away at a convention. You gave Marquetta the keys so she could feed your fish. I stopped by with her one evening before we went out to dinner. I have to admit, we weren't nice. Marquetta showed me around. You know, gave me an idea of the intentions you had for women visiting your pad." Barbara giggled.

Todd remarked, "Markie, I don't believe you sometimes. You've been over plenty of times; even without calling, I might add. I never bothered you or should I say…displayed my intentions then, did I?"

Marquetta laughed, then apologized, "I'm sorry. It wasn't nice of me. You're right, you never approached me in that way whenever I came by, but are you going to deny your intentions for the design and set up of your townhouse?"

Phillip replied, "She got you on that one. But I don't understand, why didn't you approach Marquetta while she was there if the place was hooked up for that kind of entertainment?"

"Do you think she would've continued to come over to visit me if I did? Man, I had to make a choice. Move fast and lose her or take it slow."

"Man, it took you ten years! I'm smart, Barbara and I have been seeing each other seriously for one year. I knew what I had to do and I'm doing it."

"Phillip, you don't understand. He still had to bring women to that townhouse that would respond to the set up. He didn't want to give that up, and after meeting Sam and knowing how much Todd listened to him, Todd probably got the idea he could change my mind."

Todd queried, "You think you're so smart, don't you, Markie?"

"Let's just put it this way; you learned it was best to do things her way in this instance. Just think, that will make Saturday afternoon all the sweeter," remarked Phillip.

Excitedly, Todd replied, "How right you are!"

"Phillip, you mean Saturday night. Remember we have a flight to catch to Florida, plus board the ship, and with the reception moved to the mansion, we'll probably be longer than originally planned. So, Saturday afternoon is out of the question," stated Barbara.

Todd exclaimed, "Wait a minute! What is this about the reception being held at Earl Smith's house? Markie, what's going on?"

"I meant to tell you but not like this. Anyway, let me tell you about the call I received from Juanita. She informed me that my Uncle Earl understands we're having a small informal wedding with immediate family and close friends, but he wants our reception at his house. He'll be responsible for everything. He has his people on standby, waiting for our answer. Juanita will coordinate it, so we can relax and just do what we need to do personally to prepare for the wedding. We don't have to pay for anything."

"I don't think it would be fair for Barbara and I not to pay something. We have family coming, too," commented Phillip.

"Look, Phillip and Barbara, you two were getting married first and we intruded on your marriage plans to include our own. The least we can do is be responsible for the cost, especially if it includes a small reception afterwards. Phillip, you'll meet Earl and Bob Smith and can talk to them about business if you want. Barbara, we can tell our children that our reception was held in a mansion. This will also give Juanita something to do. What do you say?"

"Just say yes. You know Markie. She'll keep it up until you agree," commented Todd.

Phillip replied, "No cost, okay!"

Marquetta said, "No cost and, Barbara, we meet with Juanita tomorrow."

"Great," responded Barbara.

Phillip queried, "Speaking of Juanita, how are she and Sam doing? Is she still holding her own or has he broken her?"

Todd laughed and replied, "Phillip, let's go play pool and I'll tell you about my brother." Todd got off of the swing and began walking to the doorway as he continued talking. Phillip followed. "You're not going to believe it, Man. I've been eating smoked fish since Monday. I think she's breaking him."

"Oh no, so soon. You fought for ten years and look at him," remarked Phillip.

Todd, still at the entrance of the doorway, turned to Phillip and said, "That's because I did what I thought he would do in a similar situation. Man, was I wrong."

"I want to hear, too," responded Barbara. "Don't go to the rec room." The men decided to go back to their seats and let the women in on the conversation.

"I know a little of it. But I want to hear about Sam's behavior from Todd," said Marquetta. Then she asked, "Juanita's getting to him, isn't she, Todd?"

"I think so. He bought food, champagne, roses…and still no action. I think he's surprised at her changed behavior but respecting her for it. She told him she liked him and would like to continue to see him, provided he understood that there would be no sex in their relationship unless they got married. She also told him that he could sleep with other women if he needed to."

"Oh no, not that routine," remarked Phillip.

Barbara asked, "What do you mean, routine?"

"You know what I mean. You wait until we get tired of sleeping around and have no choice but to come back to you," commented Phillip.

"You only come back if you want to. It's your choice. So it's not a routine," stated Barbara.

Phillip replied, "I don't know but it worked; I'm marrying you aren't I?

Barbara queried, "Because you want to, right?"

"Yeah," said Phillip.

"Phillip, don't try to figure it out. It must be love. We're with whom we're suppose to be. After ten years, I'm not questioning anything. I'm looking forward to the wedding night."

"You almost made me forget. Thanks Todd, you reminded me. No reception. I have to have you, Baby, as soon as we're legal. I don't want to wait until we get on the ship. We'll probably be, too tired to enjoy it."

"Phillip baby. We'll be married! We can make love anytime. So if we wait until the next day, it won't matter."

Phillip replied, "Yes, it will. I want to make love to you that day! I've been looking forward to this Saturday for a long time. I want my marriage consummated that day!"

"I hear ya, Man—me, too. Those things can last for hours. A friend of mine told me he and his wife were so exhausted after the wedding celebration, all they wanted to do was sleep," commented Todd..

"No way am I just sleeping on my wedding night. Why do you think I wanted the wedding so early? I figured by afternoon, we'd be finished with all the activities and have the rest of the day to ourselves," said Phillip.

"Phillip, you and Barbara are catching a plane to Florida and a ship from there. How much time do you think you're going to have to yourself that day. You will probably be exhausted, but what difference does it make? You'll have the rest of you life to enjoy your wife," remarked Marquetta.

"That's true, Phillip. We can make love anytime after we're married," stated Barbara.

"If we don't have a reception, we can have time, at least, for a quick one."

"Not with me on my wedding day, you won't," replied Barbara. "I don't think I'll be in any condition for a quickie. Phillip, we discussed that earlier."

"I'm sure we can work it out," said Todd. "Phillip, If we can come up with something that would be satisfactory to both of you, will you take part in the reception?"

"Yeah," answered Phillip.

"I have an idea. If it works, that will be my present to you," replied Todd.

"Speaking of presents, since Marquetta gave us a cruise to the Caribbean, we decided to give you a trip, too." Phillip handed an envelope to Todd. Todd opened it and smiled.

Marquetta noticed the smile on Todd's face and asked, "Where?"

"To the Caribbean. They gave us a cruise to the Caribbean. Thanks," said Todd. "You really want me to understand the importance of the reception issue, don't you?"

Phillip laughed and said, "Literally. We fly to Florida and catch the ship from there. We decided it would be fun to give you two the same gift. Although I don't think you will be seeing us much, and don't look for us, either!"

"My sentiments exactly," responded Todd.

"Who am I going to get to run SCI in my absence?"

"That's right, I'll be with you," commented Barbara.

"No you won't. You'll be with me," replied Phillip. "We just happen to be on the same ship. I want you and Marquetta to understand that, without any question. Todd and I will not be sharing you two."

Todd put his hand around Marquetta's waist, pulled her to him, kissed her, and queried, "You understand, don't you?"

"Yes, Todd, I understand no communication with Barbara on our honeymoon. I mean really. You two are ridiculous. I think we should be allowed to speak to each other."

Barbara laughed and said, "They'll be all right after the marriage is consummated."

Phillip inquired, "Todd man, how could you kiss her? I can't involve myself in any form of affection now. We're getting down to the wire and my body recognizes it."

Todd laughed and replied, "The kisses are what keep me going or I would be climbing the walls right now."

Marquetta decided she had more important matters to concern herself, and said, "Todd, I need someone to run my office. Who can I get?"

"Your mother; she seems bright enough. If she has any problems, she can call your father or your uncles."

"You know, she might do it. I'll call her now. Excuse me." Marquetta jumped off of the swing, leaving Todd swinging slowly from her momentum, and walked into Phillip's family room, which was closest to the veranda, and picked up the phone. She decided to take a seat near the phone after she finished dialing the number.

"Hello," said Margaret when she answered the phone. Margaret had just finished her nails when the phone rang. She picked up the receiver very carefully so she wouldn't ruin her nails.

"Ma," responded Marquetta.

Margaret knew Marquetta's voice tones very well. She knew she needed assistance. "Yes, Marquetta, what's wrong?"

"Nothing really…I mean…Barbara and Phillip gave Todd and me a cruise to the Caribbean for our honeymoon. Now I need someone to run my business. Do you think you could do it? I don't have anything that's pressing and I'll show you around tomorrow, if you agree."

"Thank you for asking me. I wondered who you were going to get. So, you think your mom can handle it, huh?"

"Todd suggested you and I think so, too. If you have any problems, you can ask Daddy, Uncle Earl, or Uncle Bob to help you."

"Marquetta, do you think only your father and your uncles can run a business?"

"No, Mom, I just thought…I'm sorry. You encouraged me. I know you know what to do. You gave me ideas on how to set up SCI. I don't know how I could forget. I think I've taken you for granted. Juanita reminded me of that today, and now Todd. You are a very bright lady. But sometimes, I only see you as my mother. Uncle Earl told me I looked and acted like you. I'm warning you, don't do too good of a job; I may try to keep you around."

"I like what you're doing so I will help you, but you're paying me. I'll have an agreement prepared by tomorrow."

Marquetta laughed and said, "Ma, I don't believe you. Thanks for being there for me. I love you."

Margaret replied, "I love you, too, Marquetta. Although you're getting married, you'll always be my baby girl."

"I know, Ma. But thanks, I needed to hear that. You know, you're really getting to Juanita, too."

"I love her, too. She acts like Earl more than she realizes. I'm so glad she's going to stay with your father and me for a while. I think it will be good for all of us. I think she's going to win over Todd's brother, too."

"I know, Ma. I think Juanita will marry him, too, especially if she keeps getting help from you."

"Thanks for the confidence. I'll see you tomorrow."

"Thanks Ma. Tell Daddy, Grandpa Tom, and Grandma Kate I said 'hi' and I love them. Good bye."

———

The birds were chirping outside of the window where they were dressing for the wedding. The brilliant rays from the morning sun were shining through the window pane. The clear blue sky seemed to punctuate the earth with expectancy. Marquetta looked through the window, then stated, "What a beautiful day to be married!"

"You both look beautiful," responded Juanita. "Get ready to walk in five minutes."

"Okay," replied Marquetta.

"Let's say a prayer before we walk," suggested Barbara.

"That's a good idea," remarked Marquetta.

Barbara led. "Father God, we thank you for this day. Please forgive us for our sins. Thank you for giving us the strength to stand on our beliefs. You have blessed us to be married. We thank you for the men who will be our husbands. Let us be the wives that you would have us to be. Please continue to help, lead, guide and protect us, dear Lord. In Jesus' name. Amen." Tears flowed from their eyes in thankful humility. They dried their eyes and walked.

As Marquetta stood in the reception line greeting guests, she thought back to the wedding ceremony and how she felt after the Pastor pronounced her and Todd husband and wife. She determined, *I'm Todd's wife." Before she could comprehend want that meant to her, she laughed because she remembered how quickly Phillip got them to the mansion for the reception. Also, the fact that no pictures could be taken until after the reception, as* determined by *Phillip and Todd amused her too.* Marquetta thought, *I still don't see how Phillip is going to make love to Barbara before we arrive on the ship tonight, unless he knows something I don't know.* At that instance she noticed Todd giving Phillip something in an envelope. She thought, *I wonder what Todd gave Phillip? I'll ask him later.* Phillip and Barbara left the reception line and the room. Marquetta determined to find out what that was all about, turned to Todd to ask him, but some guests came up to greet them. Marquetta reasoned she and Todd greeted more guests than they invited. Finally, Marquetta realized Earl Smith had invited his consortium associates. Marquetta said, "Todd, a lot of these people are members of Uncle Earl's consortium."

Todd replied, "Earl told me both our businesses are members of his consortium, so that's why he invited the other members."

"I didn't realize how vast the membership is that he has acquired. There are a lot of movers and shakers here. Uncle Earl must really be making serious money, with the type of investors he has here today." Marquetta's mind drifted back to her feet. She wanted to take her shoes off because she had been standing in one spot for what seemed like hours. She stated, "Todd, my feet hurt! Isn't it time for the line to be over? People are still coming into Uncle Earl's house. If this keeps up, we'll be here all night." Her thoughts changed to Barbara and Phillip. She contemplated, *I wonder how Barbara's feet feel about now or if Phillip has noticed how late it's getting?* Marquetta searched the room for Barbara and Phillip and said, "Todd, where are Barbara and Phillip? I don't see them anywhere. Do you think they left? After all, Juanita has turned this reception to one of the longest I've ever seen. It's a good thing she served appetizers' upon the guests arrival. Did you see the list of activities on the program. This isn't a reception, this is a serious party! She has singers lined up to sing. No one's coming through the line now. I have to take my shoes off." She, took off her shoes and placed them under the small chaise lounge in the foyer. At this rate we'll leave from here and go directly to the airport."

"Exactly. Mrs. Parker," replied Todd.

"What about Phillip? He's going to be angry."

"He's taking care of that situation right now. He and Barbara are consummating their marriage. Like we need to do, and will, as soon as they come back." That is why the greeting time has been extended. That way, the majority of the guests won't miss the newlyweds. We're out here and they're in there."

"They left?"

"No they're in one of the guest rooms."

Marquetta laughed and said, "You've gotta be kidding, with all these people in this house!"

"It's legitimate, remember. Didn't you and Barbara say, once we're married we can make love anytime. Well, this is one of those times. Markie, we're going as soon as Barbara and Phillip return, okay?"

"Todd what if somebody is looking for us?"

"That's why we, took turns." Todd's eyes looked, spotted Phillip and Barbara coming from the back entrance and said, "Good! Here they are now." As Phillip explained to Todd how to reach the set of rooms on the west wing, Marquetta felt her stomach tense up as she thought, *This is it. It's not my first time. It's just like riding a bike. It'll be all right. I love Todd. I want to do this. It's just been so long.* She glanced to where Barbara was standing and noticed a beautiful glow on her face. Barbara walked over to her and, as if she knew what she was thinking said, "You'll be fine. It'll be all right." Before Marquetta could say anything; Todd, took her hand, pulled her to him and said, "Come on."

Marquetta reached for her shoes and put them on quickly then, followed him, although she felt like a teenager who was sneaking away from her parents. She giggled and said, "Todd, I feel so silly and a little nervous."

"I know, stop worrying. You're with me."

"I know, and you're good to me," replied Marquetta.

As they reached the bedroom door, Todd kissed her and said, "I love you, Markie, very much." They walked into the bedroom. There was a bottle of Marquetta's favorite wine and a tray of hors d'oeuvres. The room was decorated in their wedding colors. Todd poured each a glass of wine and they sipped from them frequently as Todd talked to her. "Markie, what are you thinking about now?" He rubbed her hand trying to relax her.

She replied nervously, "That I may feel some distress."

"Markie, do you know how long and how many times I have sat in my office and tried to imagine how you would feel in my arms? Knowing that you were my wife. I will be gentle with you. But it has been a while so you may feel a little discomfort, but a lot of pleasure, too. Okay? You're my wife today. That means a lot to me. Take off your veil, shoes and stockings so you can get comfortable.

Let me take your glass." He put both glasses on the dresser by the bed. While Marquetta got comfortable, so did Todd. Todd asked, "Do you feel more relaxed now?"

"Yes a little." She leaned her head on Todd's chest and started playing with one of his hands, as they sat on the side of the bed. Todd turned her head to him, kissed her gently on the forehead and then on her nose. He lightly kissed her lips and then her neck. As he felt the tension leave her body, he kissed her teasingly with his tongue until he knew she wanted him to kiss her passionately. When he could tell she was ready to completely undress, he whispered in her ear. "Let me undress you." As he undressed her, he examined every inch of her body with his eyes, hands, or both. He enjoyed her beauty and marveled that she was his. He realized he was admiring his wife. He smiled. He took time to explore areas on her body which were sensitive to his touch. He made certain to record them mentally. Marquetta's body yearned for Todd's. As he stroked, fondled and caressed her, she uttered sounds of ecstasy. Todd kissed her passionately as he embraced her. He watched her movements until he knew her body had submitted to his touch and she was ready to receive him physically as her husband. At that moment, they became one. This new union was a beautiful and wonderful experience for them. They continued to indulge in it until they finally drifted off to sleep.

When Phillip knocked on the door, it startled Marquetta, so she raised her head quickly from the pillow. To relax her, Todd, took her hand and rubbed it soothingly as he queried, "Who is it?"

"Todd man, come on. They're getting ready to cut the cake."

"Okay, we'll be there in a few minutes. Thanks Phillip." Todd looked at Marquetta and said, "No need to jump, your Uncle Bob set this up for us with Juanita's assistance. He understood our problem. He said, "Ten years was a long time to wait.'"

Marquetta smiled, then asked, "What do you think?"

"If I knew then what I know now, I would've asked you to marry me when I first met you. But since I didn't, I can say, it was worth the wait. You can't get rid of me now, because we are married for sure."

"I don't want to get rid of you. I'm enjoying married life."

"That's good, because I love you, Marquetta Marie Parker."
"I love you, too, Todd Patrick Parker." They kissed.

## THE END

Printed in the United States
42052LVS00004B/187-210